Knowledge Management in Law Firms

Expertise in Action

Consulting Editors **Luis Felipe Mohando,**
Silke Gottschalk, Martin R Schulz and **Gerard Tanja**
on behalf of the International Bar Association

Consulting editors
Luis Felipe Mohando, Silke Gottschalk, Martin R Schulz and Gerard Tanja
On behalf of the International Bar Association

Managing director
Sian O'Neill

Knowledge Management in Law Firms: Expertise in Action
is published by
Globe Law and Business Limited
3 Mylor Close
Horsell
Woking
Surrey GU21 4DD
Tel: +44 20 3745 4770
www.globelawandbusiness.com

Printed and bound by Gomer Press

Knowledge Management in Law Firms: Expertise in Action
ISBN 9781911078135

Table of contents

Introduction: knowledge management in law firms

Luis Felipe Mohando
Sorainen

When I first encountered the words Knowledge Management (or 'KM', for short), they seemed deceptively simple in their meaning yet daunting in their implications. All lawyers are familiar with knowledge. Knowledge, defined as "the fact or condition of knowing something with familiarity gained through experience or association" and "acquaintance with or understanding of a science, art, or technique" by the Merriam-Webster Dictionary, has always been at the heart of the legal profession, as an essential component of practising law involves applying knowledge and expertise to solve clients' legal problems. Similarly, many lawyers have experience of managing cases and most partners nowadays are familiar with 'management' – defined by Merriam-Webster as "the act or art of managing: the conducting or supervising of something (as a business)" – at least on a superficial level. However, these two words put together seem more difficult to grasp: what would 'managing' (guiding, conducting, supervising, moulding, herding, leading, crafting, coaching, transmitting?) 'knowledge' (all the legal knowledge, what knowledge, whose knowledge, where?) imply or even mean?

I will not try to give a complete answer to that here, as the different chapters in this book will give many perspectives on how to address those concerns. In contrast, I would like to offer some brief remarks regarding how it makes sense to engage in KM in the context of the business of a law firm. I hope that such remarks would serve to introduce the general ideas to those that are new to KM in the legal market. However, readers should bear in mind that definitions of KM and conceptual models of both KM and the legal business are quite varied – if not heatedly debated – and the ones below are my own, based on my personal experience and understanding. Other authors, including contributors to this book, may (and do) have different ones.

The chapter starts with an account of the business of a law firm, followed by a general overview of what could be understood as KM. Section three gives an overview of the intersection between KM and the legal business. Section four gives some concluding remarks.

This chapter is based on a lecture presented at the University of Latvia in March 2016, which in turn was based on Schulz & Mohando[1] and my personal experience

1 Martin Schulz and Luis Felipe Mohando, "Precedent databases and knowledge management", in H Knott (ed), *Risk Management in Law Firms: Strategies for Safeguarding the Future* (Globe Business Publishing, 2014).

as a law firm knowledge manager. As it is intended as a mere introduction, citations and references have been kept intentionally to a minimum.

1. What do law firms do?

Lawyers, as operators of the legal system, perform an important social function. However, it is possible to also analyse law firms as businesses offering their services in the marketplace. As such, how could we characterise the 'product' that lawyers sell? Typically, clients may have a legal problem; maybe they have been sued and need representation, are negotiating a transaction and would like help with drafting the agreement, or plan to set up a new business and need to know the regulatory framework. Clients would then approach the lawyers that they trust and tell them about their issue so that they could provide a solution. This solution is the product. What do lawyers then do? They apply their talent and expertise to come up with solutions, present them to the client, and if the client trusts the lawyers' judgement, help them implement the solution.

From the above description, I would like to highlight three key elements that characterise the services lawyers are offering in the market and that would differentiate them from their competitors: (i) intelligence, talent or brainpower, the ability to discover and think through legal solutions, (ii) experience and expertise, the knowledge of the law and the legal landscape as well as the capacity to understand whether a solution would work in the real world, and (iii) the trust between clients and lawyers that moves clients to bring them legal problems, accept the solutions presented and implement them. These three elements are reflected in the way business lawyers tend to charge for their services: an hourly fee ('brain' hours) based on the seniority, experience and prestige of the lawyer doing the work (proxy for talent, expertise and trust), further negotiated on the basis of the particular relationship with the client (trust).

With these elements in mind, let us think about the development of a law firm and its scalability. Let us imagine a small law firm. Provided there is no shortage of work from its clientele, what would be the firm options if it wanted to expand and increase its revenue?

The first general way of increasing the revenue that I would point out is increasing the amount of hours worked and billed to the client – that is, increasing the brain hours. Keeping overall hourly rates constant, more billable hours mean higher revenue. Within this route there are two main options. One is to make existing (experienced) lawyers work longer hours. However, there are physical limits to how many billable hours each individual can produce. Conversely, the firm could hire more lawyers that could multiply the availability of brain hours. This option has downsides also: at the outset, there are costs involved in identifying talent and enticing it to join a firm. Beyond that, and crucially, new recruits, even talented ones, may not have the same level of experience or expertise as the current lawyers. Thus, unless and until they are trained and acquire the necessary expertise, they are unlikely to generate the same trust or the same work quality, or command the same hourly fee as the more experienced colleagues. Overall, as headcount, total billable hours and revenue increase by the addition of new (junior) lawyers, the expertise may become diluted, and the general work quality and average hourly rate may decrease.

A second general way for increasing revenue is providing a better service for clients and charging higher hourly rates. Keeping the amount of billable hours constant, a higher hourly rate means higher revenue. Increasing expertise and providing better resources to lawyers may help achieve the delivery of better service to clients that would enable higher hourly rates, through speed, efficiency and quality. For instance, the firm may try to make billed hours more efficient, so that the same work could be done and delivered faster. If a contract could be drafted with one hour of work instead of two, that would allow the firm to produce two contracts instead of one, and charge its clients accordingly. More experienced lawyers who have access to better resources may be able to do things faster and more efficiently. Leaving aside efficiency, better expertise and resources may have a positive effect on the quality of the solutions devised for clients, which would also justify increasing the hourly rate.

From this we can deduct that knowledge is not only a necessary component of the legal advice, but that its management is a crucial part of the growth of any legal firm beyond the small and solo practitioner level. Knowledge and expertise are assets of the law firm; albeit immaterial, they are as real and important as any other in the operation. Small companies can operate out of a garage and a laptop with minimal or no organisation or management, but as they grow and more assets and resources are brought in, organisation and management become a necessity. In the same way, once a law firm reaches a certain size, managing all assets, including knowledge and expertise, becomes a necessity.

2. What is KM?

Knowledge is central to most human endeavours, so it is natural that there are a myriad of definitions of what its management is, from many different industries and points of view. However, it is possible to make a general illustration of the concept by paraphrasing Collison and Parcell:[2]

- KM is very difficult to define. However, we could say that it involves applying management principles and techniques to knowledge (an intangible asset) as you would to other assets.
- KM is about capturing, creating, distilling, sharing and using knowledge or expertise.
- Knowledge is both explicit ('written down' somewhere, that is, incorporated into a reproducible medium and transmissible) and tacit (in somebody's head).
- Knowledge is not just know-how ('the processes, procedures, techniques and tools you use to get something done'), it is also know-what ('the facts required to complete a task[,] the information needed in order to take a decision [and] the things you need to collect together before making

2 Chris Collison and Geoff Parcell, *Learning to Fly: Practical Knowledge Management from Leading and Learning Organizations* (Capstone, 2004).

something'), know-who ('knowledge about relationships, contacts, networks, who to call on for help'), know-why ('strategic insight – understanding the context of your role, and the value of your actions'), know-where (the 'ability that some people have for navigating through and finding the right information') and know-when ('the sense of timing – to know the best time to do something, to make a decision, or to stop something').

- KM is not just about books of wisdom and best practices, but communities keeping knowledge alive by sharing what they know, building upon it and adapting it for their use.
- Knowledge is not a snapshot of what is known at a point in time, but the evolving set of know-how kept current by people who regularly use it.

Based on these concepts it is easy to see that all law firms, in one degree or another, practice a form of KM. As mentioned above, the practice of law itself involves the application of the lawyer's knowledge of the law and expertise as operator of the legal system to offer answers to a client's legal issues. What makes a good lawyer has everything to do with knowing what the law is, knowing how to plead cases and negotiate contracts, strategic thinking, finding the right precedents, resources and authorities, knowing the right experts and how to engage with them, knowing when to take different legal steps, and so on. The challenge, however, is transposing this implicit internal KM that makes an individual lawyer great to all the appropriate law firm members and in that manner supporting the growth of the firm.

3. KM in law firms

KM initiatives and departments will be important for law firm growth and consolidation, but how could they be characterised? This depends on a myriad of factors, including the size and maturity of the firm and the legal market, the firm culture, and the status, organisation and standing of KM initiatives in the firm. Nonetheless, some broad characteristics could be drawn by looking at the general nature of the legal work and the KM functions in law firms in different places around the world.

3.1 The cycle of matters

When thinking about KM in law firms, I find it useful to explore the life-cycle that client matters and assignments have within a law firm business and its relationship with expertise. This could be divided into five stages.

First, a client decides to retain the law firm for a matter and the firm accepts the assignment (and in firms with more than one lawyer, the matter is assigned to a lawyer or team). Secondly, the designated lawyer or team analyses the matter and the applicable law and reaches a certain understanding of the legal status of the matter and the possible solutions. Thirdly, the lawyer or team develops the solution, presents it to the client and, if applicable, assists the client in implementing it. Fourthly, on the basis of developing, presenting and implementing solutions, the lawyer or team can learn valuable lessons and gain experience and expertise on the matter, in particular if successes and failures are reflected upon. Fifthly, the experience gained from providing satisfactory solutions to the client matter can be used to foster trust in the market and enhance the possibility of getting further similar assignments from the same or other clients. If the firm is perceived as having prior experience in the field, clients may be more inclined to retain it for matters in the same field, starting the cycle again.

Graphically, we can represent the cycle like this:

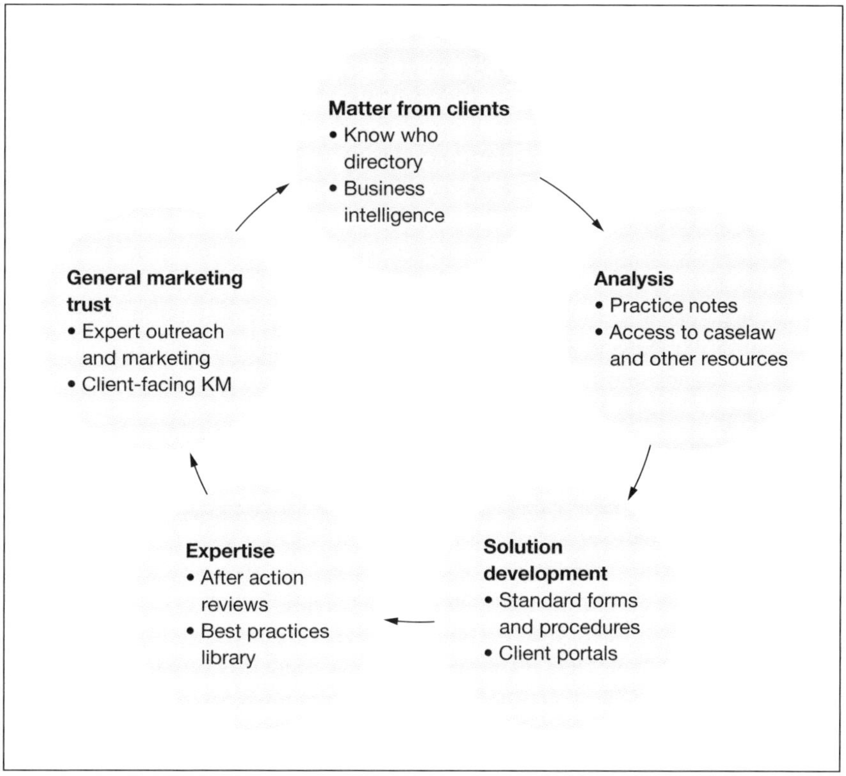

3.2 KM focus and sharing culture

Each stage of the matter cycle has implications for knowledge and its management, and the graph mentions some examples of KM tools that firms use in each stage. However, a basic premise of KM in law firms will be to harness the expertise created by working on matters so that it can be used in other stages. Expertise gained in a matter can affect whether to accept a matter or whom to assign it, how to analyse it, what kind of solutions are feasible or reasonable, how best to structure, present or implement a solution, which prospective clients may be interested in similar solutions, and so on. That said, the nature of the legal business makes KM particularly important in ensuring that the expertise gained in a matter is readily available at the analysis and solution development stages of future matters, so that the lawyers can have the best possible understanding of it and provide the best possible answers to the challenges the matter poses. Moreover, the availability of expertise should enable lawyers to reuse efforts made and solutions crafted in prior matters in analysing and finding solutions for new cases, 'avoid re-inventing the wheel', and deliver solutions faster and more efficiently.

Thus, a primary function of KM in any law firm will be to find ways of providing, within the firm possibilities, the highest level of expertise and knowledge resources to all firm lawyers, so that they have the best possible knowledge necessary to provide solutions for the client matters assigned to them. This entails maximising:

- the flow of information from external resources (legislation, case law, doctrine) to all lawyers;
- the flow of expertise from experienced lawyers to new recruits and juniors, and
- the flow of expertise from experts in one area: field, industry, transaction type, country, etc to other realms.

There is no single right answer on how these flows could be enabled and maximised, as this will not only depend on the firm, but also on the situation and the particular persons involved. However, all these flows have in common the ability and willingness to communicate and share among lawyers.

In fact, most of knowledge flow could (and in many firms does) happen spontaneously. When lawyers do their legal research for a certain matter they normally share it with other team members. When senior lawyers instruct their junior colleagues about a matter they indicate what, when and how to research, draft documents or deal with proceedings. Lawyers love to comment on their successes and tell war stories to their colleagues.

Thus, the ability and willingness of the firm lawyers to share their experiences (both good and bad) with other colleagues, and the ability and willingness of these colleagues to listen, trust the source and make use of the knowledge shared, will be crucial for knowledge management in that firm. This could be called the 'sharing culture' of the firm, and is the starting point and focus of legal KM in many firms around the world. For such firms, the role of the KM is to maintain and enhance the firm sharing culture, through creating and maintaining communication (sharing) channels, creating and maintaining central points of storage and retrieval of materials, promoting the contribution to such channels, ensuring the quality and reliability of the materials, creating and monitoring content creation and curation systems, and a wide variety of other actions.

As the legal markets mature and consolidate and firms become larger and expand over many jurisdictions, the need and characteristics of legal KM also evolve. Also, the legal culture of the particular jurisdiction, and its membership of a particular legal family, will shape the kind of initiatives that will make sense in the particular circumstances. In the UK and the US, for instance, the KM function grew out of librarians, which, given the common-law context, have always had a large role in law firms. All big firms have had big, well-staffed libraries and wide access to advance legal databases, things at the heart of legal KM, for decades. Moreover, the large headcount, team size, geographical distribution and matter volume of the leading law firms allows for a much higher investment in KM. In contrast with smaller markets and firms, larger firms in mature markets typically divide legal staff (above paralegals) between fee-earners and professional support lawyers (PSL), who are senior experienced lawyers that instead of doing client work perform knowledge functions in each team. These knowledge functions include 'current legal awareness' (legal trends follow-up and legislation and case law update), precedent vetting and curating, creating and maintaining standard forms and practice notes and training new arrivals. In smaller firms, by contrast, PSLs tend not to exist and these tasks are generally shared among all (fee-earning) lawyers. In any case, mature market firms tend to treat KM departments as an important support function, just like Human Resources or IT.

3.3 The use of ICT in legal KM

KM in law firms, as well as the legal market and the entire culture for that matter, is profoundly affected by technology. In particular, technology can make possible knowledge flows that would have been impossible otherwise: for instance, smartly searchable databases containing all possibly applicable legislation and case law on an area of law, available anywhere from a tablet computer that a lawyer can bring to court is nothing short of a miracle. Few KM initiatives will be successful without embracing the possibilities that ICT offers.

Nonetheless, ICT should not be seen as a panacea. Modern technology offers magnificent tools to enable communication flows, but tools alone will not work if the sharing culture is lacking due to the lawyers' unwillingness to share or listen to colleagues. Moreover, excessive reliance on technology may lead to other problems, like information overflow or decay in other sharing channels that are more suitable for certain circumstances, as well as problems between colleagues that belong to different generations or have different attitudes towards technology. Few computer engineers are as familiar with the law as lawyers are, and many lawyers are suspicious or unrealistic about ICT projects and systems. This brings one interesting angle in which KM departments act in many law firms; due to the KM department affinity with both worlds, it can act as a bridge between them even in projects that do not actually pertain to the knowledge flow between lawyers.

3.4 Benefits of legal KM

As mentioned before, given that knowledge is central to the legal business, the effective management of knowledge has the potential to provide significant benefits to a law firm. No general account of legal KM would be complete without a list of the benefits, but a comprehensive list would not be possible within the confines of this article. Let me conclude this section, following Gottschalk[3] and Schulz and Mohando,[4] by mentioning some of the benefits that KM could provide to law firms.

One first general idea is that legal KM could benefit law firms in the area of

---

3 Silke Gottschalk, "Benefits of Knowledge Management – What efficiency gains and risk reductions can come from KM?" (unpublished presentation, IBA Annual Conference, Vienna, 2015).

4 See n 1 above.

efficiency gains. Implementing legal KM could help lawyers to get the right answers to their questions at the right time, enhancing quality and responsiveness, and avoid reinventing the wheel (ie, doing research or developing solutions already done for a prior matter) by reusing existing knowledge, which may translate into using less hours and personnel to produce the same solutions, increase profitability and liberate personnel to have more idle capacity in case urgent matters arise.

Another general idea is that of the creation of an effective learning organisation. Around this idea coalesce concepts like the creation of 'one firm' culture, regardless of the different offices, regions and team that constitute it, the fostering of a knowledge sharing culture, the incorporation of continuous improvement philosophy into the firm processes and the empowerment of support functions.

A third way of thinking about the benefits of KM is seeing it as a quality management tool. The systematic way of managing knowledge as an asset can be instrumental in ensuring consistent quality across the firm, building 'client centric' legal services, can become a profitability driver and give an advantage over competitors.

Finally, KM can be instrumental in improving risk management, by increasing the availability and consistency of documentation, enhancing the recognisability of risks, and by directly reducing and improving the resilience of the organisation in the face of risk. Effective KM can reduce malpractice risks by reducing the risk of knowledge deficit (eg, not knowing a piece of legislation or case law on point in the matter) and through better understanding of possible conflicts of interest. It can reduce the risks associated with inconsistent quality and advice (an often overlooked risk of reinventing the wheel is that it may not be round every time), as well as enhancing the predictability of resource usage and reducing budgeting and forecasting shortfall risks. KM can also reduce the risk of losing knowledge equivalent to a loss in intangible assets, including the implications of experienced lawyers leaving the firm.

4. Concluding remarks

Knowledge management seems an obscure and intimidating concept, but at its core is based on common sense and so is its usefulness in the legal business context. We can think about it from the point of view of an average lawyer that has just received an assignment from a client. What should this person do? He should get all the relevant information from the client, get to know all the applicable legislation and case law, apply his knowledge to the facts, come up with a solution, communicate the solution effectively to the client, and he needs to do it fast, efficiently and without errors that would give grounds to malpractice liability. A modern law firm infrastructure should to cater to these needs. Together with other support functions, KM is a central part of such infrastructure.

In sum, knowledge and expertise are part of the law firm assets. A higher level of knowledge allows a firm to deal with more complex and profitable cases, enables higher hourly rates, reduces risk and makes efficiency gains possible. As any other asset, it can and should be managed to achieve the firm goals. In small firms such management is done spontaneously, but larger firms need to establish KM policies and practices more formally. What KM does varies in different firms, but generally involves current awareness, capturing, curating and storing precedents, creating standard forms and in general fostering know-how sharing and a sharing culture.

Implementing knowledge management strategy in practice

Allie Lustigman
Charles Taylor

1. Introduction

This chapter breaks down the practical steps for the successful implementation of the Knowledge Management (KM) strategy into three parts. After a review of current models for implementation, the first section focuses on how to effectively create a knowledge sharing culture. How much work needs to be done in this area is dependent on how embedded KM is within the organisation. For companies in which KM is a new direction or service, you will need measures to ensure that employees understand the concept of KM itself, as well as the strategy objectives. For all firms, however, there must be sufficient buy-in and incentives for the implementation to be successful. Many of the tools that you may need to employ are part of the principles of Change Management, and indeed, you may wish to appoint a Change Management consultant to assist with this. The second part of the chapter concerns the Knowledge Manager and his or her team, focusing on how to manage the logistics of implementation; the budgetary decisions; time management; resourcing; and tracking your progress. Put another way, these are part of a Project Management approach, and by undertaking these steps you will ensure your implementation goes smoothly, and can be replicated. The last section of the chapter will then take a more practical approach, as it delves into the importance of piloting a knowledge tool, and how this can assist in your overall implementation. Interspersed throughout the chapter are some case studies from different firms outlining the strategies they used to implement a knowledge tool or initiative, which should provide further practical examples for implementation.

This chapter assumes that the groundwork in planning and creating the KM strategy has been done, and in particular, that two important aspects have been carried out: a full audit of the firm's knowledge tools and capabilities, and a decision on the most appropriate initiatives to implement in the firm.

Every firm is different, with varying cultures and levels of enthusiasm concerning KM. Therefore, this chapter is largely from the perspective of a firm that is relatively new to the concept. Not all firms will need to utilise all of the techniques and ideas laid out in this chapter, but at a basic level, these are important approaches to get right for successful implementation.

2. Models for successful KM implementation

There have been many studies on the key success factors for implementing KM.

These are worth reading and give some clear and sound implementation steps to follow. This chapter takes influence from, and incorporates many aspects of these models. In Chong and Choi,[1] they list various steps:

> *From the analyses of the models, it was found that several studies have proposed several key variables for successful implementation of knowledge management. For example, Davenport et al. (1998) have identified eight knowledge management success factors such as (1) technology infrastructure; (2) organizational infrastructure; (3) balance of flexibility, evolution and ease-of-accessibility to knowledge; (4) shared knowledge; (5) knowledge-friendly culture; (6) motivated workers who develop, share and use knowledge; (7) means of knowledge transfer using various information technology infrastructure; and (8) senior management support and commitment. Ryan and Prybutok (2001) propose five success factors such as (1) an open organizational culture; (2) senior management leadership and commitment; (3) employee involvement; (4) teamwork and (5) information systems infrastructure. Perhaps the most comprehensive list of success factors has been presented by Moffett et al. (2003). Ten key components to successful knowledge management were identified: (1) a friendly organizational culture; (2) senior management leadership and commitment; (3) employee involvement; (4) employee training; (5) trustworthy teamwork; (6) employee empowerment; (7) information systems infrastructure; (8) performance measurement; (9) benchmarking and (10) knowledge structure.*
>
> They then go on to list their top critical success factors for implementation:
>
> (1) Visible top management leadership.
> (2) Employee training.
> (3) Employee involvement.
> (4) Spirit of teamwork.
> (5) Employee empowerment.
> (6) Information systems infrastructure.
> (7) Performance measurement.
> (8) Knowledge friendly culture.
> (9) Benchmarking.
> (10) Knowledge structure.
> (11) Elimination of organisational constraints.

Guidelines have also been listed by James A Albers,[2] which seem more project or practically oriented, and focus on the knowledge strategy and audit:

- Select knowledge management team.
- Establish knowledge management strategy and business case.
- Perform knowledge assessment and audit.
- Perform information technology (IT) assessment.
- Develop project plan and measurement systems.

---

1 Chong & Choi, "Criticial Factors in the Successful Implementation of Knowledge Management" (2005) *Journal of Knowledge Management Practice.*

2 JA Albers, "A Practical Approach To Implementing Knowledge Management" (2009) 10(1) *Journal of Knowledge Management Practice.*

And Davenport and Prusak[3] also list some key factors to implementation:

- A knowledge-oriented culture.
- Technical and organisational infrastructure.
- Senior management support.
- A link to economics or industry value.
- A modicum of process orientation.
- Clarity of vision and language.
- Non-trivial motivational aid.
- Some level of knowledge structure.
- Multiple channels for knowledge transfer.

This chapter draws on the above models but focuses on the implementation steps needed after the knowledge strategy has been created, and in the specific context of a corporate or law firm environment. Additionally, it splits the steps into three groups; first, customer focus and creating a knowledge sharing culture, secondly is the knowledge team focus and utilising key implementation techniques, thirdly the practical focus on implementing a pilot project.

3. Customer focus – creating a knowledge sharing culture

"There is a general agreement that a knowledge-friendly culture must be present or nurtured in order for knowledge management implementation success" (Chase, 1997; Choi, 2000; De Long *et al*, 1996; Galagan, 1997; Greengard, 1998; Gupta *et al*, 2000; Jager, 1999; McDermott & Dell, 2001; Ribiere, 2001; Ryan & Prybutok, 2001; Skyrme & Amidon, 1997; Wah, 1999; Wild *et al*, 2002).[4]

Outlined below are useful steps for fostering a culture of knowledge sharing; they are: buy-in, identifying knowledge advocates, communicating KM, internal marketing and incentivising.

3.1 Buy-in and identifying knowledge advocates

First and foremost, implementing any new strategy, tool or initiative needs buy-in from the top senior management, as well as employees at all levels. It could be argued that this is the most important aspect of successful implementation in a corporate organisation. Without leadership and support, projects are unlikely to get traction, basic resources will not be allocated and employees will simply not be interested. In this scenario, these issues can be described as 'knowledge barriers'. Raub and Von Wittich[5] undertook research into knowledge professionals' methods for implementation, in which they found that 'targeting knowledge actors' (senior leadership) and building 'internal alliances' (employee engagement) were key factors.

Buy-in can work from a top-down or bottom-up approach; in the former by ensuring leadership from senior management in promoting KM and instructing

---

3 T Davenport and L Prusak, *Working Knowledge: How Organisations Manage What they Know* (Harvard Business School Press, Boston, 1998).

4 Chong & Choi, see n 1.

5 Raub and Von Wittich, "Implementing Knowledge Management: Three Strategies for Effective CKO's" (2004) 22(6) *European Management Journal* 714–724.

other heads of departments to filter the strategy down. The latter involves identifying 'knowledge advocates', or those employees who understand and are willing to be involved in KM practices, to influence their peers. A mixture of both of these approaches is usually best practice, and varies depending on the tools that you are implementing, particularly if they involve large changes, new processes or additional training. Ensuring support from other teams that aid the implementation of your initiatives, such as Professional Support Lawyers (PSLs), Finance and IT teams, is also crucial for success. This is discussed later in the chapter.

In the top down approach, building a rapport with senior managers is integral, and to do this the knowledge manager should be able to instil trust and confidence. Having a committee or board set up with key managers sitting on it is another way to communicate directly and get across ideas. Ensuring that you have a good relationship with your manager and that they have a healthy understanding of the benefits of your role is also important for escalating your ideas. In garnering buy-in from senior managers you will be able to communicate your strategy, the benefits of KM, and gain support for your initiatives and implementation, which should hopefully flow through the organisation.

Another tempting option is to employ senior management to enforce a strategy on employees; this can be useful for some aspects of projects, but can often backfire. Employees with little time can come to resent being told to take on new initiatives. As Raub and Von Wittich state: "There are good reasons to argue that any attempt to exercise pressure on the part of a CKO (Chief Knowledge Officer) will adversely interfere with effective KM implementation. It will create fear and resistance and may ultimately stifle knowledge transfer." This type of strategy may work best for more practical aspects of implementation; for example, mobilising teams to produce small but integral pieces of work as part of a larger initiative. Likely the most useful advantage of having buy-in from senior management is to foster a knowledge sharing environment by ensuring that understanding and encouragement of KM is communicated and filtered down from the top level.

> *Leadership is responsible for creating the knowledge vision of the organization, communicating that vision, and building a culture that regards knowledge as a vital company resource.*[6]

Taking up more time, but possibly slightly easier, is the bottom up approach of obtaining support from employees outside of senior management. A first step is to start by identifying 'knowledge advocates'. These are people that, put simply, 'get' what you are trying to do and are enthusiastic about KM. Identifying them may come out of your knowledge audit; by speaking to people around the firm you will likely come across those that see knowledge gaps and are keen to find solutions. Additionally, keeping up a rapport with your work colleagues and working with them will also allow you to identify willing advocates. These are the people you can call upon to test tools, act as senior users, provide feedback and importantly, to communicate what they are doing with their peers and generate understanding and promotion, for further implementation. Additionally, turning a knowledge sceptic

6 Chong and Choi, see n 1.

into a knowledge advocate is a highly useful process for ensuring further buy-in around the firm. Showing someone a solution to a problem using KM is one method of gaining their support for your projects. If a sceptic can be convinced they will usually be very willing to promote KM amongst their colleagues. Some would say these are the people you should be targeting, but remember, it can take time to convince everyone, and therefore, at first, it may be easier to work with those who are more understanding of what you are trying to do, and additionally those who show apathy, to convince and effectively spread your message.

Table 1: Graphical representation of the two streams that make up practically implementing a KM strategy

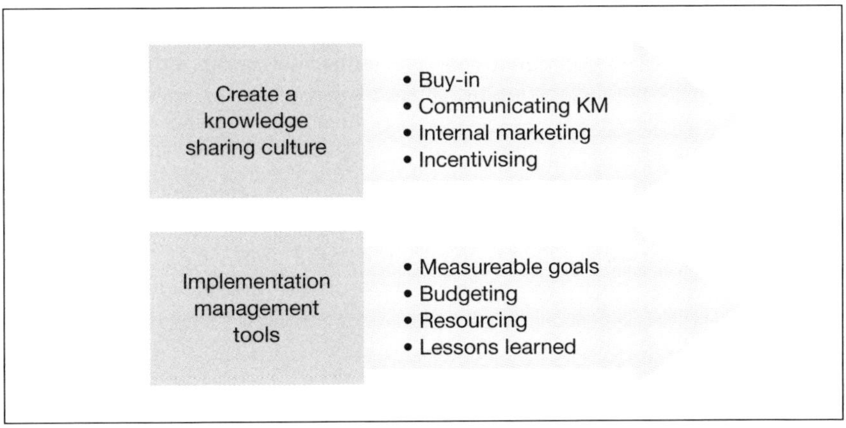

3.2 Communicating knowledge management

One crucial factor that makes implementing a KM strategy more difficult than other strategies, is the lack of understanding around KM in many firms, and the vague nature of the description of KM itself. Therefore, clearly communicating what KM is and its benefits is key to ensuring implementation. Without this basic understanding from employees, full implementation will likely fail. This communication needs to be consistent and continue throughout implementation and beyond, in order to ensure that KM becomes a recognised tenet of your firm's culture. Consistent communication is key, but think creatively as to how you do this. Simple contact with teams at departmental meetings or floor-walks is a tried and trusted method and extremely effective. The next section of the chapter on internal marketing gives more ideas.

KM is a vague term and often seen as a fad.[7] Therefore when communicating what KM is or a new KM tool or initiative, it is important not to use jargon, and to speak the firm's language.

Clarity of vision and language is crucial when implementing any change and particularly so for knowledge management.[8]

7 Raub and Von Wittich, see n 5.
8 K Eginton, "Knowledge Management – Law Firms can do it too!" (1998) 6(4) *Australian Law Librarian* 247–255.

Bear the goals of the firm in mind and always relate KM back to these. Use real-world examples taken from your company to illustrate points and ensure you give relatable and tangible benefits as to why you are implementing KM. Ensure you 'know your audience' by listening, and understanding their everyday roles and concerns, and then communicate how your initiative will assist in these individual issues.

Training employees is a clear and integral way to communicate KM ideas and methods and an extremely useful factor to implementation. Salleh and Goh (2002) insist that "if a company wants to become a truly knowledge-based organisation, it must start with quality training".[9] Whether this is part of your induction to employees or done on an *ad hoc* basis, training on KM tools and practices will ensure that knowledge sharing is employed appropriately and correctly by users, and that a good level of understanding of central KM techniques is acquired. Training can include identification of useful knowledge to be shared around the firm, the importance of metadata for search, and practical training on knowledge ICT tools.

Case study: implementing a KM system

Getting a KM project off the ground requires support from a range of people. At our firm we identified the following key stakeholders in the launch of our new knowledge management system: IT, the central knowledge team, the PSLs and the fee earners themselves. At each stage of the project we needed to convince different stakeholders of the value of the project – their buy-in was essential in order for the initiative to move forward. We were surprised to find that one of our biggest challenges was getting the PSLs to feel part of the project and to create a positive energy about the new system. We had assumed that as knowledge professionals they would automatically be supportive of the project and would understand the importance of what the new system will achieve. In practice, this was not the case and was an excellent example of how communication is essential for KM initiatives to succeed. Part of the problem was that the project had initially been managed by an IT projects team who then transferred responsibility to the central knowledge team for the system roll-out. A lack of communication during the hand-over meant that it was assumed by the central knowledge team that the PSLs had already bought in to the project when in fact they actually still needed convincing of its merits. It became clear that the PSLs felt that they had not been adequately listened to during the initial IT development phase and as a result they felt unheard. A big concern for them was that the project meant a lot of extra work in terms of transferring knowhow and precedents into the new system. We quickly realised that communication about progress on the project would be essential and that it was critical that the PSLs were fully informed about what was going on. Within the knowledge team we took a lot of time to explain to PSLs the benefits of the new system over the current system and to ensure that they felt fully supported with the work they had to complete. We also spent a lot of time

9 Chong and Choi, see n 1.

listening to their concerns and ideas and asking them questions. By listening well and communicating regularly we were able to give the PSLs the reassurance they needed and they are now completely on board with the project.

3.3 Internal marketing

Internal marketing is very much linked to communication. This allows you to consistently relay the benefits of KM, and therefore why you are implementing it. It is an important tool for buy-in and for ensuring understanding amongst employees of how knowledge sharing can assist in their everyday work.

This chapter will go into the benefits of pilot projects for implementation at a later stage, but you should note that this is an excellent way to market yourself and KM, promoting it as a practical solution to problems. Utilise internal marketing tools such as posters, messages on your intranet or customised email signatures, to effectively draw attention to new KM initiatives and lay out how they have helped to benefit users and the firm generally.

Bulletins from the KM team are excellent ways of communicating your day-to-day activities and to promote KM. These can be done on a monthly or bi-monthly basis. If departments don't have individual bulletins, tack yourself onto a bulletin that is already distributed in your company. Additionally, setting up fairs or events under the banner of KM is an innovative way of communicating your message to many people. 'Knowledge events' can consist of suppliers you invite in to talk about their products or resources, give presentations, and with added incentives of food or competitions. These events allow you to spread your message in an informal and inviting way and can be done annually to cement into the firm's culture. They also allow you to identify your team to the wider firm and ensure that employees know who you are and the services you provide.

Marketing your team is an important tool for ensuring that employees understand who to go to for information about KM, and to put a human face onto this principle. If your team is new then this is all the more reason to promote them, and ingratiate yourselves into the firm, before the changes and transitions begin as part of your KM implementation. Promote yourselves through the various communication methods above, such as fairs and floor-walks, inductions and training, as well as individual meetings, intranet pages of information and email communications.

3.4 Incentivising

The last part of this section of the chapter is perhaps the most practical in terms of how one can encourage a knowledge sharing culture within an organisation, in order to effectively implement a KM strategy. Incentivising is often mentioned as part of the key success factors to implementation and it can take many forms.

Formal methods of incentivising include performance measurement and rewards related to KM, such as ensuring that KM is integrated into employees' appraisals and yearly objectives. If KM is a new concept in an organisation, adding it to appraisals could take a lot of persuasion. However, KM objectives can be concise, SMART (Specific, Measurable, Assignable, Realistic, Time-related) and very beneficial for employees. Additionally, if managers succeed in showing how KM can benefit a company overall in terms of efficiency and profit, then these are all reasonable arguments for why KM should be included on appraisals. A major advantage to having KM integrated with performance is that it will clearly show employees that KM is an important facet of the company culture, which will encourage the use of KM tools and knowledge sharing generally. KM objectives can involve sharing a certain number of know-how documents, or communicating knowledge on a useful topic in the form of presentations or memoranda. This method of incentivising KM is a sure-fire way of ensuring knowledge creation and sharing. However, it can backfire if not implemented correctly. There should be a clear, company-wide understanding of KM and its benefits to the employee in order for this to be fully accepted.

More informal methods for incentivising KM are usually appropriate. These can include 'gaming' activities or initiatives that at first seem like another form of bribery, but actually work to embed understanding in employees of KM and how it can help them. Competitions are useful tools that embody this concept. They can be utilised when launching a knowledge tool, or to encourage knowledge sharing. For example, a simple competition could see the person who shares the most know-how to a knowledge system win a prize. This could be done on a team or firm-wide basis, depending on your organisation. These types of initiatives, if done well, create friendly competition amongst employees, and generate discussion and enthusiasm about KM. All of this benefits the knowledge manager in implementing the tool, by allowing it to be marketed and getting the adequate materials for it. Of course, competitions can have negative effects and one needs to ensure the quality of materials that are submitted as well as the quantity. Another more informal method for incentivising is simple recognition. A presentation or a small reward to an employee for a contribution to KM is very effective in encouraging more active knowledge sharing, and in fostering a knowledge sharing environment.

Incentivising doesn't always have to work through a carrot and stick approach; employees can be enthused by KM by being actively involved in the process themselves. Chang and Choi argue that employee empowerment is a crucial factor in implementing a KM strategy. Employee empowerment, which includes taking ownership and having freedom to express ideas and create or contribute to systems, fosters a culture of proactive employees who want to find solutions and do more to further themselves. Empowerment is also about trust, with senior management trusting their employees to take ownership of initiatives, and employees trusting the resources they are all helping to provide. Helene Russell[10] writes that "the key to a good knowledge sharing culture is trust". I believe that trust, coupled with employee empowerment, is extremely useful for implementing KM. Most of the knowledge generated is from the employees themselves, and by encouraging employees to generate materials, set out their own objectives, and take ownership of KM tools by informing how they will work, there will likely be much more enthusiasm for them. By facilitating this sharing and making it clear that the content and tools are owned

10 H Russell, *Knowledge Management Handbook* (The Law Society, 2012).

by the employees, they can feel empowered and more encouraged to create and share knowledge.

Case study: creation of knowledge base tool
Ownership was integral learning from the implementation of our Knowledge Base. One of the key things that has happened with our knowledge base (that we didn't predict at the beginning of the project) is that the content in it evolved into forming the basis of our expertise pages. The claims department organised itself into claims groups that then had their own expertise pages created for them with a mixture of knowhow/precedents/how to guides/useful links all on one page – so in effect a contents page to different areas of the intranet in one place. Each sector group 'owns' their page and each group has a leader who feeds back to me content that needs to be there. In this way the page is tailored exactly to their requirements rather than just being an anonymous collection of information. So the message from that is getting the users to take responsibility for the content is crucial to the success of the knowledge base – and is often the hardest thing to achieve as until they start using it they can't always grasp the benefits.

4. Knowledge team focus – implementation management tools

For successful implementation you will need to factor in how you will manage creating, launching and tracking your new initiatives. Below are the key tools, often used in project management, which will help to ensure implementation goes smoothly and meets your strategic objectives. With each of these areas, adequate planning should be carried out, much of which can be done during the creation of the KM strategy itself. The key tools outlined here are: measurable goals, budgeting, resourcing and lessons learned.

4.1 Measurable goals

Creating a proper strategy is one of the key factors to successful implementation.[11] In your initial KM strategy, you should set out the reasoning for implementing your various initiatives, or the business case. The business case should be used as a basis for more broken down, measurable goals. In order to successfully implement the KM strategy, knowledge managers must track their progress by referring back to these goals. Much like managing a project, key milestones should be put into place for individual tools and initiatives, as well as the overall process of KM implementation itself. It is only once you have clear measurable goals that can be tracked, that you can assess whether your KM implementation is succeeding, and whether it is delivering what the business needs. It is useful to break down your overall strategy into key metrics, which can then be assessed. Albers[12] lists some examples of these: "degree of access to important information, quality of content, effectiveness of knowledge flow, and efficiency of information management". Others could include

11 A Igwe, JUJ Onwumere and P Obimaka, "Building Blocks of Successful Strategy Implementation and Execution in the Management of Organisations" (2015) 5(3) *Information and Knowledge Management*.

12 See n 2.

connectivity of employees, identification of knowledge experts and retention of internal knowhow. Implementing the KM strategy is a fluid process that consists of projects and initiatives simultaneously and dynamically being carried out. One therefore needs to track progress to ensure that the overall 'mission' is being achieved.

It is also important to measure how your KM initiatives are performing in the context of the overall business strategy. Business strategies can vary and involve a number of factors. Overall, most businesses want to improve their financial performance, and while it can be argued that KM contributes to this, KM can be more effectively measured against factors such as efficiency and intellectual capital. If you can show that the KM strategy is meeting objectives, internally and in the context of the firm's overall objectives, then you will ensure that the strategy fits into your organisation, is useful for the business, and you should be able to garner more buy-in for future initiatives.[13]

4.2 Budgeting

A further project management feature that should be utilised as part of KM strategy implementation is budgeting. Each individual initiative and tool should be budgeted for and KM professionals should outline the overall cost for the strategy. This will allow you to ensure that a sufficient budget is in place for you to carry out your strategy. These can of course be estimates, but they should be backed up as far as possible with proper quotes. Costs for external tools or internal development should be laid out. Ensure you get your budget approved at an early stage when you have the most support for your objectives. You will also need to track your budget, working with finance teams and putting in necessary tracking tools to ensure you are keeping in line with your estimates as far as possible, and escalating early if the possibility of going overbudget presents itself. Essentially, knowledge professionals should be realistic in budget setting, ensure the adequate finances are in place, and make adjustments where necessary in order to successfully carry out the strategy. Always communicate with the finance team and your manager regarding the budget and be transparent if problems occur.

4.3 Resourcing

Ensuring you have the right team in place with the necessary skills to carry out tasks and projects is essential for implementing a KM strategy. This relates not only to the immediate KM team, but also the other departments that you will need to support you, such as IT, Finance and HR. The knowledge manager will need to assign the correct people to the tasks that match their capabilities. Additionally, timeframes should be mapped out to ensure that tasks and projects can be delivered in a reasonable time. If the KM team is small then this needs to be taken into account, and timeframes or initiatives adjusted accordingly, or the KM manager should look at what other teams are available to support. A communication plan should be put into place to ensure tasks, objectives and initiatives are tracked and that there is a

13 *Ibid.*

clear reporting structure. The teams should be able to communicate the progress of projects and tasks, as well as easily escalate issues to get them resolved. Shared intranet pages and regular meetings are practical ways of facilitating this communication.

KM cuts across different practices in a firm, but also relies heavily on some departments, such as IT, which KM managers will need support from and to forge strong relationships with. IT departments will likely be involved in your strategy in the form of project managing initiatives from the technology side, providing resources and budgets. Therefore, it is important to ensure you have the necessary IT resource in place for your implementation, and to maintain good relationships with IT teams. This is the same for other departments which will play key roles in your strategy implementation, such as Professional Support Lawyers (PSLs), Finance or Risk.

4.4 Lessons learned

Similar to completing a project or when launching different tools, implementing the KM strategy will inevitably encounter hurdles and difficulties. These can include initiatives not being embraced fully by the organisation, a lack of buy-in, or practical problems concerning your IT infrastructure or budget. These issues should all be noted down as lessons learned for future implementations. Your strategy should evolve with your implementation, and be a living document that is updated continuously. By seeking to understand and documenting when things go wrong, and indeed, when implementations go smoothly or are particularly successful in areas, you will be able to draw on this knowledge in future, as you roll out your implementation.

One way of noting lessons learned is by creating a clear table. Your table can split up issues encountered into themes, such as communication, resources or change management. Then you should note down what went well and what could be improved for each of these themes. Don't forget that the lessons learned document or meeting should not just be a reflection exercise. Clear actions should be attributed to each of your lessons learned and assigned to the appropriate person, to be resolved for future projects or initiatives. See appendix below.

5. Practical implementation – run a pilot project

5.1 Benefits of a pilot project

As related above, rolling out your implementation slowly, one project or tool at a time, is extremely beneficial. Running a pilot project in one team or office is an excellent way to show clearly and tangibly your KM strategy in practice, avoid the risks that come with a larger implementation group, and lay the groundwork for further implementation of your plan.

A pilot project is extremely useful in helping to obtain buy-in for you and the KM strategy implementation. A successful pilot project is a practical illustration of how the KM strategy can benefit the firm, which in turn can assist in obtaining buy-in and momentum in your implementation. Your strategy should outline where there are knowledge gaps in the organisation, and clear problems that can be solved by a KM tool. Either through piloting a large KM project or by "picking some low-hanging fruit" (Russell 2012) with smaller solutions for common problems, you should be able to solve these issues. Overall, highlighting and marketing how tools have helped the firm or provided a simple solution to a common problem eases along the implementation process, by reassuring sceptics, garnering attention, and providing further enthusiasm.[14]

A pilot project is also a useful training tool and experimentation; ensure you document your lessons learned, as outlined above, in order to understand where things have gone wrong as well as where you succeeded. Practice, as they say, makes perfect, and by learning from your pilot project, this should help you as you move on to implementing further tools. You will also gain an understanding of how best to approach the implementation for the rest of your overall strategy.

6. Selecting your pilot project

It is useful to select the right project and many factors should be taken into consideration when choosing which project to go for. Prioritising is key, particularly when thinking about whether to undertake a larger project or a series of smaller initiatives. Your original KM strategy should help you to understand the major problems the firm faces and should inform your decision, essentially giving you a plan of action for how you will carry out the implementation. Studies and my own experience have shown that quick wins are often useful to start with, as they build trust early on. This is part of a bottom-up approach, working on smaller projects that have already been started or have traction, and utilising KM to solve these smaller problems, which in turn helps to show how KM can be useful.[15] It is also sometimes easier to progress your own initiatives if you can identify similar ones around the firm and use them as a springboard for your own.

It is helpful to take into account which initiatives will produce the most value or return on investment. Quick wins are helpful but larger projects will have more impact. Rolling out an upgraded intranet or a new knowledge database will solve larger problems, generate more publicity and if successful, will be more rewarding in terms of trust and buy-in. This could be seen as the riskier project to pilot, but with greater rewards. It is useful to weigh up your options, but if possible, I advocate working on one larger project but selecting smaller quick wins to progress in the meantime, as part of the fluid implementation of your strategy. Ensure that you have the resources in place to carry this out.

There is also the decision of what type of initiative to start with; should they be IT-based or more cultural programs? Installing an IT solution is a popular tool in the KM armoury.[16] In fact, information technology infrastructure is a hugely important driver for knowledge management, as it is often technology that facilitates knowledge sharing, which is integral to implementing your strategy.[17] This is a good argument for undertaking these types of projects early on if they are not already

---

14 See nn 5 and 11 above.

15 *Ibid.*

16 P Clark, "Implementing a Knowledge Strategy for Your Firm" (1998) 41(2) *Research Technology Management* 28.

17 See nn 1, 3 and 8 above.

Table 2: Risk v Reward chart relating to decisions on which projects to select to pilot for implementation

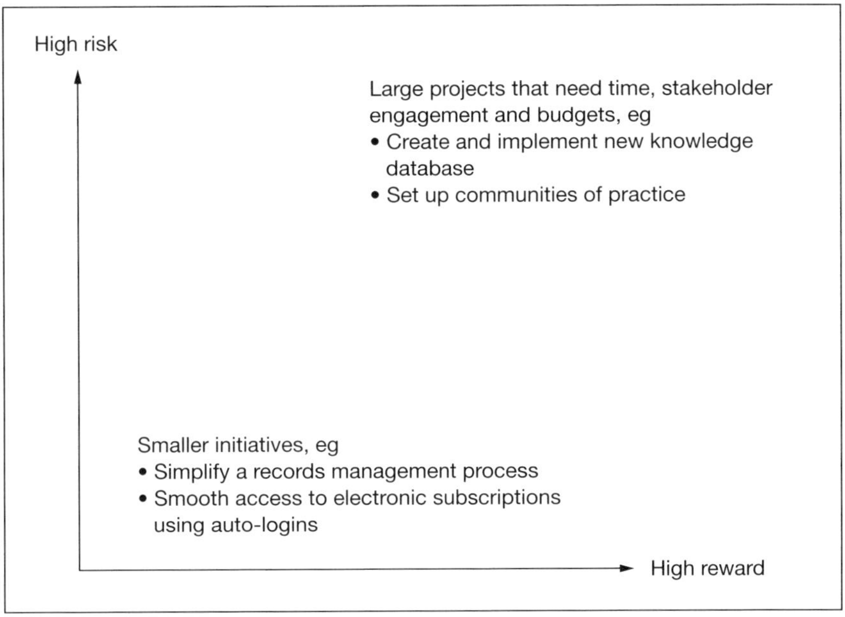

available within the firm. Corporate technology is developing at an incredible rate and is a staple in law firms today, being taken up in a swift and unprecedented way. KM has been able to utilise technology to enable efficient storage, search, sharing and accessing of knowledge in new and innovative ways. Popular KM tools include knowledge databases, Intranets and employee specialism directories that connect people quickly and efficiently.

Case study: intranet upgrade

High user acceptance is essential for any KM project. In implementing our new intranet we ensured that the requirements gathered and subsequent work were based on user needs and feedback. With the proliferation of technology in our everyday lives, people are used to fast and easy information gathering, and they expect this of corporate technology too. If usability is lacking it is very likely that take-up amongst users will be low. Therefore, our intranet project focused on ways to improve information search and retrieval, and we designed a modern and clean, user-friendly interface. We ensured that that it was the users who informed the project from the beginning and every step of the way. We used surveys and focus groups to gather requirements and ideas for the new structure and look and feel. We then called upon the business users for feedback further into the project, to consult on usability and functionality during user testing sessions, and again after our roll out and launch.

ICT can be the obvious choice for a first project. However, an important point to note is that people knowledge transfer is still one of the best ways to communicate knowledge. Structures such as Communities of Practice or informal learning sessions are excellent KM initiatives, and could be considered as projects to pilot as part of your implementation. Communities of Practice build and foster a knowledge sharing environment in an organisation, and so are highly useful initiatives when first implementing the strategy.

Most of our respondents [saw] the creation of communities of practice as a hallmark of successful KM implementation. CoPs lead to more effective knowledge sharing and pave the way for a knowledge-centric culture.[18]

Setting up these programs should be worked out, tracked and project managed in the same way that one would manage the implementation of an IT tool.

6.1 Replication

Once you have rolled out your pilot project in whatever form, whether it is a small project of improving processes, or a larger IT implementation, it is then time to do this again with your next initiative, and so carry on with the overall implementation of your strategy. Utilise your lessons learned to improve your processes, but equally, no implementation is ever the same, so ensure you keep logging your learnings. Build on the groundwork that you create in your pilot project, such as the working relationships you have fostered, the confidence from management and your peers, and the project planning tools you put into place. Utilising these and furthering them in the next iteration will make it all the more easy.

If you are new to your organisation and still need to get to grips with the firm culture, the level of enthusiasm for new tools and the amount of resistance to change, this staggered implementation approach will be very useful to you. By implementing smaller tools and deepening your understanding of your firm culture, you will eventually know how best to approach your implementation in relation to crucial cultural factors, such as the identification of key influencers, the understanding of how much publicity is needed, and so on.

It may be that tools need to be implemented in offices internationally, or in different departments around your organisation. It is far more straightforward to oversee all aspects of implementation when you are working on a tool in your office, rather than one overseas. If you conduct a pilot project in your own office you will be able to replicate it more easily in overseas offices by utilising your lessons learned, already having processes and tools in place and tried and trusted methods laid out. It is important to note, however, that different offices may have different cultures and habits in relation to knowledge sharing. There have not been many studies on the topic of overcoming cultural differences in organisations for implementation. However Desouza and Evaristo[19] outline three approaches to rolling out KM globally, which essentially vary in degrees of ownership and control for individual offices. The

---

18 See n 5 above.

19 K Desouza and R Evaristo "Global Knowledge Management Strategies" (2003) 21(1) *European Management Journal* 62–67.

moderate approach consists of the headquarter office setting out the programme and broad policies but leaving execution to the regional offices. This approach fits in with the idea of employee empowerment, and it will allow offices with different cultures or technologies to take on the overall KM idea but also streamline it into their working practices, by managing the technologies or objectives for the tools themselves. It is best, as part of your buy-in exercise when identifying knowledge advocates and growing your knowledge sharing culture, to also think about employees in other offices, and find out how their practices and culture differ from yours.

By rolling tools out in one office or area of the business at a time, and learning from these as you go, you will refine the process and ensure it goes more smoothly at each iteration. The same goes for the different facets of your strategy, don't try to roll everything out all at once, particularly with larger tools or initiatives. By implementing and launching one tool at a time you can learn as you progress and refine your process.

7. Conclusion

Implementing a KM strategy is a rolling and fluid process. It involves initiating and launching projects and tools little by little, and building on the groundwork laid from each of them to begin the next iteration of your strategy. Many factors come into play for successful implementation, which can be split between focussing outwardly on creating a knowledge sharing culture in your firm, and then looking inwardly at your and your team's processes. For the former, ensuring you have support and buy-in, that KM is communicated clearly, that you incentivise and that you market yourself and your projects appropriately is key. For the latter, working on more tangible factors such as measuring progress, resourcing and budgeting and documenting lessons learned must be undertaken. Overall, practically implementing KM is made up of change management and project management in order to overcome knowledge barriers and successfully achieve your strategy's objectives and aims.

8. Appendix

Example of a Lessons Learned table

No.	Theme	What worked well	What can be improved	Task Owner
1				

KM governance for law firms

Porcia Newell
Licensed attorney
Anthony J Rhem
AJ Rhem & Associates, Inc

1. Introduction

Knowledge management (KM) is becoming more prevalent within law firms as well as legal departments as the practice of KM has become more mature. KM governance in law firms ensures policy adherence and the successful maintenance and management of content (information and knowledge). In the case of KM, governance provides controls to guarantee that the content stored provides the best value for the organisation.[1] Governance will detail how the various types of content including, but not limited to, legal briefs, precedent/case law, internal and external firm publications, outside legal knowledge bases and repositories will be managed. It describes the policies, procedures, roles and responsibilities, as they pertain to processes and workflows that must be executed in order to ensure governance occurs as intended. Effective governance planning and the application of the governance plan are critical for the ongoing success of the law firm KM program.

The governance plan will establish the processes and policies to:

- Avoid content proliferation.
- Ensure that legal content quality is maintained for the life of the KM program.
- Provide a consistently high quality user experience by defining guidelines for content creators.
- Establish clear decision-making authority and escalation procedures so policy violations are managed and conflicts are resolved on a timely basis.
- Ensure that the solution strategy is aligned with business objectives so that it continuously delivers business value.
- Ensure that content is retained in compliance with legal/law firm retention guidelines.

Benefits of good legal KM governance include:

- providing a business-wide common infrastructure for legal related content;
- providing more reliable and relevant searches;
- ensuring that KM delivers relevant content to its users in an effective way;
- employing best practices that will improve usability and findability of content; and

1 AJ Rhem (2015). "Organizational Issues and KM Governance: Setup options for big and small Law Firms, Keeping knowledge relevant in the face of change" [PowerPoint Slides]. International Bar Association Annual Conference.

- providing the capability to lower total cost of content development and management through increased efficiencies of content use and management.

2. Defining your content governance framework

A holistic approach is needed to properly manage and protect a law firm's client and legal business content. A holistic approach will support the firm's capability to mitigate risks, improve client service, and reduce the cost of managing content needed to bring efficient delivery of legal services.[2]

This approach includes a program that will also:

- enable lawyers to meet their professional responsibility regarding client content;
- recognise and respond to regulatory and privacy requirements that apply to firm and client content; and
- rely upon a culture of participation and collaboration within the entire firm.

2.1 Governance Board

The Content Governance Board (the Board) is responsible for establishing long-term strategic goals related to customer content that reflect the business aims of the organisation. They manage and maintain content standards ensuring any approved changes strengthen and improve the organisation's goals. The Board will be responsible for coordinating efforts across the law firm. Each area of the firm will remain responsible for standards and categories for its specific area, creating consistent messages will depend on coordinating through the board on:

- identifying and codifying new categories and standards, including communication between stewarding areas via representatives from the Board;
- handling deviations between areas in which standards or categories may be in conflict;
- agreeing to which stewarding area is the final decision maker on conflicting topics that emerge when managing content across channels; and
- determining timeframes for intentional refreshing of categorisation tools and deliverables.

The Board will consist of leadership level employees with decision-making responsibility (manager level) for content standards and KM processes and/or repositories within their area of the firm. These individuals will participate based on job responsibilities. So, for example, if a director or manager responsible for content standards in their area changes to a new role, the Board responsibility will shift to the new manager who assumes content standards responsibilities.

The Content Governance Board should comprise leadership from the following areas within the firm:

- administrative management (HR, finance, marketing, etc);
- business intelligence.;
- information security and privac;
- ethical/legal compliance;

---

2 *Ibid.*

- firm intellectual property;
- IT system administration/infrastructure;
- KM;
- litigation support;
- records and information management; and
- risk management.

With the support of senior executives this board will guide all aspects of content creation, use, retrieval, maintenance, storage, and disposition by the firm.

2.2 Governing Content Best Practices

The governing of content for the law firm environment should implement the following best practices:

- Use workflows and approval for document centres and site pages wherever official documentation is stored.
- Use version history and version control to maintain a history and master document.
- Use content types with auditing and expiration for document libraries to manage document lifecycle.
- Use site-use confirmation and deletion to manage site collection lifecycles.
- Identify important corporate assets and sites that contain personally identifiable information to be sure that they are properly secured and audited.

3. Establish your law firm KM governance model

To establish and execute governance of law firm knowledge assets it is important to follow a holistic governance model. The law firm KM governance model illustrates the various aspects of KM governance within law firms, see Figure 1: Law Firm KM Governance Model.[3] The model begins with an understanding of creating, sharing, accessing, discovering and delivering legal content (which includes information and knowledge). Sharing of information and knowledge occurs through many areas within the firm. Much of the sharing is facilitated through the law firm's knowledge repositories. Laws firms also have to account for the need to access outside research repositories. These repositories include sources such as WestLawNext®, LexisNexis®, and VersusLaw®. Once the content is accessed, pertinent content is discovered and then delivered to the right legal personnel to be leveraged by the law firm.

In the centre of the law firm, governance model content governance occurs. Content governance provides the policies, practices and procedures to optimise cost and risk both from the perspective of creating, sharing, accessing, discovering and delivering content with the system's capabilities to store, protect, secure and preserve the law firm content. The bottom component of the law firm governance model information technology (IT) systems are represented. The systems within the law firm provide the mechanisms to store, protect, secure and preserve the law firm content.

3 *Ibid.*

Figure 1: Law firm KM governance model

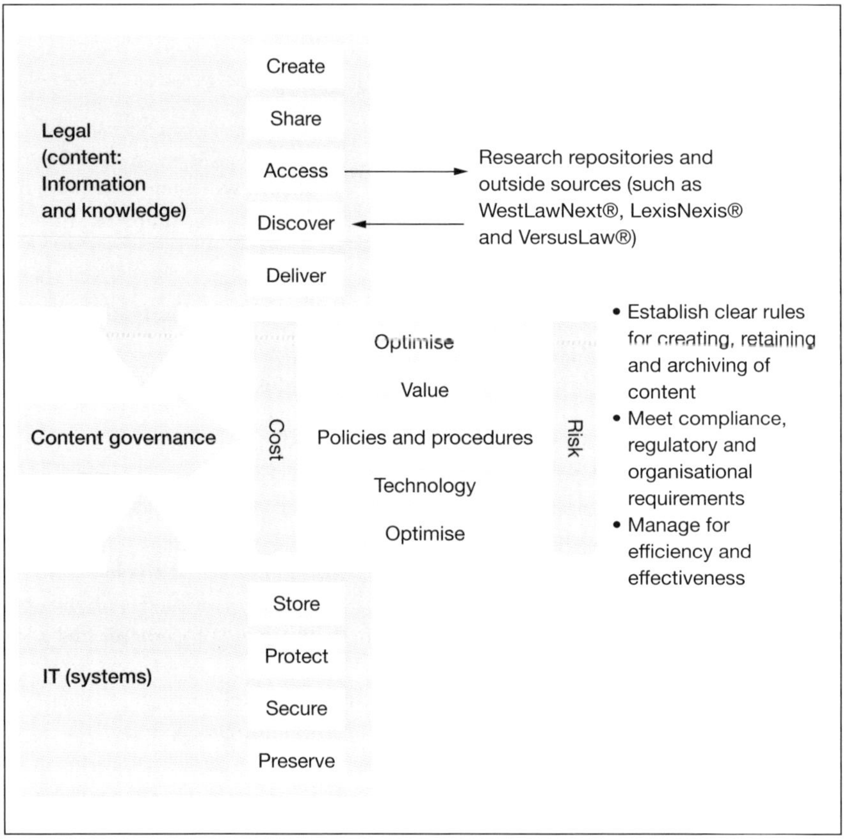

The model illustrates the following aspects:

- The need to ensure synchronisation between content stewardship and management.
- The connection to governance where policies and procedures are applied.
- The establishment of rules for creating, retaining and archiving content.
- Applying compliance, regulatory and organisational requirements.
- The alignment with the various systems that store, protect, secure and preserve the content.

Effective content governance adds value to law firms by providing:

- compliance and regulatory adherence to satisfy auditors and regulators by developing data management environments leveraging technology and process;
- enhanced business intelligence capabilities as high-quality content drives opportunities to cross-sell and retain existing customers;
- reduced environmental complexity; and
- improved business flexibility and accelerates strategic initiatives by providing

comprehensive and predictable content environments that support effective business decision making.

4. Governance policies and benefits

4.1 Policies

Policies define rules for use; standards describe best practices. From a governance perspective, policies are usually driven by statutory, regulatory, or organisational requirements. Users are expected to meet policies without deviation. These standards are established to encourage consistent practices. This policy should be revisited yearly to identify potential changes to this retention policy.

The governance plan describes the policies, procedures, roles and responsibilities as they pertain to coordinating content governance across the entire law firm. Effective governance planning and the application of the governance plan are critical for the ongoing success of content and KM. The governance plan must have strong management support and cross-functional involvement from all areas of the firm. This will ensure regular communication with the business to promote content management capabilities and to proactively identify ways that content management can benefit the firm. This will support a coordinated governance effort across the law firm and provide the structure to enable a clear governance reporting structure.

Coordinated governance is critical. If content is flowing through processes that are not coordinated through design, then the foundation upon which content is built needs to be consistent. With all of these varying factors, content governance represents the use of best practices to coordinate standards, categorisation and processes to ensure the output created through any stewarding process is built upon consistent information which positively impacts on the overall brand experience.

Content governance coordination includes:

- identifying and coordinating dependencies between standards, content management systems, and processes;
- ensuring that content strategy artefacts (content model, taxonomy and metadata) are maintained and available for use;
- creating processes for requesting, evaluating/prioritising, making and communicating any changes between content stewarding/communication channel areas; and
- new standards or categories for verbal or visual messages need to be communicated between content stewarding areas and/or content management systems for awareness and to proactively identify potential conflict.

Coordinated governance benefits law firms by providing:

- a forum to discuss best practices and build consistency across channels for the benefit of customers;
- a cross-channel common infrastructure for all content;
- greater ability to search existing content effectively;
- content artefacts (content model, taxonomy and metadata schema) which remain relevant to users;

- clear decision-making authority and escalation procedures so issues or deviations are managed and conflicts are resolved quickly;
- greater efficiency in content development and management processes throughout the content lifecycle;
- improved client services: access to content that improves lawyer productivity, enhances knowledge sharing and collaboration, and results in faster service delivery to clients;
- risk mitigation: policies to protect content and ensure compliance with legal and ethical requirements, reducing the firm's malpractice exposure; and
- cost containment/reduction: cost reduction in the areas of real estate, human resources, discovery, litigation and legal and regulatory penalties through immediate access to pertinent, relevant and up-to-date content.

5. Executing and enforcing content governance

Policies define rules for use; standards describe best practices. From a governance perspective, policies are usually driven by statutory, regulatory, or organisational requirements. Users are expected to meet policies without deviation. These standards are established to encourage consistent practices. The following sections describe specific policies and standards that should be established for the law firm to ensure and execute governance of their information and knowledge resources.

5.1 Governance roles and responsibilities

Roles and responsibilities describe how each employee as an individual or as a member fulfilling a particular role within the law firm is responsible for ensuring the success of content governance. The following are the primary roles that contribute to defining and administering governance within the firm.

Role	Key responsibilities
Executive sponsor	Serves as the executive level 'champion' for law firm governance. The primary responsibility of the executive sponsor is the strategic positioning of governance as a critical mechanism for achieving business value and helping to communicate the value of managing and maintaining corporate knowledge within all management levels of the firm
Governance Board members	The members of this body perform oversight and enforcement of the policies, procedures, rules and requirements concerning governance of content represented by the various areas of the firm
Content Governance administration	Serves as the administrator of all Content Governance Board activities and meetings

5.2 Maintaining navigation and search

The core benefit of KM is the ability to classify, retain and find critical knowledge. Metadata and organisational structure play an important part to insure navigation and search on the applications that deliver content (ie, knowledge management system (KMS), content management system (CMS) and/or document management system (DMS)) work as designed. Navigation and search are also important for long term adoption and success of KM because they are the framework by which users find the content they are looking for. If users are unable to find the content they need, the value to the user is almost entirely lost. The KM navigation can be changed based on recommendations of the user community.

5.3 Maintaining metadata

Metadata are those elements which are used to describe, organise and administer content. These elements include but are not limited to: title, description, topic, subtopic, create date, refresh date and archive date. Any user may suggest metadata changes. This request needs to be vetted and approved before moving ahead. Metadata reuse is highly recommended. This means that metadata values should be enforced during the content creation processes. It also means that determining metadata values and their quality should not be one area's view of values. Critical metadata values will reflect the overall content structure within the law firm's knowledge repository. Metadata quality in the repository is a direct reflection on the effectiveness of content that is attainable now and in the future. The effectiveness of metadata should be measured by evaluating search relevancy, seeking inputs from law firm associates and proactive monitoring.

Measuring effectiveness is a key component of governance. Metrics are a component to measuring overall adequacy and effectiveness of the knowledge repository. Initial rollout of the knowledge repository will take some time across the firm. Experience shows even then that adoption takes time. Measurements at the beginning, middle (during adoption) and end (fully matured) can be different. The following presents practical examples of why KM governance is important to law firms.

6. Practical considerations for KM governance

6.1 Attorney-Client privilege (ACP)

A major issue facing in-house attorneys in legal departments of large institutions is how to maintain ACP. Take large financial institutions, for example. With over 200,000 employees and millions of customers, there are bound to be human resource-related issues and contentious customer service issues that require internal investigation by in-house counsel. Hence the need for confidential information gathered during these investigations to remain privileged.

(a) Hypothetical scenario

A bank teller is servicing a particularly obnoxious customer. In her haste to finish the transaction, she makes an error while processing the items. The customer then proceeds to go on an expletive-laced tirade against the teller, who is eight months pregnant. The teller calls for her manager, who does not respond and provides no assistance. The customer continues to say the vilest things imaginable to the teller. By this time, other staff members have stepped in to complete the botched transaction. The manager finally appears and asks the customer to leave. Feeling threatened and upset, the teller calls her husband and tells him what just transpired. The husband just happens to be in the area and high-tails it over to the bank to defend his wife's honour. The husband and the obnoxious customer exchange words. The obnoxious customer produces a baseball bat from the trunk of his car. Not to be outdone, the husband responds by wielding a tire iron. A scuffle ensues in the parking lot between the teller and the obnoxious customer, and the police are called.

I know you are wondering what this sad scenario has to do with legal KM. In fact, KM plays a huge role in sorting out and responding to the myriad of issues presented here. In this hypothetical situation, the customer threatened to sue the bank for the parking lot assault and the botched transaction. The teller threatened to sue the bank as well. She alleged that her manager did nothing to put a halt to the hostility that she faced, and claimed that she suffered emotional distress. Would the bank take disciplinary action against the teller for instigating the fight? Against the manager for failing to act appropriately? And what about the obnoxious customer? What would be the result of exiting the relationship with this customer? A cast of many investigators, attorneys, executives and paralegals from different lines of business will need to be engaged to resolve the issues presented here. And believe it or not, legal KM will be a major factor in closing this case.

(b) Attorney-Client privilege in a pre-litigation context

Fact finding in a pre-litigation context means that employees have to be interviewed, and documents and electronic communications need to be gathered. In the hypothetical scenario above, the branch associates must be interviewed; the teller, the manager and the entire staff will be questioned by the bank's corporate safety and security team, as well as by local law enforcement. The human resources department will undoubtedly be involved, as they will be conducting their own investigation into both the teller's and the manager's behaviour. The deposit operations group will need to be involved to evaluate the impact of dumping the obnoxious customer.

Gathering facts and collecting statements from a large number of people across different lines of business can be challenging, and keeping that information under ACP is daunting. We don't want an email chain containing proprietary information or even worse, admissions of liability, to become discoverable. Another major challenge is getting the importance of ACP across to lay-people, who may not understand that they 'break' privilege by forwarding or copying someone in on a privileged email chain. For example, if the manager in the scenario above has no understanding of what ACP is or why it is important, he may not take care to maintain it. If he is leaving for vacation in the middle of the investigation, he may forward emails or share documents related to the investigation with his assistant manager, thinking that the assistant manager can cover for him while he is out. What the manager has essentially done, is destroy ACP by forwarding privileged emails and sharing privileged documents.

KM in legal departments helps alleviate concerns around ACP. If only certain employees are given access to the KM folder for a particular matter, the number of people who have access to privileged information is limited, and the likelihood that privileged information will become discoverable because it was inadvertently shared, is diminished. KM allows employees to send relevant documents directly to the appropriate location in the KM application, reducing the likelihood that privileged information will be intercepted by unnecessary parties.

KM systems allow in-house legal professionals to conduct investigations more efficiently, maintain information, and distribute information on a 'need to know' basis. This is essential for in-house litigation practice. Furthermore, having a document collection process that can be followed by non-legal people is easier than trying to explain/maintain ACP outside of the KM application. Finally, KM systems allow attorneys to efficiently create privilege logs.

6.2 Document preservation

KM also plays an important role in a law firm's or in-house legal department's ability to preserve documents. The capability to preserve documents and store them in a central location is essential when conducting internal investigations within an organisation. Banks, for example, need to collect and store documents and electronic communication relevant to internal investigations; either to evaluate whether or not to litigate, or determine how to manage an in-house investigation. In a pre-litigation context, documents collected in anticipation of litigation are, again, protected by attorney-client privilege. In cases of associate theft, conflict of interest, or other misconduct, legal department KM capabilities will allow HR and other decision makers to efficiently make appropriate personnel decisions, because all of the relevant documentation will have already been submitted to the KM application.

(a) Preservation notices

When a Bank or other large institution receives a notice to preserve evidence, they have a continuing legal obligation to preserve and protect information and evidence which may be relevant to pending litigation. KM applications provide a centralised repository for collection and storage of documents, email communications, video surveillance and photographic evidence. The KM application will allow this information to be managed on a case-by-case basis, and access to the file can be restricted to in-house and/or outside counsel.

(b) Work product management

An attorney's brief bank, template letters, legal research, legislative updates and contracts are all extremely important documents. In-house counsel can use KM applications to manage these kinds of documents efficiently. For the in-house attorney, KM applications allow legal department personnel to organise state-specific template letters and contracts, for example. This capability is essential because large organisations which conduct business nationally or even globally, must maintain content which meets state and/or country-specific legal and compliance requirements.

(c) ***Business considerations***

Perhaps the most important reason that large law firms should have KM capabilities, is the fact that most legal departments of banks and other large corporations will not even hire a law firm that doesn't have KM capabilities. Large institutions want to know that their matters are being handled efficiently. If both the law firm and the client have the ability to share materials across the same KM platform, the cost to produce and ship documents will be reduced. If a firm can tout reduced billing costs because this particular technology allows them to offer their services more efficiently, large corporations are more likely to retain the firm that can do that.

From a practical standpoint, KM applications allow the firm and the client to communicate securely. If the KM application allows the parties to send encrypted information, the corporation's privacy policies are maintained, and customer information is protected when communicating with outside counsel.

6.3 KM governance challenges for law firms

Understanding where to find the right content which is buried deep within your firm's thousands of research repositories and outside sources (such as, WestLawNext®, LexisNexis®, and VersusLaw®) is a challenge for all law firms. Having an understanding of who in the firm has knowledge of specific content and wondering if what you have in your repositories is up-to-date and relevant is another essential challenge to overcome. Multiply that by the number of trial and appellate briefs, memoranda, pleadings, depositions, emails, letters and spreadsheets prepared by inside and outside counsel alike and the challenge becomes even more daunting. Without incorporating governance your firm runs the risk of paying for research over and over again.

All firms will rely on continuous communication and education to drive adoption of new policies and procedures that will govern the use and storage of content. These policies and procedures govern content from client representation records and administrative information from key business units (eg, HR, accounting, marketing, conflicts, firm management, etc).

Some of this content firms have within official repositories and/or shared drives and it is organised in a meaningful way (ie, law department, client, matter). All of this content is in dire need of a structured, multi-year plan to address its management and maintenance.

Today's increasingly tech-savvy associates and partners want access to content from any mobile device or cloud storage. This has created security challenges and concerns. While some firms establish policies that don't allow employees to sync their smartphones, others do with provisions, including the ability to remotely clean all content if the device is reported lost or stolen. When it comes to cloud-based services, the cloud creates an environment where the firm's content must be secured, managed and maintained based on increased privacy and security policies. This becomes even more challenging if the firm doesn't know exactly where the content is located (for example, if a cloud-based vendor does not have all of its servers located in the United States).

6.4 Retention policies

Another governance challenge for law firms centres around retention policies for all content including email and transitory files. The firm must have policies to determine whether content can be archived or deleted. In order to delete information, you need to know its relationships. It is vital to develop an organised repository for firm content, which includes both client and administrative so it can be managed throughout its lifecycle. Then, develop a retention schedule that is ideally tied to the closed date of the matter for client records and the legal requirement or business need for administrative records. As firms examine email retention, it is understood that email retention is typically based on age; for example, emails in the inbox or sent items may be retained for a pre-determined amount of time and deleted or archived if not filed into the official repository by that time.

Prior to implementing an email retention policy, it will be necessary to address legacy information and provide custodians with an opportunity to file email records before they are permanently removed. Depending on the size of the firm, some forecast that auto-deleting email older than three years, for example, could free up more space. Leading-edge firms are also beginning to adopt an automated matter-closing process, effectively applying retention policies across all repositories. This helps to keep firms compliant as clients and partners join and leave over time.

Also, there is a need to have retention policies regarding transitory files. This includes voicemail, instant messaging (and text), and electronic dictation, as firms typically do not want to retain these file types for the long term. Some have set retention standards for the manual transcription of voicemail messages or implemented auto transcription technology for electronic dictation. With the increasing use of voice over internet protocol (VoIP) and voice and email integration, firms have the need to plan a policy surrounding the retention of voice audio files in advance of implementation.

Retention schedules for the applications themselves are imperative. Retaining voicemail for up to 30 days before deleting automatically, or opting not to retain instant messages once the conversation window has been closed are just two examples of managing this type of information. Some firms use instant messaging software that automatically saves conversations in the user's mailbox, where they would be retained based on the email retention schedule.

7. Summary

KM is becoming more prevalent within law firms as well as legal departments as the practice of KM has become more mature. KM policies, procedures, techniques and technologies have been proven in other industries to the point where legal entities are taking notice.[4] Governance for law firm content (information and knowledge) is essential for the success of any firm or department. From defining the content governance framework and governance model, to identifying, executing and enforcing governance process and policies; content governance is a complex discipline to implement. This complexity presents challenges for the firm which they must address in order to be successful.

4 AJ Rhem, *Knowledge Management in Practice* (Boca Raton, FL: CRC Press, 2016).

Attorney-Client privilege presents challenges for managing and maintaining sensitive content. It is the policies, processes and procedures of the firm that will make the difference in ensuring the firm maintains client trust. Document preservation is akin to retention; both support the firm's continuing legal obligation to preserve and protect information. Meanwhile, work product management enables the firm to execute specific governance on the organisation's localization-specific content to meet state, region, province and/or country-specific legal and compliance requirements.

To realise the potential that KM governance offers to law firms, a holistic governance plan that includes a board to execute and monitor the management and maintenance of content must be implemented. The KM governance details that have been presented in this chapter provide the roadmap and consistent structure for implementing governance in law firms. All content developed and accessed by the firm needs to take advantage of the firm's governance processes, policies and procedures. Deploying a KM system, content management system and/or document management system must incorporate the necessary governance of digital assets to ensure they are kept relevant, accessible and up-to-date.

Knowledge professionals in law: demonstrating value and retaining talent in a changing legal environment

Tara Pichardo-Angadi
Norton Rose Fulbright LLP

Writing about a career in law in 2016, albeit the highly specialised career of the knowledge professional, means having to consider how disruptive legal technology and other changes to the legal market might impact on such professionals.

Consider the prediction that we may soon enter the era of artificial intelligence based legal problem solving, where an online service containing the underlying legal material could understand the legal questions asked of it by a user and analyse and classify the fact pattern of the question before giving the user an answer delivered by way of legal advice.[1]

A knowledge professional whose role is limited to carrying out basic research might see that role taken over by such an online service. Regardless of the timescale of such a tool being developed, there are reasons, inherent to the structure and content of knowledge roles, which make this scenario unlikely.

Knowledge professionals carry out a huge variety of tasks, ranging from the legal research described above to training lawyers and clients, developing templates to bring greater quality and consistency to legal documents whilst improving profitability, developing client products to showcase the expertise of their area of practice and much more, as will be discussed in this chapter.

Many developments in legal technology will actually make knowledge professionals more central to our business than ever. This is true whether the technology, such as document automation or e-learning, requires the input of content, which will often fall to our knowledge lawyers. It is also true when the technology requires lawyers to consider possible applications to their area, such as predictive analytics for case management tools, logic tools developed to deliver legal advice in certain areas. Also, in a changing profession, where a more diverse workforce is developing, including contract lawyers, alumni, apprentices and so many others, having a strong knowledge team devising bespoke training and tools will ensure the consistent quality which law firms need more than ever.

1 R Susskind, *Tomorrow's Lawyers* (Oxford University Press), p49.

1. What do we mean by knowledge professionals?

1.1 Professional support lawyers or knowledge lawyers – what's in a title

A few decades ago, London-based law firms created the role of the professional support lawyer. This title was used to describe lawyers who, after an early career as fee-earners[2] or operational lawyers, move into a role supporting their practice area as a senior technical adviser. The role evolved and morphed over the decades and the purpose of this article is to give some insight into the scope of knowledge roles as they currently exist in many international, regional and local law firms. We will look at the competencies required for people in knowledge roles as well as the potential career development for lawyers in these roles.

Before we start discussing the range of roles that come under the knowledge banner, there is a preliminary point to note relating to the title of the professional support lawyer. Firms have given people in this type of role different names over the years: knowledge management (KM) lawyers, practice development lawyers, professional resource lawyers and my personal favourite (well alright, I might be biased!) knowledge lawyer. Can we learn anything from this lack of naming convention? Probably that the constantly evolving scope of this type of role has encouraged firms to be more creative in knowledge lawyer[3] titles than in their 'fee-earning' counterparts. The changes also reflect a shift in how the profession has wanted to be perceived, moving from the more passive 'support' to a more active 'management' or even a simple 'knowledge' focus.

1.2 Knowledge managers and other supporting roles

Alongside knowledge lawyers, the need for support at a junior level is often expressed. Knowledge lawyers are a relatively expensive resource and one which should be used carefully and shielded from too many administrative tasks. Enter the paralegal or non-legally qualified executive assistant, whom I will refer to as the knowledge assistant. The range of tasks performed by such knowledge assistants will depend on whether they are legally qualified or not but could cover tasks such as training administration, simple precedent updates, current awareness, database management and intranet management.

In some cases, these knowledge assistants go on to become knowledge managers as they gain seniority; sometimes the knowledge managers perform a different role altogether, especially in cases where the knowledge manager is actually managing the knowledge content of a whole office or region. This brings me to the distinction between those knowledge professionals who produce content and those who manage content produced by others.

1.3 Content, process or a mix of both

Predictably, only those professionals who are lawyers are on the content producing

---

2 Many professional support lawyers and other knowledge professionals record their time to client matters, making this distinction irrelevant.

3 I'll stick to this denomination from now on.

end of the spectrum. However, not all knowledge lawyers produce content. Those knowledge lawyers who are relied on by their teams to produce content (training, precedents, client material) will generally have significant experience in their area of expertise. They are able to add value by acting as technical advisers to their team. Sometimes, a knowledge lawyer might be appointed outside of his area of expertise and his role will often in that case become more of a hybrid.

On the other end of the spectrum, many knowledge professionals only manage the content produced by others. Actually, this is very much the norm outside of the legal industry. We seem to be the only ones who have developed this role of technical expert within the knowledge function – in most industries for example, the technical experts are in the operational business units and the KM team is in charge of ensuring that these experts share their knowledge with colleagues through collaboration, knowledge retention and transfer and other KM tools and techniques.

In any event, even those knowledge lawyers who are on the content producing side will generally also have a role in managing the content produced by their team. It will be their role to ensure knowledge developed by their team in a matter context percolates into the products they develop and maintain: an illustration of the virtuous circle will see the partner call on the knowledge lawyer to advise on a particularly thorny legal issue in a transaction concerning a new area of law, the knowledge developed through that query will then make it into a guidance note and will be used to update training on the topic.

1.4 Systems and other project focused roles

Many firms have knowledge systems teams, working alongside IT departments to act as business advisers to IT and decipherers of technological needs supporting the firms' KM and sometimes practice management. These roles may be held by lawyers and non-lawyers alike – their common attributes are being technologically savvy and understanding business needs of lawyers. These roles are crucial to the success of knowledge IT projects but more importantly, they are often a first port of call for lawyers' requests regarding new tools. Of course, these roles might equally be filled by project-specific business analysts or other similar roles within IT departments. The important feature of all these is that they can serve as catalysts of changing business needs to feed a law firm's IT function.[4]

1.5 Other models?

(a) Partners

Some law firms have opted for a knowledge partner model, whereby certain partners are given responsibility for knowledge content in certain areas. These roles will generally require knowledge lawyers and others working alongside the partner to support them. In other cases, the knowledge partner will have a role managing the knowledge team. Having strong knowledge champions at partner level is a huge

4 See also later development on lawyers involved in legal technology.

advantage in getting buy-in to knowledge projects and shows great commitment from the firm to knowledge.

(b) *Research lawyers' billing time*

One final category which might come under the label of knowledge professional is a type of fee-earning lawyer I have come across in Canada: the research lawyer. Research lawyers act as the technical experts, honing in on particularly important and/or urgent legal research in another lawyer's matter. These research lawyers will come in and out of matters as the need for specific research or advice emerges. I have not seen this category of fee-earner carry out the other traditional tasks required of knowledge lawyers.

1.6 Outer reaches of knowledge: legal project managers, practice managers, process improvement lawyers?

More recently, other categories of non-fee-earning lawyers have emerged to support the changing practice of law.

In addition to knowledge and compliance/general counsel teams where non-fee-earning lawyers have been embedded within law firms for decades, there are now pockets of lawyers working on legal process analysis, legal project management, legal technology projects and wider practice management roles.

It is probably useful to say a few words about a few of these roles as there are closer connections between them and the knowledge roles described above.

Legal project management and legal process analysis roles can be treated together. At the outset, when looking at improving the efficiency on a particular type of matter, a legal process lawyer will need to analyse the matter and disaggregate it into component parts, each of which might be further analysed to consider how best to structure the work and resource it. Further down the line, with project management tools and techniques to hand, a legal project manager will be able to ensure the matter progresses and the work product is delivered seamlessly to the client, regardless of how it was resourced.

Legal technology development requires lawyers who are technologically astute and who also know about their area of practice and its potential needs. To give a practical example, a lawyer in my firm has developed our Court Intelligence Database,[5] which allows for the easy search by a variety of factors of banking litigation currently proceeding through the English courts. In developing the process by which the vast volume of content was input into the tool, this lawyer used his knowledge of statistical analysis to model the reduction of 'big data' to manageable proportions.

As the description of all these roles shows, there is a wide variety of roles which might live within a knowledge function. The main thing to remember here is that there is no one size fits all, what counts is having the right people in the right place doing the right thing. This will depend on a law firm's overall strategy, size and

5 Adam Sanitt, Knowledge Of Counsel and our Head of Disputes Knowledge developed this tool, which at the date of submission had been nominated for the 2016 Legal Week Innovation Award.

financial performance among other factors. Whatever the context, the resourcing model should allow flexibility so the roles can evolve as the business needs do.

2. What does 'good' look like? Knowledge professionals' competencies

Now that we have set the scene with a compendium of the roles which could make up a knowledge team, we should look at what 'good' looks like. Given the wide diversity of roles described, we will focus on the knowledge lawyer for the remainder of this chapter.

2.1 What's in the role? Define this before setting competencies

In order to assess a knowledge lawyer's performance, we should start by defining what is in and out of scope for his role. This will depend on what other resources you have to support your knowledge efforts.

Let's assume a mixture of internal and client-facing focus covering the range of activities from current awareness, precedents, client updates, internal and client training and technical fee-earner support. This mixture will vary from role to role with add-on tasks such as business development or practice management support depending on the needs of the user group.

2.2 Assessing competencies

Each of these tasks can then be assessed according to a scorecard showing what is expected at any given level of seniority. This can be done by setting competencies for the knowledge lawyers in much the same way as competencies might exist for other categories of lawyers in the firm. This will allow knowledge lawyers' technical knowledge and professional and other skills to be assessed in a consistent way across the firm.

In addition to setting competencies for the knowledge lawyers as a whole, individual key performance indicators might be set on an annual basis as part of the performance review. These can be set specifically to cover the projects of the knowledge lawyer in question. This will allow the knowledge lawyer's deliverables to be assessed based on criteria which have been agreed in advance. Setting these can be challenging: it may be difficult to reach the right balance between the quantitative and the qualitative. Examples of quantitative KPIs might include on the client-facing side numbers of visitors on your knowledge pages, attendance at client training, and potentially fees generated by your paid-for knowledge products. Internal quantitative KPIs could include hours of training delivered, numbers of precedents developed or maintained, and hours recorded to matters in relation to queries. Qualitative KPIs will revolve around positive feedback from clients and internal users, success stories of knowledge products leading to client instructions, and risks avoided thanks to quality knowledge products being available. The right measures will largely depend on the level of maturity of your firm, your knowledge role job descriptions and competencies and what your management structures need to see as a result.

2.3 Case study on a knowledge lawyer competency framework

When it came to first setting our competency framework alongside the knowledge career structure, which I will describe later, we took as a starting point the associate competency framework which a lot of thought had gone into and which was well bedded down in the firm.

Certain elements were added to reflect the different focus of the knowledge lawyer, but as a general rule we found that much of the competencies which we expected of our associates were also expected of our knowledge lawyers. The main headings of our competency framework are therefore very similar even though the detail differs to reflect the specific requirements in a knowledge lawyer role.

To illustrate this, let me break down one of our key competencies around applying and developing legal and technical competence. Core to this, we would expect a knowledge lawyer to: demonstrate exceptional technical and intellectual ability, be commercial and practical in their application of the law, have sound drafting skills, be able to develop and deliver effective training, understand and develop systems to capture and share knowledge, and promote a knowledge sharing culture. Each of those skills will then show some examples of what 'good' looks like at the various levels of a knowledge career, much in the way of a balanced scorecard.

3. How to retain talent? Knowledge professionals' careers

3.1 That was before – a relatively young profession

When I embarked upon the second part of my career as a knowledge lawyer, there was no recognised path for knowledge lawyers to progress upon. There was a very flat structure and an assumption for many that this was the end of the road.

The result was that for many of the more ambitious amongst us, taking up a knowledge career was a risk as there was limited visibility of what the future would hold.

This started changing over the course of the noughties and by the time we had our first round of promotions to Of Counsel,[6] the wheels had been set in motion for the design and implementation of a new knowledge career structure.

3.2 How to stand out and be noticed? Promotion is the name of the game

At this stage I can only talk to my own experience and that of the peer groups of knowledge lawyers who have been promoted during my current mandate as regional head of knowledge.

Once competencies and KPIs have been set, knowledge lawyers will know what to work towards and how their deliverables should be assessed to demonstrate their true value. This should be part of an ongoing discussion around what will be expected by the business to support a case for the knowledge lawyer to be promoted.

The assessment can be made objectively, based on common criteria applicable across your entire team.

---

6 In 2010 we appointed our first round of four Knowledge Of Counsel, with another two in 2014, three in 2015 and again two in 2016.

Of course, as in many other careers, there will often also be a large element of self-promotion which will come into play. Talent may be recognised *per se*, but a promotion will often be the result of the knowledge lawyer in question being consistent in informing management of their achievements.

3.3 Case study on knowledge career structure

We embarked on the journey of introducing a career structure globally back in 2012. The project team included representatives from various regions and practice areas. Our first step was to map out the various job titles which existed in knowledge to find where our team was at the outset. Once we had decided that we wanted our knowledge career structure to mirror the associate career structure we had implemented previously, our job was simplified and we had the benefit of our associate competencies to help us develop the knowledge competencies.

We decided on job titles for consistency: on the qualified lawyer side the entry level is the knowledge lawyer, which is roughly equivalent to our senior associate. The next step is the senior knowledge lawyer, which is equivalent to a more experienced senior associate. Finally, our Knowledge Of Counsel are our most experienced knowledge lawyers and recognised go-to advisers in their area. On the systems, administrative and less experienced or unqualified lawyer side our knowledge assistants may move up to knowledge manager status when they have acquired the requisite experience and competencies.

Finally, we mapped our existing roles into the new structure. This was of course preceded by communications around the project and followed by individual meetings to explain the changes to team members.

The more fundamental change in our case was the increased expectation that knowledge lawyers would have a strong client-facing role and would increasingly be seen as go-to experts in their field. This was adopted by our knowledge team with some trepidation but much enthusiasm – the career structure had been long awaited and we were able to retain our talented knowledge lawyers and hire a number of excellent candidates, of a calibre we might not have been able to attract previously.

All in all, this was a success for our firm and one which I am personally very proud of.

4. Conclusion

In the current context of change in the legal services market, flexibility is the key to future proofing knowledge roles. After our initial focus on ensuring knowledge lawyers were more consistently client-facing, we have been focusing on efficiency and using knowledge as a tool to ensure greater profitability. Some firms have dedicated process improvement teams but in others, this is an additional role which might be taken on by the knowledge team. In many cases, knowledge lawyers are playing an increasingly important part in technology and practice management type projects. This adaptability is a sign of the knowledge professional's agility in this world of constant change. It is the sign of a career with a future.

Taxonomy, informal tagging or both: master data, processes and benefits

Jonna Vainikainen
Castrén & Snellman Attorneys Ltd

1. Introduction

Can good content management be a key to a better client experience? Many companies collect data like antiques – not knowing what to do with it. The ability to capture, process and reuse knowledge is extremely important. Law firms are impacted by changes in technology, the growing volume of information, big data, social networks and even robotics. This means the role of knowledge management (KM) is changing too.

Companies grow and become more complex. Data can be stored easily in many different places and systems. The volume and velocity of information is snowballing. In many cases data is unstructured and cannot be used to benefit business. With data volumes growing exponentially, law firms need to be able to search and analyse information quickly. Employees need to adopt new approaches and technologies to manage their workload. This will put increased pressure on information quality and sourcing, efficiency and consistency, flexibility, knowledge sharing as well as training and learning new skills. All of this is also a challenge for KM departments.

The main question I will be looking at in this article is, do law firms need a formal taxonomy in order to cope with these changes or is it possible to use only informal tagging?

2. Taxonomy

2.1 What is a Taxonomy?

Taxonomies have been used in many fields for a long time. A taxonomy is a traditional hierarchical vocabulary in which all the terms are agreed and they constitute a common language within the organisation. With a good taxonomy users can search information using standardised names and metadata as well as drill down from a general category to a more specific one. Information can be divided by importance or relevance and it can be viewed from different angles, for example from a client or assignment perspective. The key is to organise data logically and consistently into categories and subcategories, finally creating taxonomy.

2.2 Stumbling blocks in taxonomies

Typically, taxonomies have been used in library systems, document management systems and later in various search engines. One problem that firms confront is that taxonomies are not congruent, which means that they can be different in different systems, which I believe is the main reason for not implementing enterprise search tools. It is just too complicated, expensive and time-consuming to unify the standards of the organisation when older systems may not even support the adding, modifying or re-naming of fields. There is taxonomy management software on the market, but the biggest issue is not the software, but agreeing the standards within the organisation. This is because taxonomy is much more than IT, it is 80% people and processes and only 20% technology. Before actually developing the taxonomy, you'll need to define your scope, purpose and types of content formats.

3. Tagging

3.1 What is tagging?

If taxonomies are too time-consuming and expensive, could informal tagging do the trick? Due to the growth of social networking, tagging has become more popular. Who hasn't seen a hashtag in which metadata is marked with an #. This form of tagging is used in microblogging and social networking services such as Twitter, Facebook and Instagram. In tagging, users can create and add the tags and can include links to other items. Today's tagging takes the meta keywords concept and recycles it. Simple and easy.

Tagging allows unlimited possibilities to classify an item. Instead of belonging to one category as in a traditional taxonomy, an item may have several different tags. Compared to a hierarchical limited taxonomy, users can classify each item as they wish. In a typical tagging system, there is no explicit information about the meaning or semantics of each tag, and a user can apply new tags to an item as easily as applying older tags.

Hierarchical taxonomies can be cumbersome and slow to change. The flexibility of tagging allows users to classify knowledge in the ways that they find useful, but the personalised variety of terms can create challenges when searching.

3.2 Knowledge tags

Knowledge tags are valuable for preserving organisational intelligence that is often lost. This intelligence is often stored only in the minds of individuals and even if the knowledge is captured it is typically isolated and unharnessed by the organisation and disconnected from information resources. In the past years, the legal market has changed. Clients have become more demanding; they want more for less. If law firms can capture the valuable knowledge of lawyers, process it and reuse it efficiently, this will intensify work, reduce costs and create efficiency; requirements that clients already take for granted.

Knowledge tags are more than traditional non-hierarchical keywords or terms, they describe aspects of information and allow users to create a cross-resource base of knowledge. Knowledge tagging is generally more flexible than other KM classification systems. Knowledge tags add additional value, context and meaning to the information. Knowledge tags capture knowledge in the form of, for example, notes, comments, descriptions, classifications, guides or references that are collected in tag profiles. Conceptual knowledge tags describe procedures, lessons learned and facts that are related to the information resource and anecdotal knowledge, a memory of a particular case that may not surface without a specific context or situation.

3.3 Tacit knowledge

Personal, or tacit, knowledge is the information of an organisation or its employees. It is highly connected to the actions, procedures, routines, values and feelings of individuals. It is very personal, which means that it is often difficult to collect and transfer. Learning by doing and learning together is the best way to share tacit knowledge. In this case it is critical to share knowledge and know-how and to create new information, not necessarily to document it.

3.4 Stumbling blocks in tagging

When users can freely choose tags the result can be incoherent and inefficient. If the tags create metadata that includes homonyms, which means that the same tags are used with different meanings, synonyms and even different inflections of words, the user may experience navigation and searching difficulties.

4. Master data management

In this next section, I discuss a particular type of taxonomy, master data management. In many firms, data management can mean 'copy management' and people still spend a great deal of time searching for relevant information. The ability to exploit data requires consistent information specified in every system – or at least in the most important information of the organisation.

4.1 Master data management in general

Master data management is defined as a technology-enabled discipline in which business and IT work together to ensure the uniformity, accuracy, stewardship, semantic consistency and accountability of the organisation's official, shared master data assets. Explained more simply, it is a collection of responsibilities, processes, practices and tools that are used to describe and govern and ensure the quality of an organisation's relevant information. The most important thing is to know what terms are used for the same information in different systems.

Organisations do not need a monolith system, the main thing is to have a strong standard for the information that is used throughout the organisation.

4.2 Data governance

(a) Processes

Organisation data governance is a control system to ensure that the data entry meets the agreed standards. This is a process not a department or function, even though it involves various departments and functions. The fundamental process is to 'fulfil the client's need', and an organisation's goal should be to provide services through client experience. This is crucial, because master data management, data modelling, processes, analysis and continuous improvement begin with identification and

Figure 1: Master data management elements

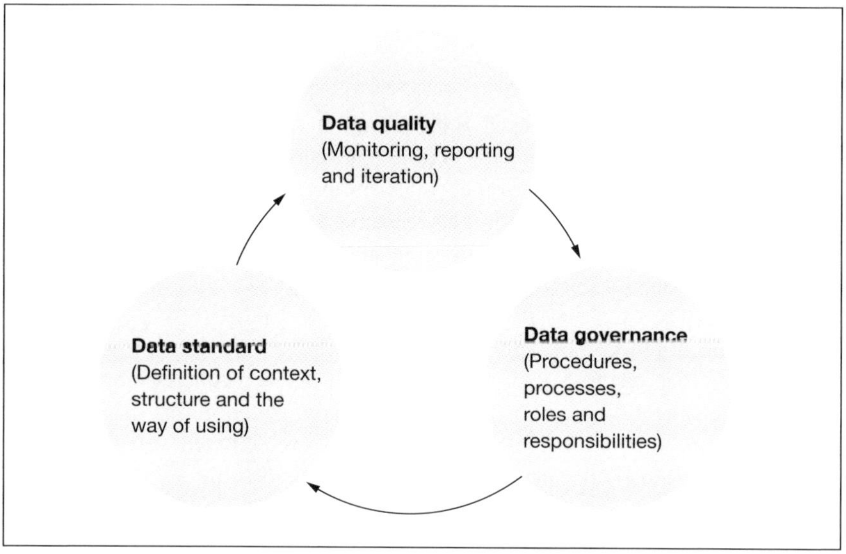

scoping. Start with the end in mind: what will fulfil the client's needs. The expected result needs to be clarified before diving into the data, modelling and process activities. The result is initially the most important part to comprehend, because the purpose of a business process is to produce a specific result. A client's need could be 'receive a client-oriented proposal' and the partner result could be 'send an offer to the client'.

Processes are the 'DNA' of the organisation. It is good to remember that everything we do in our daily jobs is part of the process – we are the actors of the process. This is true even in law firms, though not everybody would like to admit that.

Describing an organisation's processes is a key part of master data management. When doing this, it is worth taking the effort to really think about the names given to processes. Here are three tips for good process names:

- The process name must indicate the result.
- Name the process from client's perspective.
- Name the process in the singular.

(b) *Procedures and training*

Even though the processes are the DNA, users need procedures and training in order to ensure the process runs as intended. Processes and procedures are often confused. A procedure is a set of instructions for the completion of a single task. You can align processes and procedures, for example by linking them together. The above picture depicts a complete process with tasks and responsibilities. By clicking a single task, you can drill down to the guides relating to that task, which in this case can be found in the organisation's SharePoint intranet. This is, in fact, a form of knowledge tagging.

New processes and working methods require that personnel be trained. Firms

Figure 2: Process chart linked to intranet instructions

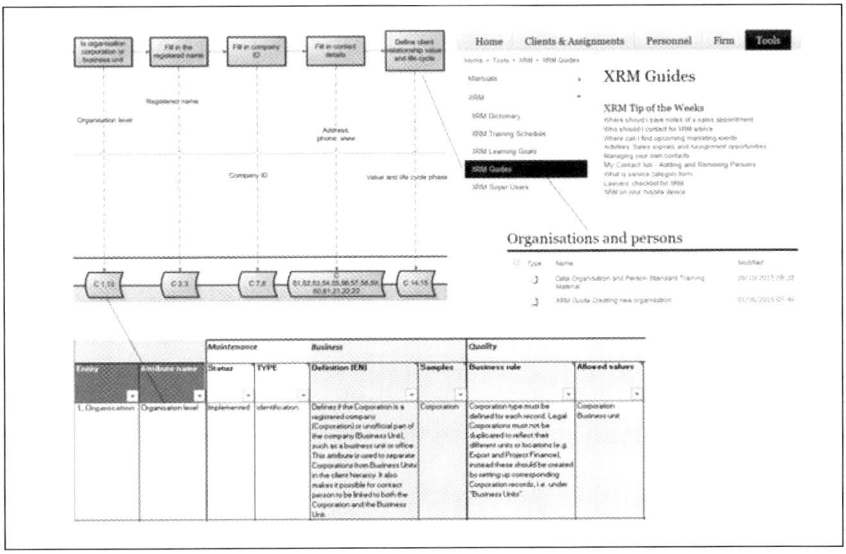

need to provide time for learning, too. The problem of the decade seems to be a lack of time. Employees need time to learn new skills and systems to succeed in their tasks. One way to help learning can be knowledge tags, which give users the possibility to add information to help others. This can be factual knowledge, for example the kind found in books and data; conceptual knowledge; expectational knowledge, which includes individual expectations, working hypotheses and beliefs; and methodological knowledge, which is derived from reasoning and strategies. These forms of knowledge often exist outside the data itself and are derived from personal experience, insight, or expertise. An example of a situation in which this kind of knowledge can be very important would be a document automation system at a law firm. In a document automation system, the most important thing is not the automated document itself (even though the system speeds up the drafting work faster), but the knowledge that senior lawyers put into the document to help others draft or negotiate the content of the document.

(c) ***Risks of poor processes***

Before going into more detail on some best practices concerning processes and master data management, I want to spend a moment going over what risks can arise if processes are not working well. From a law firm's point of view, the risks can be:

- weakening of client experience;
- loss of sales and decrease of revenue;
- increase of costs;
- weakening of quality;
- inability to fulfil statutory requirements; and
- dissatisfaction of employees.

(d) ***Roles and responsibilities***

In master data management it is important to define the owners of information and processes and responsibilities in creating and updating the information, what information to update and where. It is also important to recognise who the information is for.

In a master data management project, develop strong partner and user relationships, include subject matter specialists, for example experts in insider information, conflict checks or anti-money laundering, in the project. Try to take a user-oriented perspective. Many times developers make the mistake of 'talking IT'. It is better to give the users the possibility to deliver the message. However, it is important to remember that communication is now seen as an important part of a knowledge manager's skills, and good communication can be the key to success.

4.3 Data standard

(a) ***Why standardise?***

As mentioned above, the volume and velocity of data is constantly increasing, which is putting accuracy to the test. KM departments are coming under pressure from the growing demands of the rest of the organisation. The challenge is how to maintain quality and accuracy while responding more quickly. Data volume from an increasing number of sources is creating major challenges.

What is the danger if an organisation doesn't standardise data?

- Poor data quality can hinder the organisation's business.
- Information is hard to migrate and integrate.
- IT projects can be delayed.
- There are challenges in reporting.
- Risk management is difficult.

Data standardisation is the foundation for efficient data combination and distribution throughout the organisation. It is relevant because, for example, client information (categorisation such as value and role, sales, assignments) is needed to optimise the relevant measures for each individual client. One important thing to think about is fulfilling legal requirements, such as anti-money laundering, data privacy and insider information responsibilities, not to mention enabling sufficient reporting and analytics for the management cannot be forgotten.

(b) ***What is master data?***

Not all important information is master data. It is important to identify and define the most important information of the organisation. Master data is static information that is the essential and shared information of the organisation. It has a jointly agreed structure, content and meaning. This key information can include, for example, data about clients, products, places and employees.

(c) ***Definition of content and structure***

To standardise data, an organisation needs a defined data standard that:

- constitutes a common, understandable and unambiguous language for business critical key information (master data);
- defines what the master data organisation needs to collect and maintain from their business processes;
- represents the agreed meaning, structure, content and quality requirements for master data;
- is an essential basis for reliable reporting, exploitation of data and communication between different interest groups; and
- eases business development and implementation of new systems.

Figure 3: Data standard benefits

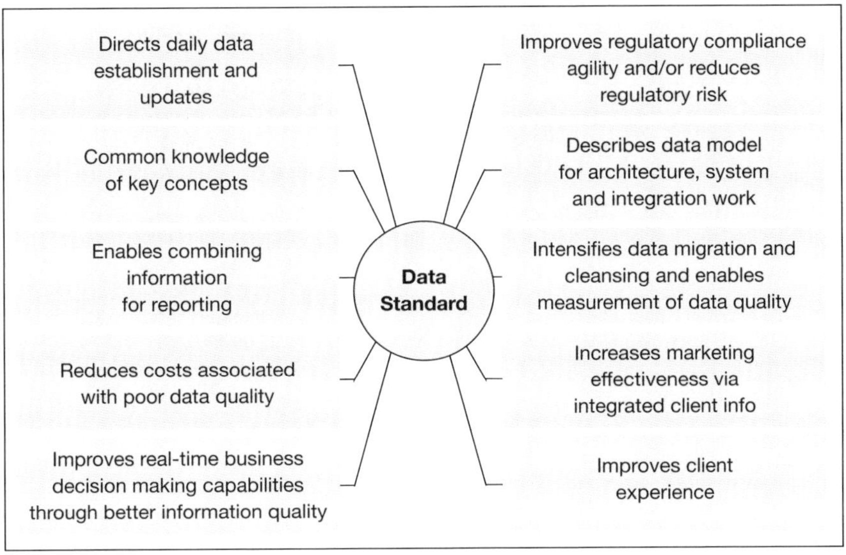

A data standard contains:

- definitions of key entities agreed throughout the organisation (eg, what we mean when we use the term 'client' or 'office of the client');
- relations and dependencies between key entities (eg, we need to establish a registered organisation above each office);
- client grouping and classification, which is based on the requirements of operative activities and reporting;
- definitions of attributes (eg, what do we mean by 'organisation trade name');
- examples of content;
- technical meta-data of attributes (eg, what alphabets to use);
- reference values of attributes (eg, standardised country pick list);
- quality requirements for entities and attributes (eg, registration number is mandatory and it needs to be filled in a specific format);
- owners for entities and attributes; and
- rights to create, update and read (CRUD) data in attribute level.

The above list presumes that an organisation has defined its master data maintenance processes and lifecycle model.

Figure 4: Entity diagram example of organisational master data

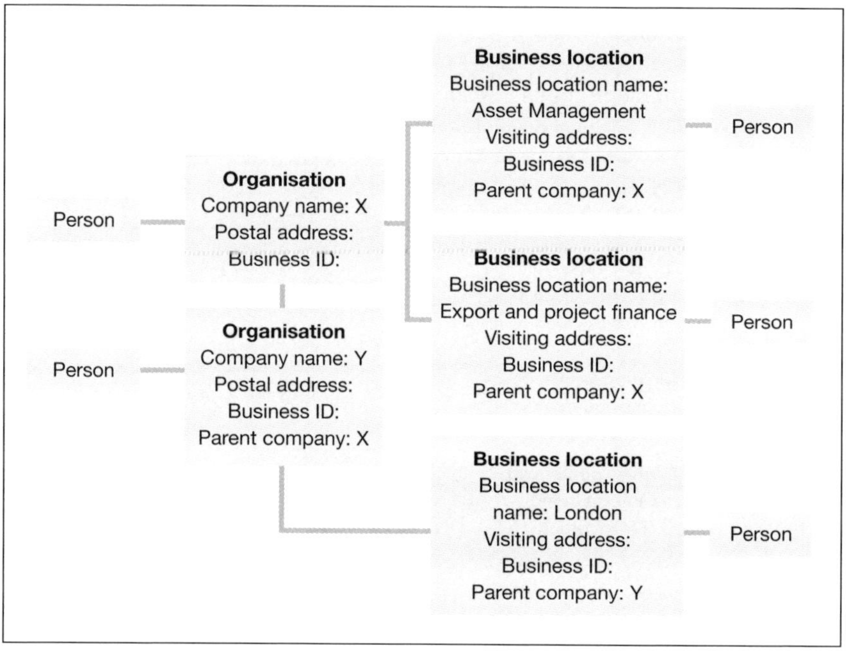

4.4 Data quality

(a) *Data quality in general*

We all know that if you're organised and systematic with your belongings, it's easier to keep your home nice and tidy, and you can find your belongings in no time. This same rule applies to the world of data as well. A lack of quality normally leads to problems in integrations and lots of manual work. The same information can be found multiple times in various systems. Poor data quality can be caused by, for example, non-uniformity of fields in different systems, a lack of important client or contact information, old information not being updated and relevant information being mixed with irrelevant information.

The system should track changes made at the entity level. The entity level, needs the following tracking information:

- time stamps for creation (created date); and
- last modification (modified date) including:
  - the creator (created by); and
  - the user who last modified the entity (modified by).

For some important fields, there should be a mechanism to track the value history at the field level. The value history includes information of the previous value, modification timestamps and the modifier reference. This information is relevant, for example in regulatory issues. As a law firm we have a statutory duty to identify the clients we assist and know their background sufficiently well to satisfy ourselves of the legitimacy of the client's assets and their purpose in using our services. Another example is the requirement to maintain electronic insider registers and enable sufficient reporting to authorities.

(b) *Data quality management process*

Once you have quality data, you need to maintain it. Data quality management also needs a specific process. It is not enough to cleanse company information once, it is crucial to define feasible processes to create, update and eventually delete the information when there are no longer any grounds to keep it. Firms need a reason to collect information and to report it and also need a means to delete the information, even on the level of a single field. After that, people need to be trained to ensure that only relevant data is updated in the system. Good data quality enables information management, good management processes and continuous improvement.

All employees can benefit from consistent and up to date information.

5. Benefits of master data management and processes

The goal of master data management is to gain business benefits throughout the organisation. There are three main direct benefits of master data management. First, consistent information saves time and money, because it intensifies work. Secondly, it enables reporting, business intelligence and analytics. For example, it can enable a 360-degree view of the client and of cross-selling between different practice groups. Last but not least, it reduces business risks and increases legal compliance.

5.1 Mapping business benefits and creating user stories

The kinds of benefits described above may not always be apparent to members of the organisation, and it is often important to be able highlight the benefits by mapping them out. One way to map business benefits is to use concrete user stories built from three factors:

- role;
- need; and
- benefit.

A role could be, for example, partner. That partner's need could be to see a 360-degree view of the key clients, and the benefit could be to create a better client experience for the client and revenue for the firm. This partner's story could be:

I am able to manage my own contacts, share information on sales activities, sales signals and assignment opportunities. I am able to manage and monitor the marketing and sales activities of the services and clients I am responsible for. I am able to draft key client plans, record planned activities and implement the planned activities. I am able to follow assignment referrals from different perspectives. I can create offers and exploit price lists. I can follow price estimates and compare them to the realised costs. I can create new framework agreements and exploit client price lists when making a new offer. I can examine and exploit financial information relating to the client and assess client value based on previous transactions and future potential.

5.2 Initial assessment of the quality of the process

An equally important part of communicating the benefits of master data management is to communicate in a clear and compelling way why the process has to change. This can be done by completing an initial assessment for the as-is process, that is, what will happen if the process is left as is? You can complete an initial assessment by answering the following questions:

Employee:

- Is there a documented process and if so, are there process tasks that are of no use?
- What parts of the process do not work and what would you change if you could?
- Do you have the necessary tools and do you get appropriate training and support to fulfil your tasks?

Process owner:

- Does the process increase or reduce client experience and satisfaction?
- Does the process use appropriate resources?
- Does the process increase or reduce employee satisfaction?

You must also provide a sense of direction by defining the goals and objectives of the to-be process. You can divide goals into subjective goals and measurable goals. A subjective goal can be the feeling "the client will love this process because..." Measurable objectives are specific targets in format:

- topic (what will be improved);
- target (what is the measurable object); and
- timeframe (when the results will be realised).

6. What about the client?

6.1 Strategy

- Strategy – what we do and how are we different?
- What clients do we serve?
- What are our clients' needs and what gives added value to them?
- How do we manage our offering to serve the clients' needs?
- What are our competitive advantages or why choose us?

6.2 Client experience

Cost efficiency, reliability and comprehensive services are taken for granted today. They have become what are called hygiene factors and they no longer bring added value to clients or make firms more client-centric compered to competitors. Clients want more. Factors that can really give added value to clients are emotional and symbolic:

- focusing on client experience and understanding the touch points – the points of contact or communication between us and our clients;
- emotion management and personalised experiences – how does it FEEL to work with us;
- storytelling – a blog can be a great tool for this;
- traditions;
- differentiation by visualisation – more pictures and graphs, less text.

It is important to think about what actions could improve your company's client experience and, at the same time, your company's competitive advantage. Here are some examples:

- Learn to be even better in understanding your clients and their businesses, and share this information more actively and systematically with others.
- Focus on finding more common benefits and touch points for our client and your firm; this will drive client loyalty.
- Improve the thinking about how your work affects your clients' daily routines and what to do to help the client feel happier.
- People want to buy from places that make them feel good. That is why it important to create an experience that keeps your clients coming back for more.
- Learn to be even more interactive with clients.

Also ask questions from a client perspective:

- Are there too many touch points?
- Do you feel happy about the process and how does the process affect your daily routines?
- Can your work be located within the process?
- Are you the person that connects the process steps?

When you start to see processes through client experience, you will see processes in a different way than they are traditionally thought of. For example, if processes don't work, what are the risks from the client point of view?

- low (causes dissatisfaction);
- medium (causes dissatisfaction and if continues can be the end of the client relationship); and
- high (immediately causes the end of the client relationship).

There are four typical obstacles to success: vision, value, execution and commitment. To make all this happen, the whole firm needs to work together towards a common target. It takes confidence and perseverance. It means continuous improvement and a willingness to learn and change.

7. How can master data and tagging help?

How can master data help us succeed in these goals? When data is well maintained, it can be used for the benefit of the clients.

Interaction with a client can be, for example, the possibility for the client to access relevant assignment information in real time. It can be done via several channels, for example, extranet, mobile, web. The feeling can be created by giving key clients added-value content, customising web page services according to the client's industry or providing clients with a visualised international network map. Only our imagination is the limit.

In this context, it is also possible to exploit tagging, for example in social media content. Many lawyers blog, and many blog systems allow authors to add free-form tags to a post, along with placing the post into categories.

The picture below is of an international network map that combines master data and tagging. For example, business partners are master data, and this is combined with locations, which is done by geographical tagging (tag for the geographical longitude coordinate).

Figure 5: Example of master data exploitation

8. How to get started in master data management

Figure 6: Master data management project lifecycle

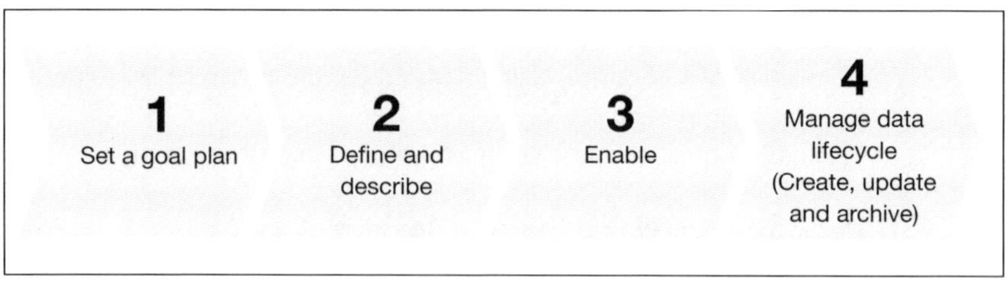

8.1 Set a goal and plan

A master data management project is not an IT project. Business is strongly involved. Set a goal and plan the project. The project manager needs to know the information and business needs. Understand your target audience and their requirements. Establish ownership of the master data and processes, organise workshops and use different channels to give the business side the possibility to be involved and give comments. Involve partners, department heads, process owners and support personnel from across the business who can represent end-user interests and who understand the business. It is critical to ensure ongoing support, so build a common language.

8.2 Define and describe

When you have set a goal and planned the project the next step is to define and describe. Keep the data standard as simple as possible to enable easy updating. Focus on the most important data first and complete it later if necessary. Know the content and the subject areas it covers:

- Define what master data is.
- Define a master system.
- Categorise the information and list information elements.
- List data sources.
- Define the person responsible for the information.
- Create a data update process.
- Combine the data.
- Update automatically.

8.3 Enable

Define who will be responsible for maintaining master data and processes. At the project phase, it can be a good idea to assign a project team with the responsibility for ongoing management, maintenance, and further development. It is also important to establish governance processes and a change control process.

8.4 Manage data life cycle

At this moment it is time to think about the change control process. When the master data project is finished, the work is not. It is important to agree how to handle the change control process. Why, who and how to review, approve and implement the necessary changes. Periodical reviews of the content and processes are required to see if there's a need for development. Master data and processes need to change over time to remain current and of value. It is also important to recognise new business opportunities that can affect current processes.

When master data is integrated into many systems, it is especially important to have a process for managing version control. For example, will the data standard be updated as new terms are added, or will there be a regular update cycle? Coordinate updates with other information systems using the master data.

8.5 Stumbling blocks in master data management

As stated above, a master data project cannot be carried out as an IT project, it needs a business driver. This ultimately boils down to communication and managing change, and the owner of the project needs to be from the top level of the organisation. Technology is set to play an even greater role in making information distribution more efficient as the range of organisation and market data continues to

Figure 7: Master data management project steps

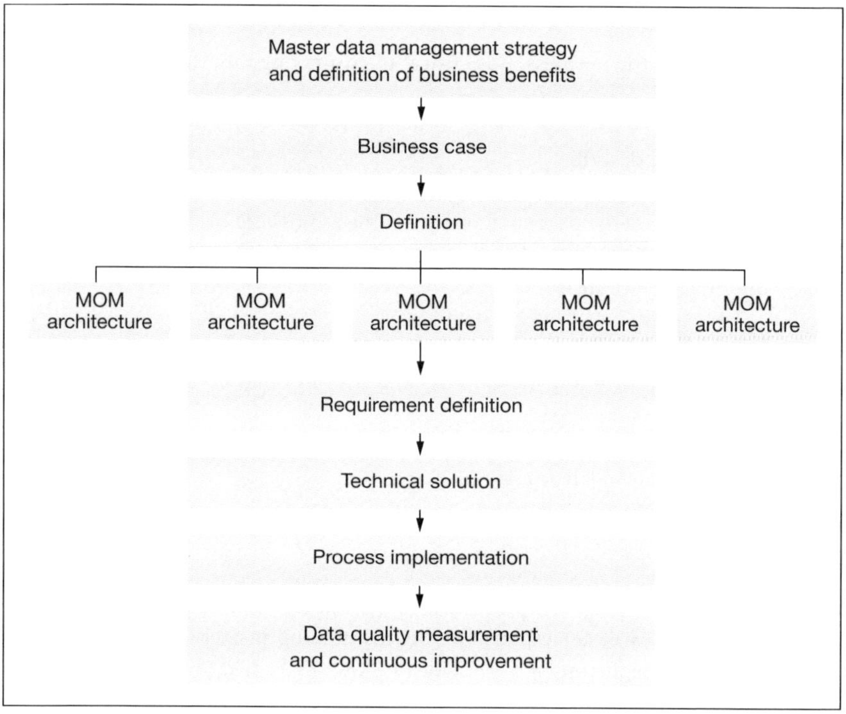

grow. Multiple channels impact the ability of KM to respond. It is also a challenge to communicate in such a way that the changes are not seen as a technical issue. Doing things consistently matters more than in what system we do them in.

In a master data management project, many people lose their freedom to do things as they wish. Employees need to change their ways of working so that the data remains consistent and at the same time learn new skills. Sometimes employees find these changes annoying, and sometimes changes mean more work for individual employees.

9. Summary

The world is changing rapidly, clients want more for less and information volumes continue to grow. In this context, what are the benefits KM can provide to law firms and lawyers? The benefits can include, for example, the ability to:

- Promote the organisation's skills to improve innovation, efficiency and performance and continuous development.
- Manage and expand the talent and experiences of lawyers at the firm.
- Introduce the relevant state-of-the-art tools and promote personnel development by providing training.
- Help system owners to develop the organisation's business systems, process owners to develop and execute core processes and manage master data.

- Identify relevant information, reuse, store and share both external and internally developed knowledge assets such as research findings and case history information.
- Get business involved and deliver information in the right way and format to the right persons to capture the attention.
- Reduce risks.

As mentioned before, a master data management project is not an IT project, but a business project. It is about managing change, and master data management and processes are a living and growing entity. The work is never finished. On the other hand, you do need to know when to stop. If possible, establish a specific role or roles under KM to get enough visibility for the importance of it. It is also of great importance to notice where master data is not needed. Tagging is a great way to capture the knowledge of different individuals and it shouldn't be limited too much.

Plan for the long term. Don't collect data just for the sake of it. Have a vision and a strategy for information management as a whole. Capture, process and reuse the knowledge to benefit the client. Keep the goal in mind: what brings value to the client and makes them happy. Good content management can be one significant factor to a better client experience!

TOP FIVE things to remember!

- Reverse your thinking (take a client's perspective).
- It's not the data itself, it's how you exploit it.
- Doing things consistently matters more than what system they are done in.
- Be close to business and create a strong relationship.
- Be innovative!

Implementing enterprise search in a law firm

Silke Gottschalk
Luther Rechtsanwaltsgesellschaft mbH

---

1. Enterprise search systems in law firms

Over the last decade, law firms are facing up to an explosion in the number of electronic documents related to case work. When performing client work, lawyers need to organise massive amounts of electronically stored information, such as client and matter details, precedents, forms, correspondence, contracts, memos, databases, emails and attachments. Therefore it is typical for law firms that this information resides in different distributed systems. By searching this scattered information, lawyers waste time and money and weaken productivity.

Enterprise search is the practice of making content from multiple enterprise-type internal and external sources searchable to a defined audience by a search engine which operates in compliance with pre-defined security and data retention regulations. In contrast to public search systems which apply search technology to documents sources on the Internet and desktop searches which apply search technology to resources of content of one single computer, enterprise search systems describe the software of search information within an enterprise, for example a law firm. Enterprise search systems automatically index and categorise data and provide a single search interface that works across multiple systems, databases and knowledge repositories such as library catalogues, firm databases or online legal resources to provide lawyers with the most relevant answers to searches in a matter of seconds. With enterprise search systems lawyers can find relevant documents and content they did not know existed before. For providing high end legal expertise towards the client it is not enough for the information to the searchable, it needs to be findable. An enterprise search solution creates a central point for finding the information needed. For a law firm, this might be a major revelation that goes to the heart of better management and leverage of knowledge for lawyers.

When implementing an enterprise search system in a law firm, a variety of issues have to be addressed. Indexing of scattered legal resources, defining business requirements for performance of the search system and defining levels of security in accordance with internal firm compliance, professional regulations and legal requirements are the decisive factors for successfully implementing enterprise search systems within a law firm.

2. Advantages of enterprise search systems for Knowledge Management (KM) in law firms

2.1 Higher level of client services

Within knowledge management, enterprise search systems are part of KM information governance dealing with security, acceptable users and retention as enterprise search systems retrieve the relevant information through standard connectors to a variety of applications, thereby analysing and processing the information and providing it to all authorised users.

In the context of a buyer's market for legal services, client demands for efficiency, predictability and cost efficiency, regulatory changes and the need for better project and process management are the key business factors for a law firm to implement enterprise search systems. With a mature, customised enterprise search system profitability can be enhanced and efficiency in client services can be maximised to deliver high quality legal services to the clients.

Enterprise search software helps law firms to uncover value in 'big data'. Unstructured data is difficult to manage and cost intensive. Law firms need to find the seeds of value hidden in their stores of unstructured data – or risk being overgrown by the competition. The key is adding structure to this data to make it accessible, searchable and findable.

The ability to search, store, share and analyse knowledge by using enterprise search systems technologies allows a law firm to exploit unique knowledge to gain competitive advantage, set up teams of specialists for legal advice and facilitate the provision of specialised high end legal knowledge by enhancing productivity and efficiency. Enterprise search systems allow a law firm to produce certain documents, information, precedents or forms more efficiently, thus resulting in a higher level of service.

Enterprise search systems make law firms independent of changes in human resources. For a law firm, lawyers leaving the firm usually means the loss of legal knowledge. If specialist legal knowledge is captured in a legal document, precedence or form, enterprise search systems may enable the law firm to capture and maintain this knowledge independent of any changes in human resources.

2.2 Source of origin

Another business advantage of implementing enterprise search systems in a law firm is that the source data remains in the place of its origin. Apart from indexing the source of origin, enterprise search systems do not convert, alter or change the source data. One major feature of enterprise search engines is their ability to deal with, and compatibility with, different document formats. Within a law firm, source documents are usually stored in different file formats. Apart from standard software applications, law firms usually provide customised individual database solutions that might contain relevant data for things such as time reporting, client and matter details. Data remains within the application of origin and will be captured and analysed by the enterprise search system. Thereby it is irrelevant whether data is structured or unstructured. As it is characteristic for law firms that knowledge exists and becomes embedded not only in documents and repositories but also in organisational routines, processes, practices, files and norms spread in a variety of internal and external databases, the fact that in enterprise search systems the source data stays in its place of origin supports and facilitates the creation and development of future knowledge within the law firm.

Mature enterprise search systems are able to deal with all kinds of database formats. In this respect, finding the different database sources and indexing them for the enterprise search might be the biggest challenge. In the end, users should be able to search all key systems within the firm from one easy-to-use interface.

2.3 Semantic search routines

Enterprise search systems use semantic search routines. This means that enterprise search systems can distinguish context and implement it in the analysis and structuring of the data searched. During the lifetime of the system constant improvement takes places which results in better search results the longer the system is in use in the law firm.

2.4 Ready to use

As enterprise search systems are available as standard appliances for law firms, they are ready to use within short notice and are already capable of dealing with the major issues law firms are confronted with regarding client privilege, access control and search routines. Data which is added to the source databases will be automatically integrated in the search routine without any further changes of the systems necessary. As databases in law firms tend to grow rapidly in content, for example client databases, if properly implemented, enterprise search systems are able to cope with changing data pools, are fully automated, self-learning and require low maintenance.

3. Key factors of implementation

When implementing enterprise search systems in a law firm, certain administrative options and technical requirements have to be met. The enterprise search software should be highly configurable, customising the search results by tweak clusters, modification of search results and fine-tuning of the system until the search provides the best possible results. As a consequence, a constant process of review and assimilation of the search results and the search routines based on firm policies, business needs and clients' expectations has to be established.

To effect performance and stability of the system, fault tolerances and back-up, storing facilities and item repositories have to be implemented within the system. Effects of time and money in client service are the result of pre-set search routines and elaborate storing facilities that enable people to connect searches to files, share of search results and pre-define updating routines to safeguard the relevance and accuracy of search results.

Another key factor is the establishment of a level of security for the search to safeguard so users can only find information or documents they are entitled to have access to. Therefore, the ability to create multiple categories of users with different permission levels is an essential requirement for successful implementation of enterprise search systems.

3.1 Establishment of business requirements

The establishment of business requirements according to the individual firm's needs is an essential first step on the way towards the implementation of an enterprise search within a law firm. This includes determination on how search is currently used in the law firm, the expectation of the users and where knowledge and information currently resides in the existing system. When it comes to creating and implementing an effective enterprise search strategy, the anticipation of what end users derive from their everyday experiences when searching for the right information is crucial.

In this respect, the needs and information landscape of the law firm has to be analysed first. If one of the relevant factors within the law firm is the search for precedents, information tagging by key words is relevant and has to be focused on when customising the enterprise search. On the contrary, if users of the enterprise search system within the law firm spend considerable time in tracking down financial information on client performance or billing, deploying an enterprise search engine that is able to cluster the relevant information, for example, according to client or file numbers, is decisive for the successful performance of the system.

To safeguard the consideration of all relevant business needs, it is useful to categorise and rank the business requirements from 'essential' to 'nice to have'. Such a category of rankings enables the law firm to find out how well the particular search engine meets the defined business requirement. Furthermore, with a detailed rank of business requirements, performance of the enterprise system can be easily assessed after implementation of the system.

When implementing enterprise search systems it might be recommendable to start with a limited approach by focusing on the most relevant business requirements and knowledge management needs within the law firm. To minimise faults and limit costs it might be better to start initially with a defined search routine for limited tasks, for example finding precedents connected to pre-defined key words. As soon as corporate executives within the law firm see the benefits of enterprise search software in action a broader implementation tailored to the firm's needs can be envisaged.

As part of that process, pointing to examples where finding information faster would have translated into increased revenue for the law firm is recommended to successfully demonstrate the advantages for investments in enterprise search technology. This implies the focus on promoting specific use case to help illustrate the technology's potential.

3.2 Content

Enterprise search is all about content and establishing a suitable search routine to analyse, categorise and submit the relevant content to the user. The understanding of content in this respect has to be bilateral: it refers not only to the content of the source of origin that has to be searched but also to the quality of the content within the search results.

3.3 Scattered information

Scattered information means content in a variety of sources of origin. It is necessary to establish and categorise the type of content the law firm has. Law firms usually have many different databases and content management systems scattered across different networks. The source system containing the content might not even be available to an enterprise search engine. The ability to analyse unstructured content, such as web pages, emails, forms and precedents and more is one of the key features of successful implementation of enterprise search systems within a law firm. With such analysis, patterns and relationships can be found during the search. Lawyers are enabled to see a unified picture of the data relevant to them, and it helps to understand the patterns and correlations that data contains.

Scattered information usually goes along with different levels of security to navigate. Within a law firm, there might be a number of sensitive documents that currently exist but are essentially hidden because the current search tools are inadequate, for example 'security through obscurity'. Within the search, documents will come up to the surface that contain sensitive information and are subject to special security. To handle this security issue, the categories and classes of content/documents have to be identified before they are integrated in the search tool. This implies a look at where the content is stored and who the creators and contributors to such sensitive content are. In this respect, knowing the content means knowing what to present to the user. Within a law firm, this implies that security issues have to be handled at a different level according to the databases indexed for enterprise search.

3.4 Financial information

Financial information on clients and individual performance of the partners or the firm is a sensitive content area to deal with when implementing enterprise search systems. Indexing the accounting system for enterprise search requires the law firm to make policy decisions as to who will be able to see what content. This means that financial data has to be categorised according to the source of information and corresponding level of security. There might be categories of information that are publicly available and fully indexed with a low level of security, for example, available for all users within the enterprise search system. As an example, balances of accounts of law firms incorporated as capital companies that are subject to disclosure obligations in the German commercial register can be regarded as information searchable and viewable by the users of the enterprise system within the law firm.

On the contrary, partner compensation or remuneration, account balances designed for tax issues or account balance sheets of individual partners are sensitive information within a law firm that require a pre-defined level of security. In this respect, it has to be kept in mind that when implementing an enterprise search tool within a law firm, sensitive content that was formerly stored in unsecured, password-free databases or document management systems within the firm may now become present as it may be found by the search device when entering the right keywords. Typically, this content has not been subject to a level of security within the law firm as until that point users would have been unable to find it.

To overcome this issue and avoid a complicated process of document retention and categorisation, one way to start finding and securing sensitive content when implementing enterprise search systems within a law firm might be to draw up a 'blacklist' of keywords that are subject to a special security, for example 'partner compensation', 'partner/staff bonus' or 'partner admission'. Such 'dirty word' lists require constant reassessment and improvement, based on the firm's business performance and requirements.

However, it has to be considered that an absolute level of security employed on such 'blacklist' words may lead to difficulties in the search results, as these words may be contained in emails, memos or other legal documents without referring to sensitive issues. As an example, in a labour law case, a legal statement dealing with internal partner issues of the client may well contain a number of 'dirty words' such as 'partner remuneration' that have to be seen in a different context. To solve this issue, a 'blacklist' of words has to be defined in connection with the source of origin of the document, for example 'dirty words' contained in precedents or memos to clients should be classified as searchable, whereas 'dirty words' contained in internal documents of the law firm should be subject to a level of security. Likewise, checking with the accounting or human resources department or the law firm's managing partner before defining blacklists may eliminate unwanted search results and disclosure of sensitive information through enterprise search systems.

3.5 Time entries

Another sensitive issue to index is time entries. Time entries themselves may be regarded as sensitive documents whereby the explanations and narrations may provide relevant information, for example to show internal expertise or case management. One way to deal with this issue might be for the firm to decide to index this data without displaying the actual content. In case the search determines relevance for the search results, the user is required to contact responsible accounting staff to get more detailed information.

3.6 Professional regulations

Professional regulations, data protection issues and client obligations may impose special levels of compliance and security on legal advice given in sensitive cases and handling of client details and names. In this respect, an enterprise search system for a law firm should incorporate policies and levels of security for the following issues:

- safeguarding of attorney-client privilege;
- special duties of confidentiality imposed by strategic clients;
- avoidance of conflicts of interest; and
- security issues with regard to legal advice in insider trading cases.

With regard to security issues relating to client details, the observance of professional secrecy is one of the general professional duties for lawyers as set out for example in Section 43, Para 2 of the German Federal Lawyer's Act: "An attorney has a duty to observe professional secrecy. This duty relates to everything that has become known to the attorney in professional practice." Any violation of the duty of confidentiality is subject to various consequences, varying from loss of clients accompanied with financial loss to more serious consequences of sanctions for breaches of duty imposed by the Lawyer's Disciplinary Court, or even criminal prosecution. This means that when implementing enterprise search technologies within a law firm to index client names and details, the accidental release of relevant documents via executed enterprise searches to unauthorised personnel may lead to serious consequences for the individual lawyer and the whole law firm. The setting up of policies for different security levels, the use of smart filters within the search system and access controls to the search systems are suitable tools to consider when dealing with client security issues. With regard to access controls, Single Sign-On technologies within enterprise search systems allow the allocation of individual levels of security for each user. Logging in via an HTML form may be easier to use but means disadvantages with regard to the allocation of individual levels of security.

For the avoidance of conflicts of interests in client acceptance procedures, enterprise searches may be a powerful tool to find and assess conflicting engagements that may prevent the law firm from accepting the new engagement. Usually, for accessing potential conflicts of interests within law firms, access and evaluation of all kind of sensitive client and in-house information is required. This means that matter descriptions, client lists and correspondence relating to engagements should be indexed within the enterprise search system.

On an advanced level, the ability to extend the enterprise search system beyond the law firm's resources to include legal industry websites such as LEXIS NEXIS, FINDLaw.com or BECK-ONLINE enables the law firm to implement additional external information to assess any conflicts of interest.

As conflict checks searches are usually name-based, for example searches for client names or employee's names, 'exact match' search facilities limit the amount of search results to a reasonable number.

Enhanced flexibility in entering the search terms within the enterprise system offers more possibilities for finding matching results. Mature enterprise search systems support keyword, natural language, phrase and Boolean search input. Boolean searches allow the searcher to combine words and phrases using the Boolean operators such as the words AND, OR, NOT and NEAR to limit, widen or define the search. With grouping operators, such as the use of grouping and nesting operators by using parentheses, the interpretation of the search results can be specified.

Categorisation of search results enables the firm to categorise conflicting engagements found by the enterprise search system. Smart filters allow the user to refine the search results by selecting from multiple filters based on taxonomy values of the law firm. In this respect, taxonomies are groups of categories based on metadata fields of documents that are stored in structured views. In the user interface, smart filters appear under the heading 'narrow results by'. Some of the most important smart filters to refine search results for conflicting engagements are:

- document properties;
- authors, editors and recipients;
- client and matter properties;
- phrases and tags; and
- dates.

For easy filtering and navigation, a manual filtering and navigation system that can be executed flexibly on the search results allows for narrowing down of relevant content. This implies that pre-set search routines can be executed, for example, for conflict searches with regard to conflicting engagements, key words and document sources can be pre-set. Search terms should be highlighted in the results list and within the documents found to easily select relevant search results. Search results can be sorted according to 'most recent' to 'most relevant' results, thereby eliminating irrelevant content.

Document previews, saved searches, pinboard facilities and export functions allow the processing of search results.

As conflict searches are usually executed by a conflict check department within the law firm, access controls with Single Sign On technology for the use of the enterprise conflict search system are required. It has to be carefully assessed which databases are indexed and categorised for the system. Mature enterprise search systems allow for the build-up of different user categories, depending on their affiliation to different departments within the firm.

Client acceptance procedures also imply the checking for listing of clients or matter parties on sanctions lists or anti-money laundering procedures (eg, US or EU sanctions lists, PEP (politically exposed persons), beneficial owners, etc), the possibility to index external databases within the enterprise search system is an important advantage of enterprise search systems for law firms.

Thereby, enterprise search systems offer the possibility to search and open an external document in its native format by 'open document' functions without changing the content or source of origin of the document. The repository can be shown in its native format. Any matching search result within the decisive search should be evaluated in the original application to assess the relevance of the search result for compliance with the law firm's internal client acceptance and matter management policies.

The legal rules governing insider trading, for example trading of a company's stock or other securities by individuals with access to non-public information about the company, may also impose obligations on lawyers advising the relevant companies in mergers, joint ventures or other legal affairs implying the knowledge of insider relevant information to the legal advisor in the course of the transaction. The rules governing insider trading are complex and vary significantly from country to country. Under German Law, legal advisors in insider trading cases are required to set up 'insider trading lists' where the relevant knowledge and the names and addresses of the legal advisors are stored and documented by the law firm. Furthermore, law firms have to safeguard that no insider relevant knowledge is spread within the firm to lawyers or other employees not advising in the case and prohibit the trading of the public company's stock by specific insiders. In this case, enterprise search systems can be a valuable tool to administrate the firm's security policies, to safeguard the prohibition of unauthorised spread of sensitive information. Sensitive engagements may be categorised as 'highly confidential', thereby safeguarding the observance of the necessary secrecy, for example by preventing document previews or the use of certain search criteria within the search.

To allow legitimate users, for example a conflict check department within the law firm, access to the relevant details of the insider trading case or to enable them to specifically find engagements falling under the respective legal rules smart filters, preference searches or keyword searches can be defined within the enterprise search system.

4. Reminder system

The handling of confidential information, sensitive accounting and HR data and legal advice falling under special professional regulations should be subject to a reminder system once the system has started. Post-roll out the safeguarding of the duties of confidentiality and non-disclosure of legal advice to certain clients in sensitive matters should be tested in the 'live system' to find data leaks. Particularly in the first months after the launch of the system, reports of the search terms users have been using may determine whether users are using search terms not thought of that might turn up sensitive documents. Information security, data protection and access controls ensure that business-critical information never gets beyond those authorised to manage and review it.

5. Which technology provides the right support to resolve the KM issue

When entering the world of enterprise search, there are at least several dozen products available on the market. Choosing the right product for your law firm involves evaluating the types of products, establishing a requirements list and performing a proof of concept test.

Basically, enterprise search products fall into three categories. First, specialised search vendors that address specific user information needs or provide specialised solutions for the legal market. Vendors include Recommind, Attivio or Sinequa. Within the specialised search vendors on the legal market Recommind is the key player. The search engine has an intuitive user interface and is easy to install. Text within documents can trigger security groupings, a feature important for law firms that almost no other vendor offers. Recommind's system can assign permissions or access rights to specific users and groups of users. Security groupings can address the ability of the users to view, change and navigate within documents.

Secondly, integrated search vendors such as Autonomy, IBM and Microsoft merge robust search facilities with other information management functions, such as website management. One of the major advantages of such search systems is that the search system can draw on many adjacent technologies of the provider's big software family. Nevertheless, law firms need to evaluate whether the provider's roadmap of the search engine and associated products suits their future business needs and expectations. Likewise, integrated search systems may require significant resources in terms of consulting and customisation to adapt the search engine to the specific needs of the law firm.

Thirdly, detached search vendors like Google offer stand-alone systems that include both software and hardware. They focus on ease of deployment and flexibility but may not be able to address the specific needs of law firms regarding security and categorisation of search results.

6. Obstacles when implementing enterprise search

When implementing enterprise search systems in a law firm, some major obstacles have to be addressed as early as possible. Obstacles may be heterogeneous repositories, for example file shares, email, cloud information which requires different access, crawling rules and technologies. Right at the beginning of designing an enterprise search system within the law firm volumes of data in the repository should be identified. Big data volumes may require key wording and indexing to make this data searchable and provide the best search results. Access rights (such as access to documents, user rights) have to be addressed sufficiently as unsolved access issues may lead to missing or incorrect search results. The time horizon for the successful implementation of enterprise search varies according to the data volume, business requirements of the law and responsiveness of the search vendor but should not be underestimated. A realistic time horizon may be 6 to 12 months for designing and starting the system in the law firm. Adaptation and customisation of the system will be an issue even after the implementation of the system as within the use of the system more business requirements may come up. As an example in our law firm after implementation of the enterprise search features for client and email files, a specific enterprise search system adapted to the needs of the conflict check department was implemented.

7. Performance and scalability

After implementing any enterprise search technology, performance review, scalability and setting up of internal support requirements are necessary aspects to deal with. Apart from reviewing and monitoring security policies and access to documents, fault tolerances and backup should also be subject to constant monitoring routines. Fault-tolerant describes a computer system or component designed so that, in the event that a component fails, a backup component or procedure can immediately take its place with no loss of service. Fault tolerance can be provided with software, or embedded in hardware, or provided by some combination.

8. Summary

Enterprise search systems enable large, information intensive organisations such as international law firms to search, manage and retrieve information stored in internal and external data repositories according to the pre-defined business needs. Law firms may use enterprise search systems for different tasks, for example client acceptance procedures or conflict check searches. Thereby issues such as compliance with professional regulations can be addressed. As enterprise search systems enable the law firm to index internal and external databases in different file formats, relevant information can be easily retrieved by one single search system. When indexing repositories for enterprise search systems, law firms have to address security issues, user policies and access controls to meet professional regulations, legal compliance requirements and duties imposed by strategic clients. In this respect, the prevention of unauthorised use of privileged information is one of the key issues to deal with when implementing enterprise search systems within a law firm. With enterprise search systems, law firms can benefit from cost savings and increasing productivity by making relevant documents and information instantly available and locate experts in particular legal areas throughout the firm to assemble specialised teams for better client service.

Knowledge management and HR: evolving together for positive growth

Stephanie Abbott
Janders Dean

The most effective legal KM functions have never lost sight of the 'people factor'. Although there have been strong temptations to limit operations to what can be seen, measured and controlled with relative ease – usually systems and concrete knowledge 'assets' – legal businesses are fundamentally people-driven organisations. The people factor – and its dynamic, evolving nature – remains central to deriving value from KM.

Most strategically-focused legal KM functions are now orienting themselves to draw closer to the firm's clients, collaborating more closely with client relationship specialists and repositioning as partners in client service delivery (as opposed to 'behind-the-scenes' infrastructure). Although this has resulted in a subtle shift from inwardly-focused projects and activities to a more outward-looking, client-centred view for the knowledge function, the people factor is just as pivotal. Legal KM functions continue to have a vital stake in how the individuals in the organisation exploit existing knowledge to deliver client value and how they explore new knowledge to unlock the potential for innovation[1] – this means that effective collaboration between KM and HR is as important as ever.

The interplay between KM and HR in law firms is complex and multi-faceted. Regardless of the structural nuances from firm to firm, in practice most effective knowledge and HR functions share many common goals and interests, and collaborate closely to achieve them.

In our engagements, we see many aspects of the relationship between legal KM and HR functions. At their most effective, both KM and HR are engines for organisational development – that is, creating changes in individuals, teams and across the organisation for positive growth. While the precise focus may differ, a shared sense of purpose, conscious and planned points of collaboration and a commitment to delivering on common goals ensures that each function maximises its value to the firm and its clients.

The scope and responsibilities of legal KM functions are broad and varied, and the process of evolution is accelerated in today's rapidly developing market. However, the typical strategic touchpoints between HR's core functions and the

1 The concept of the dual focus on exploitation (of existing knowledge) and exploration (of emerging knowledge) comes from Henley Business School's White Paper on knowledge, organisational development and human capital management: C van Winkelen and J McKenzie *An investigation into human capital management and the ambidextrous organisation* (Henley Business School White Paper, 2011).

services that legal KM functions tend to provide remain relatively constant, despite stark differences in the detail of what is being executed and how.

Primary areas of shared focus between HR and KM:

- culture;
- organisational design;
- organisational learning;
- change management;
- collaboration and global service delivery;
- competency management, standards and capability building;
- talent and succession;
- workforce planning[2]; and
- internal mobility.

When translating areas of shared responsibility and focus into concrete measures to deliver value, firms tend to focus on the following:

- The firm's overall operational efficiency and its ability to respond to cost pressure through its service delivery model.
- Quality standards associated with client service delivery.
- Securing and extending competitive advantage, including through the ability to anticipate evolving client expectations through innovative service design.

This in turn translates to specific joint activities, geared at delivering particular business outcomes. These include:

- introducing measures to maximise and streamline efficient and reliable development of capability and expertise:
  - accelerating learning on the job;
  - minimising error and risk;
  - identifying future skills and capabilities and preparing to develop or source them;
  - developing consistent competency and capability on foundational skills, and to a reasonable extent within areas of specialization;
  - directing supervisor time away from basic proficiency and information transmission towards high context, high value knowledge sharing;
- ensuring efficient completion of work by the most appropriately skilled resource to the necessary level for client satisfaction and professional standards:
  - resourcing client work at the correct level – with staff working at the top of their range and expertise (in order to maximise client value for billable hours) rather than more senior staff time being consumed by lower level work (and risking write offs);
  - ensuring appropriate technical and operational support is in place to

---

2 Although this area has been a point of shared concern for a long time, its importance has substantially increased recently with a renewed focus and discipline around process analysis and improvement – unlocking firms' ability to approach staffing and production differently.

  - direct employee effort to the most valuable application of their skills and expertise (direct link to employee value proposition and engagement);
  - minimising wasted or duplicated effort on particular matters and across matters and teams;
- facilitating succession and buffering the firm against the departure of experts:
  - smoothing transitions through 'just in time' exchange of expertise and experience (for example, around graduate/trainee rotations through practice groups, during significant career progression points, and in and out of client secondments);
  - facilitating the transmission of significant organisational knowledge and expertise prior to staff departures;
  - ensuring orderly transitions of client work as staff move through the firm;
  - helping design and organise succession measures in anticipation of staff departures (for example, in preparation for the eventual retirement of an expert in a particular speciality);
  - protecting against risks to the firm's intellectual property and professional responsibilities associated with staff departures;
- developing means to support, facilitate and maximise collaboration.

1. KM, learning and training: from asset creation to driving capability

There are as many structural models of the interplay between legal KM and HR functions as there are law firms. However, we've observed that some common models have emerged. It is very rare for there to be full functional integration of HR and KM functions – with standalone KM functions, or integration with IT or risk/compliance-related functions more common. That said, the combination of knowledge with learning or training functions (now long-established in some of the world's most successful firms) is an increasingly common approach. The operating models for these integrated functions may range from allocating responsibility for technical legal training to KM (for example, design, delivery and administration of internal CPD or CLE programmes) through to responsibility for all formal professional development of legal staff, to broad responsibility for training and professional development of all staff firmwide. There may be a model of explicit co-ownership and collaboration or there may be a more defined delineation of responsibility, with an understanding that necessary information and administrative support will flow between the functions as required.

In the early years of KM, many firms directed their focus and investment heavily towards the creation, capture and re-use of 'knowledge assets' – that is, technical and practical information, analysis and insight distilled into documentary form and made available for access and use by staff as needed.

This was driven by an appetite to improve the efficiency and consistency of certain legal processes, including the creation of some standard or model legal documents, while keeping within certain standards for quality and efficiency. Although many firms had a high level appreciation of the breadth of potential of other elements of KM to deliver benefits, the creation and maintenance of knowledge assets and their storage and delivery systems was a time consuming exercise demanding the bulk of knowledge time and resourcing.

Despite the demands of content creation, though, many firms consciously reserved some knowledge time and energy to contribute to skills development and training, particularly for junior legal staff. Once the work involved in analysing the technical, commercial and practical aspects of legal processes and documents in order to arrive at consistent best practice is completed, there is an obvious next step. This material can then be extended to give greater structure and depth to an existing body of insight and expertise. This can be shared in the form of structured training or just in time coaching and assistance.

The underlying knowledge assets also themselves represent powerful learning resources, providing:

- orientation or 'topographical' information about the interplay between different areas of technical legal expertise;
- knowledge about the transaction (technical legal issues, and how they relate to client goals and preferences within a particular practical or commercial context); and
- knowledge about a process (including chronology, ancillary processes and risk dimensions).

In fact, the power of these assets as learning tools gave rise to a common concern and objection to their being broadly shared – that non-specialists with access to these materials would feel dangerously empowered to 'dabble' in areas outside their expertise, and would use this knowledge to hoard work rather than refer it to the most appropriate part of the firm. Although these objections were technically valid, in the sense that someone could indeed misuse knowledge assets in this way if they were so inclined, this risk was not so much related to the existence of good knowledge assets but to broader issues of the firm's culture concerning trust, professional responsibility and collaboration. Equally, the existence of these concerns validates the value of these tools to support the rapid development of technical proficiency expertise when used appropriately.

Once the task of knowledge asset capture and development began to reach maturity, the emphasis began to move towards current awareness – keeping up to date with and making sense of changes in law and practice – a necessary step to maintaining core knowledge assets but also an ongoing demand on individuals and teams. Many teams (rightly) suspected a high level of duplicated information and effort associated with keeping on top of (and, ideally, ahead of) legal and industry developments. They began to leverage knowledge resources to help filter, triage and contextualise some of the growing avalanche of current awareness information. Again, this converted into a wide spectrum of training and learning-related activities. Knowledge staff were freed up to focus increasingly on ensuring effective conversion of technical and practical knowledge into client service capability, and to help direct and support on the job learning. Many professional support lawyer roles included (and still include) a strong coaching component, whether formally recognised as part of the job or not. They have come to be a key element of the firm's approach to lawyer development – whether this is explicitly recognised or not.

Other critical learning-related functions that have become standard inclusions in the KM repertoire, working in concert with HR, include:

- Facilitating reflection and transmission of knowledge centred around key 'events', such as matter closure or secondment starts and finishes, graduate/trainee rotations and (increasingly) pitch and panel process outcomes.
- Identifying key 'day 1' knowledge for on-boarding and providing ongoing support for the gradual assimilation of more complex and nuanced information.
- Identifying and establishing technical (and, at times, behavioural) competency standards and devising concrete examples or assessment methods.
- Supporting the process of learning on the job as well as supplying technical know-how.
- For junior staff, addressing deficiencies and gaps in university training and practical legal training in order to accelerate time to increase proficiency and return on investment.
- Increasingly, working directly with clients and practices to identify needs, develop and deliver client-facing training.

2. Capability and resourcing: what, how AND who

The connection of knowledge to building capability has been well understood and recognised for some time, and KM functions have historically worked closely with HR on:

- analysing work tasks and required standards in order to develop technical and professional competencies;
- establishing means (including via knowledge assets, content management and collaboration systems as well as person-to-person methods) for relevant skills and knowledge to be acquired, exchanged and distributed;
- assessing technical and professional competence against defined standards.

Beyond identifying, supporting and assessing capability, there has long been a relationship between certain KM activities and process efficiency and improvement. Up until recently, this relationship has been more implied than explicit, with KM-originated 'best practice' documents such as template legal documents/precedents, checklists or practice papers/guides designed to optimise the relevant workflows and enable those involved in legal matters to run them as efficiently as possible within the existing business model.

The potential for process improvement and corresponding changes to how matters are staffed has been implicitly understood for years. However, this was not always approached in a highly conscious and structured manner. Many early attempts to record and codify transactional and process-related knowledge had a smarter, more efficient distribution of work as a goal, though it was often imagined that by creating the relevant supporting assets the process improvement would somehow naturally flow. Occasionally, early attempts to address legal project management and legal process improvement went further, but relied on repurposing existing internal resources (often from IT or KM) and did not differentiate between process improvement and project management.[3]

Without a strong strategic impetus towards broader service transformation and a coherent vision of how this change would play out across the organisation, many attempts to grapple with process remained as niche projects around early 're-engineering' efforts where particular work types were to be outsourced or automated.

Much more recently, market pressures and competition have given rise to a newly rigorous approach to process improvement within firms. This has reconnected process and efficiency-focused knowledge activities with the potential for varying traditional approaches to resourcing and staffing. Firms have been grappling for some time with the knowledge that client expectations regarding efficiency and value require much greater proficiency in project management and process improvement than ever before. They have learned (the hard way, in some cases) that it is impossible to successfully change how legal work is priced without changing how that work is done. In many cases, this extends to controlling and varying who does particular elements of the work. This has involved innovation of (and disruption to) traditional staffing models, rapid organisational learning and an emerging vision of how lawyers may need to learn and progress in future.

This means that the knowledge function is becoming more intimately connected with matters such as practice team staffing, mobility and progression. Knowledge teams must be able to work effectively with HR to understand opportunities, constraints and practicalities around these issues, as well as with partners and teams to help translate into day to day reality.

In those firms that lead in this area, HR and KM are developing much greater proficiency in coming to grips with the differing resource models required and tailoring firm responses accordingly. They are also moving away from a need for either function to claim ownership of these initiatives and are working effectively with internal and external specialists to craft new models for innovation and service delivery transformation.

3. Talent and succession

3.1 Talent, engagement and retention

As previously discussed, the most effective KM and HR functions have long worked together when it comes to identifying and articulating baseline role-based competencies within particular practices.

---

3 The depth of understanding of these disciplines across the industry has evolved significantly and continues to do so. Previously process improvement and project management were often lumped together and it was felt that the same resources could effectively cover both functions. Although they are closely related and some skills do overlap, a more accurate and nuanced understanding is now emerging. Process improvement involves analysing, codifying, reviewing and optimising the steps, actors, time, resources and systems necessary for the delivery of legal services. Project management is about managing existing processes in order to keep within required parameters for cost, timeliness, quality outcomes, efficiency and profitability – essentially a controlling and co-ordinating activity. Process analysis and mapping is a necessary precursor to both good project management and effective process improvement/re-engineering activities.

In addition, HR has found it can leverage the 'horizon scanning' role that many practice-based KM resources undertake in relation to understanding and contextualising forthcoming legal and industry developments. This can then be brought to bear on identifying and planning for likely future skills needs and demands – feeding into the firm's overall talent management activities.

Effectively, collaboration between the two functions also delivers value when it comes to talent acquisition, especially when it comes to minimising the 'turbulence' often experienced in transitioning into a new organisation or role. By working collaboratively to smooth and support staff through specific and predictable transition points, KM and HR can accelerate learning and ensure that less time elapses between joining and full productivity.

Predictable transition points lending themselves to collaboration between HR and KM to run more smoothly include:

- on-boarding new graduates/trainees;
- ensuring smooth and effective transitions through graduate/trainee practice group rotations;
- ensuring smooth and effective transitions in and out of secondments;
- on-boarding new experienced hires, in particular lateral partners (where the expectations for return on investment are high, the need for accelerated learning and integration acute and the risks to the firm of a prolonged, unsuccessful lateral hire process significant);[4]
- managing internal progression (most notably for newly promoted partners, but also for the transition from graduate/trainee to newly qualified/admitted lawyer).

The availability of relevant knowledge content as well as effective support and coordination between KM and HR results in a much improved and less turbulent experience for individuals during these transitions. This not only has concrete benefits to the firm as a whole but also directly impacts engagement and productivity both of individuals and the wider group they influence.

The significance of relevant KM (and other) support, not only at transition points but during day-to-day practice to the employee value proposition and engagement levels is validated by the nature of the questions and feedback that HR receive during the recruitment process. Although the support model that the firm offers may not be the most important consideration, it does form a key part of the overall perception of the employee value proposition for professional staff. The ability for staff to spend the majority of their working time on matters suited to their level of expertise, directly adding value to the client, rather than wasting time inefficiently searching for information or cobbling together documents (for example) has a direct impact on feelings of self-worth and career satisfaction.

Often staff will hold back from recording time spent on tasks that they know

4 Randy J Curato (Loss Prevention Counsel, Attorney's Liability Assurance Society Inc), "Hiring Laterals and Merging Practices – Examining the Professional Responsibility Issues" (2012) viewed on April 26 2016 at http://files.ali-cle.org/thumbs/datastorage/skoob/forms/BKAC1303_TAB13-Curato_thumb.pdf

could be done more efficiently with the correct support and systems in place, so the firm may be insulated from the financial and client-related consequences of inefficiency. However, time spent on non-billable work is often at the expense of personal time, which drives down engagement and increases the risk of talent mobility. In this way, effective knowledge functions have an impact on attraction and retention.

3.2 Succession planning and management

One of the imperatives driving the development of effective KM practices within law firms in the first place is also one of HR's concerns – succession. Legal KM's most visible activities often centre on explicit knowledge – that which can be documented and then curated and managed via content management systems. In addition, knowledge functions may strive to help convert tacit knowledge into explicit knowledge where this is feasible and valuable – distilling implicit knowledge of an existing process into a process map would be an example of this. However, there remains a vast body of experiential knowledge and industry/corporate memory that is tacit. This may also be the most difficult knowledge to transmit in a formal, structured way, being highly context-driven and often only making sense in narrative form. This hard-earned knowledge goes beyond technical inputs and outcomes, or facts relating to clients and so forth. It may be knowledge of tactics, success/failure factors or the reasoning behind particular positions and decisions. The value of this knowledge is often highly contextual and there is no business case for undertaking the mammoth effort involved in undertaking structured efforts to convert this knowledge from tacit to explicit just in case it becomes relevant later, even if this were practical or possible.

Unless there are other means of transmitting and exchanging this knowledge, it may remain locked up in the heads of the firm's most experienced and knowledgeable practitioners. When these people finally leave the firm, either through retirement or (increasingly) lateral movement, access to this expertise is lost.

Mitigating the risk of this loss of expertise has long been a focus of both KM and HR functions. HR has tended to focus on engagement, keeping the expertise within the firm as long as possible, identifying known future areas of concern and introducing structures to minimise their impact (for example, identifying and assisting with the grooming of the next generation of leaders in a particular practice area). KM's approach is often in relation to specific triggers such as a planned retirement or announced resignation.

Strategically focused KM and HR functions pair closely to understand in depth the nature of the expertise and experience of particular staff and to create maps of expertise and tacit knowledge that are maintained and accessed when succession issues appear on the horizon to ensure the firm is better prepared to respond.

They also work together on specific measures aimed to mitigate the impact of a departing expert. These may include facilitating departure 'interviews' (generating a coherent narrative thread to connect particular matters or events, knowledge assets, client insights and networks of internal expertise) or proactively increasing the exposure of staff to a particular expert through internal secondment or rotation.

Ironically, high turnover in HR or in KM seriously impedes the ability of the firm to respond to drains of expertise and sucession-related issues. Valuing and managing the organisational awareness and networks of knowledge and HR staff is an important step towards mitigating the functions' own succession issues.

4. Culture and collaboration: enabling knowledge to flow

KM and HR functions have a shared focus on ensuring that a collaborative and open culture relating to the firm's work, clients and expertise operates not only firmwide but within particular groups (in many cases, globally distributed).

In practice, establishing and maintaining healthy behavioural norms around knowledge and collaboration can be very challenging and requires sustained focus and reinforcement.[5] In tandem with smart organisational design and the availability of suitable systems and channels to build trust, where KM staff such as PSLs are 'embedded' within practice groups, they can work in concert with HR to establish and maintain pressure towards desirable behaviour change by networking with each other and modelling required approaches and exercising influencing skills in context through the day-to-day operations of the practice. For this to operate effectively, the KM staff must not be so beholden or exposed to the whims of individual personalities that they lose their ability to present alternatives.

5. Service transformation, innovation and change

John Kotter's work on accelerating organisational change[6] reveals the pivotal role played by agile, highly networked groups of change agents operating in parallel (and in harmony with) the change-related vision and activities driven through the traditional organisational hierarchy. HR and KM teams are among the most highly networked across their organisations and are well positioned to activate these informal, agile networks of change agents.

Over the years, many KM teams have developed skills and experience, often in an unstructured manner, in 'innovation projects' involving design thinking and change management.

A focus on design thinking may have emerged organically as a response to resolving practical challenges concerning communication and engagement around content, risk and facilitating appropriate use of knowledge resources.

Involvement in change and innovation may have begun to occur in an unstructured way, often centring around the convenient role that KM staff such as PSLs can play as 'friendly' design proxies for fee earning lawyers, particularly for technology-based internal change projects. Although different knowledge teams (and firms) have embraced this to differing extents, the change-related experience of KM teams has been building over many years, and, with some additional structure, skills development and guidance can be tapped for other purposes.

---

5 For a very helpful analysis of the structural and personal challenges to effective collaboration within law firms, and the means to overcome them, see Heidi K Gardner (Harvard Business School), "Effective teamwork and collaboration" in *Managing Talent for Success* (Globe Law and Business, 2013).

6 John P Kotter, "Accelerate! How the most innovative companies capitalize on today's rapid-fire strategic challenges, and still make the numbers" (2012) *Harvard Business Review*.

Now, when many firms are realising the need to fundamentally reinvent the approach to client service delivery, and the need to find ways to more effectively introduce skills and mindsets concerning change, experimentation and innovation, they are finding that some of their most experienced staff in this regard reside within their knowledge function. Many of these staff, while sharing common traits with frontline lawyers, have personally been operating in more open-ended, experimental contexts for much longer than their fee earning counterparts. Many team members (though not all) have built up levels of comfort and resilience in these respects that even very senior legal staff have not had an opportunity to develop. As organisations navigate industry transformation and reinvent themselves, this 'lived' experience can assist in minimising maladaptive responses to disruptive change.

So the challenge for HR teams becomes how to effectively tap, extend and support the expertise contained in these agile networks including those in the KM team. This must be done in a way that delivers results for the firm but also remains manageable from an employment and engagement perspective. Structure, guidance and control are necessary to ensure that individuals remain connected and engaged and that resource pressures are managed. HR's expertise in effective organisational design and individual/leadership coaching can be deployed to maximise the chances of success of cross-disciplinary project teams and ensure that these initiatives are positioned within the firm to maximise their influence. To the extent that some of these cross-disciplinary initiatives may not initially be conceived with strong HR involvement (merely seen as another operational department 'project') it is up to other professionals, such as KM, to ensure that relevant HR expertise is brought into the mix early on.

5.1 Adaptive v Maladaptive responses to disruptive change

Any change, particularly disruptive changes of the kind facing the legal industry at the moment, involves a transition period where individuals and organisations work out how to make sense of the change and adapt to it. How people choose to respond to change will drive behaviour that may help or harm the adaptation process. Adaptive responses stem from curiosity, hope and excitement. Maladaptive responses stem from anxiety, grief and fear. While a combination of these reactions is understandable in any change, effective organisational efforts to drive far-reaching, transformative change need to facilitate and encourage positive adaptive responses where possible (such as learning from new experiences and analysing new information to generate insights). At the same time, organisations may need to manage and guide staff away from maladaptive responses (for example – cognitive distortions, such as 'all or nothing' thinking or a tendency to over-emphasise or extrapolate from isolated negative data).

Responding to these change dynamics effectively touches on concerns that are squarely within the HR purview, as well as areas where KM teams have developed practical experience through involvement in early experimentation. Although those early experiments may not have delivered the transformations imagined at the time, they likely generated substantial learning and expertise that can be readily tapped, upskilled and adapted to more far reaching capacity building firmwide. Importantly, some of the attributes developed include the 'softer' aspects of constructive adaptation to disruptive change, the importance of which is often underestimated at the outset of a transformation initiative. These are skills in cross-disciplinary collaboration, maintaining resilience and a strong sense of purpose through rapid change and learning, discipline about learning from both success and failure and measuring outcomes meaningfully.

Through effective collaboration on these initiatives KM and HR staff also have an opportunity to make another significant contribution to organisational change – modelling adaptive behaviour in response to rapid change – an attribute likely to become increasingly critical in the law firm of the future. That said, not all KM or HR staff will display or be capable of the same degree of adaptive behaviour as others. Those with particular capability in this area should be identified and nurtured and those who struggle may need additional management or support as with any other staff member exhibiting maladaptive responses to change.

5.2 Alternative service delivery models

As changes to legal service delivery models ripple through the industry, the typical work expectations and tasks of a junior lawyer is one of the areas most in flux. New lawyers are an expensive resource – commanding relatively high starting salaries and, despite their qualifications, still requiring extensive training and on the job learning to reach full productivity. Part of the response of firms to maintaining quality and service while reducing costs has been to begin to redefine leverage to include other professionals besides qualified lawyers.

Some firms have specifically outsourced some functions traditionally undertaken by either junior lawyers, paralegals or knowledge/information staff, such as baseline legal research and analysis.

Outsourcing creates particular knowledge needs and challenges, both in terms of expectations around the creation, management and use of formal knowledge 'assets', process integrity, efficiency and consistency, standards and quality control, as well as communication and effective transmission of insight and learning.

Working with contract legal resources also creates potential challenges around knowledge transmission,[7] handovers and continuity of service standard and 'style'. Regardless of what part of the organisation controls and governs these arrangements, KM and HR can contribute significantly to maintaining quality and continuity regardless of the operating model in use through collaboration on process design, standards and quality assurance, skills and knowledge transfer, training, communication and supervision.

6. Conclusions: effective collaboration between HR and KM

The most effective models of HR and KM collaboration tend to involve some degree of functional integration, through specifically allocated responsibility for certain

---

7 In particular, this may apply to 'knowledge of client' – deep experiential knowledge and relationship-related awareness of client priorities and preferences. Bringing this knowledge back into the organisation may be a particular challenge for flexible sourcing models reliant on contract or freelance staff. A deliberate, structured approach to knowledge exchange can offset this to some extent.

functional areas with shared responsibility for particular outcomes. The most obvious area for this tends to be areas specific to learning and development. However, firms are increasingly putting some structure around shared responsibility when it comes to organisational development and change, as well as specific service transformation initiatives.

HR and KM staff are typically both incredibly well networked internally, and will usually have a good working knowledge of the identities and capabilities of a much higher proportion of the firm than the average practicing lawyer. This means these teams possess valuable knowledge about who does what within the firm, putting them in an excellent position to work together to foster and facilitate collaboration, make connections and helping others build a more comprehensive picture of their organisation. It is important that this shared capability is acknowledged and deployed to the benefit of the firm. The overall sense of industry disruption currently prevalent should not allow a pervasive sense of threat to result in internal competition for connections and influence.

Even where organisational imperatives towards functional integration in specific areas are limited or non-existent, the strategic relationship between KM and HR is a significant one that must be nurtured and developed.

Effective cooperation sees information freely transmitted and shared between the two, and a degree of co-ownership and shared responsibility for design, implementation and outcomes. Poor collaboration can result in unhelpful demarcation disputes, resulting in coverage gaps, duplication of effort or both.

This is a poor application of the firm's investment in both areas and creates confusion and disengagement among those intended to be the beneficiaries of properly coordinated support activities.

To do this well involves genuine and deep-seated respect for each other's strengths and areas of expertise and a willingness to promote one another's strengths and capabilities to others. As former lawyers are more likely to be involved in KM functions than HR functions, there is a risk that 'status'-related dynamics, reminiscent of those that can arise between fee earning and non-fee earning staff, become barriers to effective collaboration at the team level. KM and HR leaders must actively work together and model more productive and respectful approaches to minimise this risk.

As legal support operations become less siloed and more focused on delivery of value to clients overall, effective collaboration between HR and KM is key to developing true learning organisations capable of responding to and anticipating market disruption.

Getting lawyers to contribute content to KM systems and to use KM resources

Martin R Schulz
German Graduate School of Management and Law (GGS)

1. Introduction

There is broad consensus among academics and practitioners that in the information age, knowledge is the most valuable resource for most organisations.[1] As law is a knowledge-intensive business,[2] knowledge management (KM) is an important efficiency and risk-reducing tool for the legal industry, and provides other benefits such as systematic quality improvement, protection from the loss of know-how, and even a potential for innovation as well.[3] As analysed and outlined in several other parts of this book, a successful and sustainable implementation of KM requires an integrated approach including elements like creating and implementing a KM strategy, organising adequate resources and implementing dynamic processes of collecting and distributing relevant know-how.[4] The most important requirement for an effective KM system is, however, the creation and continuous fostering of a culture of knowledge sharing among lawyers and throughout the firm.[5] Only if law firm management provides a sustainable framework for an interactive exchange of knowledge and experience, can KM become a long-term success rather than a temporary phenomenon.

After describing some typical barriers to knowledge sharing in law firms and providing some suggestions to overcome these obstacles, this chapter describes some key success factors for designing KM systems in order to motivate lawyers to actively use and develop know how resources.

---

1 See eg Ross Dawson, *Developing Knowledge-Based Client Relationships* (Butterworth-Heinemann, 2000), pXV referring to, amongst others, the seminal work of Thomas A Stewart, *Intellectual Capital: The New Wealth of Organizations* (Doubleday, 1997). For KM in law firms see Gretta Rusanow, *Knowledge Management and the Smarter Lawyer* (ALM Publishing, 2003); Matthew Parsons, *Effective Knowledge Management for Law Firms* (Oxford University Press, 2004); Martin Schulz and Marcel Klugmann, "Creating a Culture of Knowledge Sharing in Law Firms" in Althoff *et al* (eds), *Professional Knowledge Management, Lecture Notes in Artificial Intelligence* (Springer, 2005), pp386–391; Martin Apistola and Petter Gottschalk, *Essential Knowledge and Management Issues in Law Firms* (Universal Publishers, 2011). Some parts of this chapter have been covered (partly in more detail) by Martin Schulz and Luis Felipe Mohando, "Precedent databases and Knowledge Management" in Hermann J Knott (consulting ed), *Risk Management in Law Firms: Strategies for Safeguarding the Future* (Globe Business Publishing, 2014), pp117–128.

2 See eg Rusanow (n 1), p7.

3 See Rusanow (n 1), pp343–356; Schulz and Mohando (n 1), pp117–128.

4 See eg Rhem's, chapter on KM governance for law firms, Lustigman's chapter on implementing KM strategy in practice, and Kuth and Schulz's chapter on organising KM in a law firm

5 See Rusanow (n 1), pp187–220; Parsons (n 1), pp96–115; Schulz and Klugmann (n 1), pp386–391.

2. Importance of a KM culture – removing typical barriers

Despite their characteristic features of 'knowledge intensive enterprises', many law firms face several barriers to effective knowledge sharing. When considering an active participation in KM projects, lawyers will typically ask themselves 'what is in it for me'? Therefore, it is important to look for and to remove the following typical obstacles, and to create a framework for knowledge sharing.

2.1 Creating awareness for KM benefits in light of dynamic developments

In view of the increasing pace in new legal developments, the dynamic business environment for all legal service providers combined with higher demands on legal services,[6] an effective KM has become an essential tool for operating a contemporary legal business.[7] On the one hand, clients constantly demand quick and efficient delivery of high quality service, and a proactive approach from their legal advisors.[8] On the other hand, lawyers have been traditionally flooded with information resulting from new legislation, court decisions or new developments in legal practice and academia, and the dynamics of legal change has significantly increased.[9] To master these challenges, a professional KM appears not only necessary, but also rather some sort of a lifejacket.

Nevertheless, many law firms have not yet fully managed to adapt their knowledge resources to current challenges. Although many law firms have introduced KM programmes, there seems to be room for improvement regarding the effective use of KM and of existing knowledge resources. The significance of an effective KM for the day-to-day running of law firms is often either not fully recognised or not taken seriously enough. Many lawyers still possess their own collection of documents, but despite these existing knowledge collections, one sometimes still finds a lack of willingness to share. In order to overcome this barrier, it is important to raise the awareness for the benefits and long-term advantages of an effective KM system. As indicated, KM is an important efficiency tool and can provide many benefits, such as the following:[10]

- By a standardisation of commoditised legal products (such as simple contract forms, checklists for legal transactions, 'Q & A' on recurring issues, etc) KM leads to more efficiency in daily legal practice. At the same time, KM increases lawyers' capacity for more sophisticated and difficult tasks.
- By providing updates on new legal developments (eg, new legislation and court decisions, new legal products developed in practice) KM forms the basis for a consistent high-quality output of legal products.

---

6 See eg Richard Susskind, *Tomorrow's Lawyers – An Introduction to your future* (Oxford University Press, 2013) describing the changing landscape for legal service providers and emphasising the relevance of KM, pp64–65.

7 For an analysis of the dynamic legal landscape and business environment see Rusanow (n 1), pp9–11; Constance E Bagley and Mark Roellig, "The Transformation of General Counsel: Setting the Strategic Legal Agenda" in Stuart Weinstein and Charles Wild (consulting eds), *Legal Risk Management, Governance and Compliance* (Globe Law and Business, 2013), pp45–66.

8 See Schulz and Klugmann (n 1), p386.

9 Leo Staub, "Ausblick: Der In-house Legal Counsel und die Rechtsabteilung im Jahre 2020 – stetig wachsende Herausforderungen im Zeitalter der Globalisierung" in Sylvie Hambloch-Gesinn, Beat Hess, Andreas L Meier, Reto Schiltknecht and Christian Wind, *In-house Counsel in internationalen Unternehmen* (CH Beck, 2010), pp33–49; Schulz and Mohando (n 1), p118.

10 For an overview of the benefits of KM for lawyers see also Rusanow (n 1), pp9–11.

- In addition to providing updates on new legal developments, KM can be used as a valuable source for business development activities (such as client briefings or training for clients on new laws).[11]
- By including current market trends in the monitoring of relevant news, KM also creates a potential for 'legal innovation' (eg, by developing new legal products such as new contract forms or new components of legal services).
- By providing a convenient information infrastructure, KM will also motivate employees and new joiners because they can avoid reinventing the wheel and will get the chance to learn faster and to adapt to new developments more efficiently.
- By providing high-quality knowledge KM can serve as a risk management tool, since wrong legal advice may lead to liability claims.
- In addition, KM can also protect the organisation from a loss of knowledge (eg, by conducting expert interviews with employees who are leading the firm).

2.2 Recognising the value-adding function of KM

In order to create an atmosphere in which lawyers are willing to contribute to KM, it is also important to point out the 'value-adding function' of KM activities.[12] For example, knowledge can (and should) be generally distinguished from mere information by its additional value, by providing a contextual framework to digest information, and by providing practical hints for daily legal practice.[13] Consequently, one of the main functions of legal KM is to create practical value, for example by selecting relevant knowledge from the daily flood of legal information, and by emphasising the practical significance of new developments. This value becomes obvious if legal news includes comments with lawyers' experience and practical insight, by including statements of internal experts from within the law firm. If management communicates the value of KM regularly, lawyers will definitely appreciate these benefits. This will, in return, increase the chances that they are willing to contribute to KM projects and activities.

2.3 Providing adequate links to the business strategy – a dynamic process

Another challenge is creating an adequate link of KM activities to the law firm's business strategy. Building and maintaining a professional KM system requires investing in resources, so it is important that all necessary steps match the business strategy of the law firm.[14] If management does not envisage such a link to the business model when developing the KM program nor implement it later on, this 'missing link' may seriously impair the effectiveness of any KM program. On the one hand, the gap between KM activities and the business strategy creates a risk that KM resources are used inefficiently (eg, KM products are not produced or adapted according to the users' needs and requirements). On the other hand, this problem

---

11 See Büchi's chapter on client-facing knowledge management.
12 See Rusanow (n 1), describing the value of KM in detail at pp338–360.
13 *Cf* Schulz, "KM strategy – Proving your Worth" (2011) *KM Legal Magazine* 19–21.
14 See Rusanow (n 1), p267. See also Schulz and Mohando (n 1), p121.

may lead to further risks of fee earners losing their interest in using the KM system and contributing their knowledge.

Therefore, it is necessary to define so-called 'knowledge objectives' for each practice area based on the areas of expertise of the lawyers before starting KM activities.[15] If, for example, small and medium-sized companies represent a large group of the firm's client base, KM should provide knowledge and experience on all matters relevant to these companies.[16] If, on the other hand, the partners have decided not to focus on an area such as consumer protection law (and to leave this field to competitors), it does not seem useful to build (or maintain) a knowledge collection in that area. It is important to keep in mind that the business strategy needs to be amended and updated regularly (due to the changing environment outlined above), and the KM strategy has to be adjusted accordingly. If this dynamic process works well, fee earners will immediately see the benefit of their KM contributions in promoting the business objectives of the law firm.

2.4 Ensuring top level commitment and a useful KM architecture

Lawyers will be willing to contribute to KM if they feel that the law firm's management authentically endorses KM initiatives, and if KM provides convenient and helpful tools for daily legal practice.

(a) Tone at the top – important signal for KM activities

If you want to get lawyers' contribution to KM projects and activities, you will definitely need top-level commitment.[17] The law firm's management (and senior partners) should emphasise the significance and benefits of KM and should strongly support KM initiatives regularly.[18] One option is signalling to all firm members how central KM is for the firm, for example by including the importance of KM in the firm's mission statement. In general, the members of the law firm's management should prove their commitment towards the value of KM and serve as role models by regularly contributing to and using knowledge resources themselves.[19] If the so-called 'tone at the top' is audible and sustainable, many lawyers will follow such role model behaviour. If senior partners and management can convince their colleagues on the importance of KM, all lawyers will more actively contribute to the KM system. Furthermore, management should repeatedly involve all lawyers and employees in identifying relevant knowledge resources for the firm and involve representatives of lawyers and employees in deciding how to organise knowledge. Such continuous involvement by the firm's members will be the foundation for continuous support of the KM system.

---

15 For the use of knowledge objectives see Rusanow (n 1), pp257–268.
16 See Schulz and Mohando (n 1), p121.
17 For strategies and tools to create an atmosphere of knowledge sharing see Rusanow (n 1), pp208–220; Parsons (n 1), pp106–115; Apistola and Gottschalk (n 1), pp196–202; Schulz and Klugmann (n 1), pp386–391.
18 *Cf* Rusanow (n 1), pp209–210; Schulz and Klugmann (n 1), p387.
19 Schulz and Mohando (n 1), p123.

(b) *Useful KM tools and open feedback – positive impact on day-to-day legal practice*

In addition, the management should initiate and ensure a 'KM architecture' which is useful for daily legal practice.[20] As will be explained later in more detail when discussing how to get lawyers to use KM resources (see below, section 3), the KM system should be able to prove its usefulness in practice. Such tools include various search options, convenient options to download knowledge items into lawyers' work streams, and options for a quick feedback. Such tools and features will generate immediate positive impacts on lawyers' daily workload, and this will improve lawyers' willingness to contribute their own knowledge and experience to the KM system. On the other hand, if using and contributing to knowledge resources appears as a complicated and a time consuming process, lawyers will not be easily motivated to contribute.

Management should also regularly emphasise that knowledge sharing requires an atmosphere of cooperation and constructive feedback.[21] Unfortunately, a rather competitive climate seems to prevail in some law firms, which may lead to a psychological barrier to sharing knowledge.[22] Some lawyers may fear criticism from their peers when contributing to the knowledge collection, especially in areas not at the core of their competences. It is therefore important to create an atmosphere of constructive feedback instead of negative criticism.[23] In the end, such an open atmosphere may even lead to the insight that KM contributions should become a regular element of every lawyers' business.

2.5 Providing various incentives for KM contributions

In order to encourage contributions to the KM system, the law firm's management should consider providing adequate incentives for those lawyers who actively contribute to and use the KM resources.[24] Unlike client-related work, KM activities often do not show any immediate and visible signs of success, nor directly quantifiable 'return on investments'.[25] Lawyers are most often very busy with client work and some of them regard KM contributions as another type of 'administrative work'.[26]

In order to deal with these kinds of problems it is important to create a system of incentives for KM contributions. Management can use various forms, from publishing rankings of active knowledge contributors, to specific KM awards.[27] An easy and somewhat underestimated incentive tool is the public praise for active KM contributors, if management (and, in particular senior partners) speak in high terms of those lawyers and other staff actively contributing to KM, such praise will be

20 For some useful features and tools of such a KM architecture see Schulz and Kuth's chapter on organising KM in a law firm.
21 Schulz and Mohando, (n 1), p123.
22 For these and other knowledge sharing problems see Rusanow (n 1), pp199–206; Apistola and Gottschalk (n 1), pp192–193.
23 See Schulz and Klugmann (n 1), p391; Schulz and Mohando (n 1), p123, with further references.
24 Schulz and Mohando, (n 1), p123.
25 Schulz and Klugmann (n 1), p388.
26 *Cf* Schulz and Klugmann (note 1), *ibid*. This, in part, rests on the misperception that KM is some kind of an administrative task.
27 Schulz and Mohando (n 1), p123.

recognised as a sign of distinction.[28] Furthermore, KM contributions should become a regular criterion in personnel reviews and ongoing assessments. Appraisals for valuable KM contributions should also play a role in the decision to promote lawyers to the next job level.[29] Other incentive systems may include bonus payments or other gratifications.

Furthermore, it is important to note that KM contributions are an option for lawyers to promote themselves as experts in a particular area of law or in a specific branch of business. Regardless of the fact that not every associate will make partner, every lawyer has an interest in promoting his career by making his individual expertise and competencies visible. Nevertheless, senior partners and law firm's management should grant awards for special or outstanding individual KM contributions, since appropriate recognition for valuable KM activities motivates lawyers to contribute to KM resources.

2.6 Introducing value based billing options to better integrate KM contributions

When aiming to motivate lawyers to contribute content to KM systems (and to use KM resources, see below, section 3) one also needs to analyse (and in some cases to modify) the traditional billing system. Since KM is a driver for efficiency and productivity gains (achieving more tasks in less time, eg, by using standard forms), the traditional time-based billing system might even appear like an obstacle. "Why should I become faster and more efficient if this will reduce my bill?" might be the question. For obvious reasons, clients will see that very differently, and under current market conditions, the right questions to ask are "How can I become more productive by using KM effectively? How can I convince my clients that their investment in my services is fully justified (not only because of my legal expertise but also because of efficient delivery of knowledge)?" In order to answer these questions convincingly it is necessary to consider and integrate valuable KM contributions in the billing system.[30] Being still the primary charging tool in most law firms, the billing system not only serves as the commercial basis for client relationships but also reflects the internal value code of many lawyers. In order to make KM contributions more attractive it is therefore important to demonstrate that KM is an asset not only in terms of internal productivity gains but also in terms of a marketing tool for clients. One option to reflect the appreciation for KM activities within the billing system would be to allow for a certain number of hours to be spent on pre-defined KM projects (considered as being of high value to the law firm's strategy), in addition to the agreed standard of billable hours. Providing a recognised option to spend time on KM projects will definitely increase the chance for active KM contributions.

---

28 Schulz and Klugmann (n 1), pp388–389.

29 *Cf* Rusanow (n 1), p212 describing KM contributions as a criterion for career progression.

30 For an overview of alternative pricing compared to the traditional billing model see eg Richard Susskind, *Tomorrow's Lawyers – An Introduction to your future* (Oxford University Press, 2013) describing the changing landscape for legal service providers and emphasising the relevance of KM at pp64–65.

3. Getting lawyers to use KM resources – providing helpful contents and features

When reflecting on how to motivate lawyers to share their knowledge, another yet related issue is the question of how to get them to use KM resources. Approaching this issue with an integrated perspective, it appears to be just the other side of the coin of the first question. Lawyers will typically use KM resources to save time and effort when starting to work on new assignments. When involved in an M&A transaction, for instance, they will search for some standard documents like a due diligence checklist or a model M&A agreement. To appear as the better alternative (compared to each lawyer's documents stored in his personal files after the last deal), KM resources should prove to be superior in terms of content variability, currency and ease of use.[31]

Since organisational issues of KM structures and KM systems are described in detail in other chapters,[32] I will give an outline of some key features which have proved helpful and relevant from a practical legal user's perspective.

3.1 Provide a user friendly KM-architecture

Assuming that some kind of KM database in which all relevant know-how (such as contracts, memoranda and briefings) is systematically stored will form the core part of the KM system,[33] useful and current content is a key success factor for getting lawyers to use KM resources. However, providing and delivering useful and current knowledge may prove more difficult than one would expect in the first place, since it requires various processes to select, refine, distribute and update resources. With regard to the selection of knowledge resources to be stored in the KM database, it is important to follow a strategic approach (as indicated above) instead of collecting each and any piece of information.[34] When storing strategically selected know-how, the KM database should provide users with a table of contents. As lawyers traditionally think and argue in specific legal structures, terms and categories, it seems useful to provide such categories when designing the KM system. Therefore, consider implementing a legal taxonomy (in addition to features like full text search).[35] The legal taxonomy can be described as a classification system organised by subject matter, for example for corporate law with subfolders on available corporate forms, questions on company formation, rights of shareholders, duties of managing directors etc. Such structured content serves as a guideline to help lawyers finding what they are looking for.[36] Furthermore, a legal taxonomy can also serve as a starting point for searches giving the user a helpful orientation about a specific area and related content. In sum, the KM database (as part of the firm's KM system) should be

---

31 For an overview of useful functions and features of KM databases see Schulz and Kuth's chapter on organising KM in a law firm; see also Rusanow (n 1), pp237–258.

32 See Schulz and Kuth's chapter on organising KM in a law firm. See also BIALL (British and Irish Association of Law Librarians) *Handbook of Legal Information Management*, 2nd edn (2014).

33 See Schulz and Kuth's chapter on organising KM in a law firm; see also the recommendations on designing a useful precedent database by Schulz and Mohando (n 1), pp124–127.

34 See Schulz and Mohando (n 1), p125.

35 See Schulz and Mohando (n 1), p125.

36 See Vainikainen's chapter on taxonomy and informal tagging.

tailor-made to the needs and demands of the users and has to provide easy access and a variety of search options.[37]

3.2 Recognise users' needs and facilitate search

One useful option is to offer a variety of search options such as full text search, or search tools for meta-data (like author, legal subject, applicable law etc).[38] As indicated above, depending on the KM budget and available resources, it would also seem useful to create a taxonomy scheme in order to classify know-how.[39] When designing such taxonomies it is important, however, to bear in mind that users may have very different approaches to classifying and grouping subjects and concepts.[40] Therefore, management should involve as many lawyers as possible in the initial design of the classification system, as well as in any future modifications and amendments of the categories.[41] If the KM system fulfils these requirements, lawyers will see KM tools as helpful in their daily practice and use them on a regular basis.

3.3 Provide convenient ways to contribute knowledge

A good KM system should provide efficient tools not just for searching but also for contributing know-how. With regard to the submission of documents (eg, examples from transactions) to the KM system, the process should be as simple and convenient as possible. If the law firm does not employ Professional Support Lawyers (PSL) or any other people helping with the storing of knowledge resources, it may be advisable to look for digital options and IT solutions like automatic tagging and classification of contributed documents.[42] Nevertheless, law firm management should emphasise that contributing knowledge and experience is an integral part of every lawyer's business, and should be integrated into regular processes and workflows. In addition, law firm management should give clear guidance on how to handle contributions to the KM database, for example by producing guidelines for knowledge contributions and by organising training sessions.[43]

3.4 Provide useful content and keep it up to date

Finally, yet importantly, useful and current content for daily legal practice is a key success factor. Based on the knowledge objectives set out in the KM strategy, management should analyse the quality and usage of all knowledge resources systematically. The lasting success of any KM system will depend on high quality and practice-oriented resources being regularly reviewed and updated.[44] Thus, law firm management should establish consistent processes of content management and

---

37 For an overview of useful components and features of a KM system see Rusanow (n 1), pp237–258 and Schulz and Kuth's chapter on organising KM in a law firm.
38 For an overview of useful components and features of a KM system see Rusanow (n 1), pp237–258.
39 See Rusanow (n 1), pp243–245; Parsons (n 1), p237.
40 Schulz and Mohando (n 1), p125. Rusanow (n 1), p243, points out that the assumption that knowledge will be described consistently across all systems and applications is a dangerous one.
41 *Cf* Schulz and Mohando (n 1), p125.
42 *Cf* Schulz and Mohando (n 1), p125.
43 *Cf* Schulz and Mohando (n 1), pp126–127.
44 See Rusanow (n 1), pp241–243; Parsons (n 5), pp161–173.

consistent quality control.[45] The primary goal of such content management is to ensure high quality and sustainability of knowledge, for example in terms of accuracy, topicality, practical relevance and reliability.[46] In order to get valuable input from lawyers when reviewing the knowledge resources, management should delegate specific tasks for updating to selected partners and lawyers (ideally also to those who originally contributed the know-how). If knowledge remains up to date and valuable, lawyers will be willing to take this responsibility as 'process owners' for updating their KM contributions.

4. Conclusion and guiding questions

The key to understanding effective knowledge management is to see it as a dynamic process rather than as a static tool. Accordingly, motivating lawyers to share their expertise and knowledge will only work if those lawyers are willing to actively use and comment on existing KM content, structure and resources on a continuous basis. Ideally, a sustainable KM culture will include shared responsibilities among lawyers, KM managers and information professionals for selecting, circulating and updating relevant knowledge. In addition to the cultural aspects, however, the question of usability of existing knowledge and information resources will play an important role. Creating an effective and sustainable KM system requires active participation of fee earners. In order to ensure their commitment and support, please consider the following questions as a guideline:

- Do you have a KM strategy and is it compatible with your law firm's business strategy?
- Have you reached a consensus on the importance of KM to help facing new business challenges (such as digitalisation)?
- Do you actively promote and foster a knowledge-sharing culture in the firm?
- Is there sufficient top-level commitment for KM projects and initiatives?
- Are there adequate incentives for lawyers to contribute to KM and to use of KM resources?
- Does your billing-system provide for value-based options in order to recognise KM activities?
- Do you provide a user friendly KM-architecture with benefits for daily legal practice?
- Is the content of your knowledge resources relevant, accurate and up to date?
- Do you keep future developments and their impact for KM in sight?
- Do you involve fee earners in all relevant KM activities on a regular basis?

---

45 See Martin Schulz, "Content Management – A Fine Art – And a Knowledge Paradox" (2008) *Knowledge and Information Management Legal* 17–20; see also Rusanow (n 1), p241.

46 For an analysis of these and other criteria see Martin J Eppler, *Managing Information Quality*, 2nd edn (Springer, 2006).

Aligning knowledge management goals to legal project management

Jonna Vainikainen
Castrén & Snellman Attorneys Ltd

Clients have changed. They want more for less: efficient processes, tighter cost control, increased transparency and good project management skills. Clients are no longer loyal to one firm as before, and firms face increasingly stiff competition for clients' business. One reason for decreasing loyalty is the development of communication technology which enables clients to easily obtain information from an increasingly broad range of choices. Also, trading is globalised. For these reasons law firms need to focus on a client-centric approach that creates added value for clients, value for which clients are willing to pay.

1. Client-centric approach

Adopting a client-centric approach is very important for those firms who want to be forerunners. This investment in a truly client-centric service approach requires a focus on learning about each client and that client's business challenges. A key factor in a successful client-centric approach is the firm's ability to learn how to provide added value which, in today's globalised legal services market, is more important than concentrating on traditional services. A vital part of providing value-added, client-centric services is to understand clients' own processes and touch points with the client. The in-depth knowledge of a client's needs allows law firms to modify their services to benefit the client's processes, and not only for clients' current needs, but also in anticipation of clients' future needs. True client understanding is exemplified by a law firm that can provide solutions to challenges that its client has not solved or even recognised yet. When combined with subject matter expertise and good project management capabilities, a client-centric approach can give a law firm a competitive advantage; if a law firm can fulfil its client's needs and even surpass expectations, it reduces the risk that the client will bid out the service and possibly choose a competitor.

To be client-centric means that law firms also need to have the ability and knowledge to serve clients via many different channels. Many law firms are developing a strategy to implement state-of-the-art tools, including various collaborative platforms and online services, as well as changing the ways in which the firm communicates with its clients. Knowledge Management (KM) connects people to people and people to information, which is why KM strategic action plans should support the development of their firms' client-centric approach and all accompanying strategic goals, and achieving this strategic support may be achieved through the following KM functions.

2. Capturing and cataloguing legal project management know-how

2.1 Data and knowledge

Data is the lowest level of information. Meaningful information is created when data is combined, analysed and processed, enabling the use of that information to benefit the business. Knowledge is created when the employee feels that information is meaningful, can be interpreted and is understandable. This allows the information to become part of the employee's data structure and to start to affect the employee's actions. The highest part of information is wisdom, which can be created when an employee processes knowledge by using earlier learned experiences and values. Possibilities as to how we can use legal data are various and increasing every minute.

In today's legal world, it is not enough to know the law; lawyers need to know clients' business as well. To share client understanding within the firm, interaction between employees is needed. Knowledge sharing is one of the most important means available to create added value for clients and efficiency in law firms. Learning from previous assignments, logical collection of information and sharing it in the right forums are also important. Retrospect is one of the most effective processes for capturing lessons after the end of an assignment from the project team. In retrospect the key knowledge and experiences developed, and the lessons learned by the project team during an assignment can be identified, collected and converted into actions and resources to benefit future projects. Retrospect can be arranged, for example as After Action Review (AAR) as Tony Rhem has described in his chapter 'What is Legal Project Management'. By facilitating a dialogue within the whole project team, you can capture the knowledge that arose from team interactions – knowledge that the individuals in the team may be unaware of, but which is known collectively by the team.

Many document automation systems can provide cost efficiency by automating document creation steps, however, there are still very few systems available that can collect the vital knowledge, in particular that of partners and senior lawyers. That knowledge would be extremely helpful for younger lawyers, who would benefit from, for example, information on how to draft documents, when and how to use different clauses and which clauses are negotiable and which are not. Technology may play a significant role in the future and maybe even today in capturing this type of experience-based knowledge. For example, there are already technologies available which can process unstructured data, such as using natural language processing to quickly extract key information from all previous documents relating to particular matters.

3. Leveraging KM in legal project management execution

During recent years KM has changed from a traditional library and information service to much broader specialist functions. One of the special areas is project management. Some of the benefits KM has for legal professionals and firms include:

- the ability, through expertise locators, to quickly build teams to address cases and client situations;
- the ability, through Search Engine Optimisation techniques (taxonomies,

ontologies and associated Information Architectures for legal information and knowledge objects), to improve retrieval of case history, enable associations of related cases and rulings, as well as to locate knowledge resources based on retrieved knowledge objects;
- enabling sharing, collaboration and storage of communications as intellectual capital and enrichment of a knowledge sharing culture;
- enhancing ability to mentor and cross train both new and experienced lawyers;
- improving management and expansion of talent and the lawyers' experiences at the firm;
- infusing Knowledge Management strategy in the management of the firm;
- the ability to reuse internally developed knowledge assets such as precedents, letters, research findings, and case history information;
- automation of routine processes; and
- reduction of risk.

4. KM drivers for legal professionals

Several drivers lead law firm employees to adopt KM practices which lead to law firms incorporating KM into the organisation's regular activities. The KM drivers for legal professionals and law firms include:
- efficiency and consistency;
- flexibility and responsiveness;
- training, learning and knowledge sharing; and
- workplace satisfaction.

4.1 Efficiency and consistency

KM can improve a firm's efficiency in meeting client demands and in improving the cost efficiency of the various services being provided.

KM, through explicit knowledge capture, produces consistent standards and forms, templates, process and procedures, thereby enabling firms to become more efficient in delivering services to clients. Creating standards and templates can be very time consuming. It can be inefficient for smaller firms, although even smaller law firms can benefit from simple templates and examples. For larger law firms, standardised processes, practices and tools are a must. Many law firms have already invested in standardising their business and legal processes, some have even optimised them. Perhaps the next step could be the use of Robotic Process Automation (RPA), in other words software robots that can automate routine processes and tasks.

KM can be a great help in the collection of information about specific clients or industries. The information could be collected in a specific platform, which requires a pre-defined process for collecting data. Collaborative platforms allow employees to work and collaborate using the systems that best meet their needs while ensuring that the resultant collective knowledge can be retrieved and utilised in a way that reduces the burden of collaboration on known experts. Establishing a knowledge portal enables individual knowledge to be captured and included as part of the firm's knowledge base from whence it can be accessed across the firm and this in turn facilitates retention of the firm's knowledge; it's intellectual capital. The quantity of information which can be automatically collected in collaborative platforms in the future remains to be seen.

4.2 Flexibility and responsiveness

(a) Project management

Project management and process improvement are just beginning to be utilised in legal service delivery, and one of the questions this new application raises is who should be a project manager in a legal project? Should it be a partner, senior lawyer or perhaps someone else with enough experience in legal project management? Many clients do not necessarily want partners to serve as project managers because partners' billing rates are typically the highest in the firm. Some law firms prefer to have lawyers who serve as project managers while also practising law in the same matter. However, it may be worth considering whether a project manager needs to be a lawyer at all. A good project manager or process improvement specialist will have spent years developing their expertise in their field, and some law firms are already utilising business professionals with non-legal backgrounds as project managers. This raises the possibility that KM departments could provide project management services to their firms' legal projects, as well as being responsible for the selection of client and assignment teams. Taking expertise locators as our example, KM would facilitate flexibility and responsiveness to client needs by assigning the right lawyers at the right time and with the right approach to address the particular needs of clients. This type of KM-based project management service would be cost efficient and would allow lawyers to concentrate on their greatest strength, namely practising law. Astute partners utilise talented people in each role on their project teams and there may be little to gain from assigning lawyers to fulfil an administrative role, such as that of project manager, for which they may have no training or experience, possibly to the detriment of that lawyer's ability to best utilise his or her legal expertise in that matter.

(b) Information services

Not every corporation has its own information services personnel; moreover, many companies have reduced their information services staff during recent years. This opens an opportunity for law firm KM departments to contribute to their firms' value-added, client-centric service offerings, and possibly even to take on an income-generating role; specifically, information services could be provided free of charge to a firm's best clients and sold to other clients as a 'bundled' fixed-price package or as an hourly-based service. This could appeal to clients as a cost-effective outsourced service. In addition, many KM departments are already also preparing and providing to clients different kinds of follow-up services such as providing timely notice of changes in laws relevant to the client's business. Information services also provide cost savings to clients and efficiency enhancements for firms by eliminating the need for lawyers to search for relevant background information themselves. These KM services could be tailored to client, assignment or industry-specific 'packages' which would provide lawyers with easy access to the most relevant information. Of course, the continued development of technology, leading to software robots which can search millions of documents in less than a second, and which may even provide better analysis, answers and solutions than human beings, does beg the question of how large the role of human-provided information services will be in the future of law firm KM.

4.3 Training, learning and knowledge sharing

Practical methods for sharing tacit knowledge are numerous. Law firms can support knowledge sharing by using various forms of cooperation such as teamwork, mentoring, senior-junior working pairs and exchanges of experience. Exchanges of experience can be done, for example, in knowledge sharing meetings as well as assignment retrospects such as After Action Reviews, as mentioned earlier, in which employees can use their wisdom to stimulate new wisdom in another person. All of these methods create interaction between employees and thus contribute to knowledge sharing. Additionally, the arrangement of workrooms can either help or hinder the sharing of tacit knowledge. In an open-plan office it is easy to ask questions and discuss issues. Private workrooms may reduce interaction and thus hamper the sharing of information. Ideally, an office would provide both open-plan offices and quiet working places, in a way that prioritises the essential possibility to interact. Tony Rhem has listed the key features that make for a collaborative office space in his chapter 'What is Legal Project Management'.

(a) Knowledge sharing culture

As knowledge accessibility, findability and relevance increase, there is a corresponding rise in user adoption. KM in particular, by implementing knowledge transfer, sharing, and collaboration processes, policies and tools, creates an atmosphere where lawyers can learn from one another, share best practices, and provide practical training for less knowledgeable associates. This creates a positively reinforcing cycle, encouraging employees to share more, supporting a collaborative and knowledge-sharing culture.

Successful KM practices, policies and tools create an environment where employees experience enrichment through collaboration and sharing. In addition, expertise management fosters the practice of lawyers being assigned to cases where their expertise can be best leveraged and this in turn helps to create an environment where the retention of employees is high.

It is also important that the employees of the law firm know one another's roles and areas of expertise to be able to share knowledge efficiently. Accordingly, networking within the firm is an important factor in successful knowledge-sharing. Such networking enables identification of who in the firm could benefit from information as well as who is best able to provide the relevant information. Ideally, all employees would know one another's areas of expertise and be able to directly contact those colleagues best able to help with their information needs. Knowing each other's roles and expertise is self-evident and automatic in smaller law firms, but not in larger ones. As real-life time and even location constraints inherent in law firm operation may impede the achievement of optimum networking, KM could easily serve a crucial function as the means to connect people to people.

(b) *Channels and forums of communication*

The most straightforward communication forum is a physical workplace, however, in some firms it can also be a collaboration platform or combination of those two. In addition to traditional designated communication gatherings, such as regular meetings and conferences, communication forums can also take the form of kick-off meetings, strategy day gatherings or face-to-face discussions. Furthermore, in addition to physical workplace forums there are many different non-physical channels of communication in law firms, such as email, intranet, instant messaging and telephone. All of these can be used for sharing information, but as noted above, successful knowledge sharing most often does require interaction between individuals.

Moreover, collaboration and innovation with our clients can be expected to play an increasingly significant role in the future. By innovating with our clients we can increase our understanding of our clients' needs and provide them with better services. Innovation can be done by using collaborative platforms, but innovative face-to-face discussions are likely to be more efficient – especially when they are arranged in an environment different from a grey meeting room. These places can be, for example, 'innovation of thinking rooms' – places that encourage interaction. But we must not forget also traditional well-tested secondments in client organisations that easily increase interaction with clients and an understanding of their needs.

4.4 Workplace satisfaction

Establishing KM practices with the goal of addressing retention of employees as well as the accessibility of knowledge contributes greatly towards workplace satisfaction. Fostering an environment which rewards sharing knowledge and open communication for collaboration will continue to enrich the workplace.

In our consideration of knowledge sharing, we must also address the issue of organisational hierarchy. Organisational hierarchies may hamper the sharing of information. An expert may worry that others negatively exploit his knowledge and expertise. Information may be withheld as a form of security, because those possessing information may believe that it would weaken their own position in the hierarchy if others have access to the same information. Organisational hierarchy can also unintentionally prevent knowledge sharing between departments and offices. Ultimately, if organisational hierarchy interferes with the sharing of knowledge, then information such as client and assignment understanding remains as a separate piece of information and cannot be used efficiently.

Barriers to knowledge sharing can also arise from an organisational culture that endorses withholding knowledge or which at least discourages openly exchanging information. For example, an organisation may have a culture which prefers that subject matter experts do their work independently and autonomously, and 'asking for help' can be seen as a sign of incompetence. Underlying both organisational cultures and organisational hierarchies which inhibit the free exchange of information may be a competitive atmosphere at the workplace. Knowledge sharing promotes a culture in which the working community values include transparency, trust and the lack of competition between colleagues. Of course, it should be noted that competition is not in itself inherently disadvantageous and organisations may exist that are at the same time competition-minded and communal. However, in some cases competition with a firm may lead to situations where useful information will not be shared, but withheld for the sake of protecting vested interests. Could it be worthwhile to think how to stimulate competition in knowledge sharing and reward that?

(a) ***Knowledge and know-how needs to be focused efficiently***

In the day-to-day work life of a law firm, sharing of knowledge often takes place in a very random way and the form that the sharing takes, its extent and other key factors usually depends on the personal discretion of the information's expert. Knowledge sharing practices also typically vary between different groups of experts within the firm. As random knowledge sharing may not be an efficient or effective way of taking care of a firm's knowledge sharing needs, firms should introduce common practices on a firm-wide level to ensure that client insight and assignment best practices are shared equally throughout the firm. At a minimum, such common practices should include what types of information should be shared, with whom it should be shared and what communication channels and forums are to be used for knowledge sharing. New methods and forums of knowledge sharing would also contribute significantly to development of an effective knowledge sharing culture. As one example of a likely effective method, employees who work with a specific client could meet regularly to discuss that client and their assignments. Another method could be some kind of internal social media where teams could discuss the client, assignments, ask questions and share knowledge.

5. Legal project management and KM challenges for law firms

5.1 Risk management/legal requirements

There are many legislative requirements in the field of law, which sometimes results in slower execution of processes when law firms need to, for example, fulfil the investigative requirements of anti-money laundering laws, conflict checks and similar legal compliance obligations. These types of delays can sometimes result in delays in the commencement of new matters. One way to create accuracy and effectiveness is to centralise these tasks with separate specialists that can do the necessary checks quickly and efficiently. Also a separate development or compliance team that follows the changing requirements and proposes actions accordingly is an asset to a law firm.

5.2 Pricing

In response to client demand, increased international competition and other factors, many law firms are reforming their offerings, reducing costs, changing their business structure and even changing the traditional roles of lawyers to meet clients' needs. Most of the drive for alternative pricing models has originated from clients.

When preparing a firm's pricing strategy, the management of the firm must first understand what outcome a client is seeking, and the scope of the assignment. Is it quick resolution, a specific outcome, certainty, predictability or something else? Additionally, the trend toward increasing transparency of law firm processes for clients can also lead to increased openness in pricing practices. As a general rule, lawyers are not comfortable having conversations about fees with clients – but more lawyers should accustom themselves to such discussions. Clients for their part, should expect to have a pricing conversation with the client manager or assignment responsible.

Many partners nowadays are realising that they need to engage in pricing conversations and increasingly partners are realising that help with this issue may be found within the firm's own business services functions, such as the finance function, or marketing and business development function. Nothing happens without appropriate staffing and managing for a pricing program. There are various different methods for determining pricing which law firms utilise; for example, whether partner compensation should be treated as profit or as cost, whether a contribution model will be used, and various other issues. Key in the development of usable pricing programs is the ability to effectively develop systems and processes, beginning with people and processes, and then adding reasonable technology.

(a) *Project scope*

Aside from understanding the client's objectives, the following factors also significantly affect pricing:

- What is the schedule for completing the matter?
- Who is on the team and who's not?
- What percentage of each team member's time will be allocated to the matter?
- What factors would result in the expenses of the matter exceeding the budget?

(b) *Changes in traditional employment contracts*

A trend in the legal services market is the increasing number of persons who work as freelancers. It is likely that companies will use more freelancers and consultants with a wider variety of skills in the future. Law departments will realise they can't afford dedicated staff encompassing all of the skills needed to do the legal work for their clients. Those departments will then build *ad hoc* teams using a combination of dedicated staff, law firms and freelancers who will work together for one or more projects before disbanding. It is possible that it will also become common for law firms to use freelance lawyers to help in a hurry, rather than hire permanent staff.

5.3 Data security

While knowledge sharing and multiple communication forums and channels likely will improve information and knowledge sharing within law firms, with a positive benefit for firm competitiveness and value-added client-centric services, such developments have also given new opportunities to cyber criminals, as exemplified by, among other things, the increase in email based malware attacks against law firms. Preventing such attacks from succeeding, and the very serious damage which could result from a successful attack, requires law firms to be very vigilant, particularly individual employees must exercise caution with email links and attachments, even normal office documents.

The increase in attacks on law firms shows that some cyber criminals have worked out how to game the global financial system. M&A deals, patent grants, patent disputes – these transactions are key to how businesses are perceived in the market. Successfully stealing access to such market sensitive information can turn a hacker into an inside trader, leveraging the real world financial system to make money and distorting market transparency. Law firms, and the companies that hire them, should take steps to ensure that company secrets remain secret, by detecting and preventing advanced attackers from breaching law firm defences. Data security issues place a significant amount of pressure on law firms to build the best possible layers of security into every communication forum and channel utilised by the firm and its employees in the performance of their work.

6. Conclusion

Clients have changed. They want more for less. Most law firms are traditional and many things are readily done in the same way that they have always been done. But law firms must change – state-of-the-art tools need to be implemented, project management skills developed, transparency of the processes increased, just to mention a few necessary changes. Knowledge sharing and collaboration is crucial and information volumes continue to grow. The field of robotics, its possibilities and its data security risks will change the future even more. Law firms need to renew and change along with their clients. There are many challenges to come, but they can be turned into advantages.

KM's role has changed over recent years from a traditional library and information service to an important function in law firms. The possibilities and services that KM can provide are almost unlimited. KM can have a significant role in the change of law firms – law firms just need to take advantage of it.

KM in legal project management

Anthony J Rhem
AJ Rhem & Associates, Inc

1. Introduction

Project management is "the process of application of knowledge, skills, tools, and techniques to project activities in order to meet project requirements".[1] Many organisations implement different projects. Projects are done in different environments such as healthcare, insurance, information technology, legal and other industries. Each project produces some sort of an outcome and every project has a beginning and an end.

2. Knowledge within projects

Knowledge is becoming one of the main assets for organisations that want to improve their competitiveness, and the legal industry is no exception. Knowledge comes from different sources within organisations, such as internal processes, projects, customers and internal staff and outside information sources. As markets evolve, organisations implement different projects to address this evolution; this leads to an accumulation of content (knowledge and information). Companies use knowledge management (KM) to create, identify and distribute knowledge and experiences arising from projects within the organisation.

As projects are completed, the challenge to efficiently and effectively capture the knowledge from projects remains. The use of KM in project environment is of increasing importance, as it increases the success of projects, although it brings the challenge of successful creation and exchange of knowledge.

The success or failure of projects highly depends on the ability and willingness of people to capture, catalogue and use the knowledge and exchange it with other people within projects and the organisation. This is the challenge facing law firms as they not only embrace legal project management, but also the need to create and foster a culture of knowledge sharing and collaboration. Culture and environment within the law firms that promote and encourage knowledge sharing will go a long way in supporting the exchange of knowledge and the effective use of legal project management.

3. What is legal project management?

Legal project management focuses on leveraging the application and concepts of

1 *A Guide to the Project Management Body of Knowledge (PMBOK® Guide)*, 5th edn (Project Management Institute, 2013).

project management in order to control and manage the business of providing legal services. Law firms working under fee arrangements such as fixed or flat fees, cost limits, and success bonuses are commonly utilising project management. Project management will provide management of schedule, risk, and cost in a more rigorous and structured manner. Legal project management is becoming standard practice for law departments and firms using hourly billing as they are faced with the need to be more efficient in the delivery of legal services (Rhem, 2012).[2]

Legal project management (LPM) can be an effective tool for improving efficiency in the delivery of legal services. LPM techniques can help identify best practices for scoping a matter, effectively communicating across the team, managing a budget, and monitoring progress.[3] However, to realise these benefits the lawyers will have to buy in and realise benefits from this right away. A best practice would be to start a pilot with a few lawyers in order to demonstrate the value of LPM and to achieve a quick win. Once some level of buy-in has been accomplished, continue implementing the LPM practice, capturing and applying lessons learned along the way.

Palomaki and Wagner[4] have indicated 10 aspects of what they found instrumental in getting lawyers to buy in to legal project management inside a law firm and they are included below:

(1) ***Embrace it, lawyers know everything.*** *Many lawyers will rightfully rebel against the notion that PM training is teaching them something new. PM includes skills and techniques that most lawyers currently know and use. Acknowledging that the attorneys already possess the basic skills and that PM techniques merely provide more structure around what they are already doing, is key to gaining attorneys' buy-in. And, if you talk to the lawyers about a time they have exceeded budget and had to explain it to a client that can be a good starting point for helping them identify what they can do better to avoid that conversation in the future.*

(2) ***Consider a bottom-up approach.*** *Many of the firms who are on the path to PM have taken a top-down approach. It is no surprise that the 'Do it because I said so' method is ineffective. Rather than dictating a one-size-fits-all tactic, consider starting with individual client or project teams. In order to help improve efficiencies, first identify what the inefficiencies are. All lawyers are not inefficient in the same way, and neither is the solution to help them. Training on a team level and helping individual teams analyze the way they work will be more effective and more successful – one team at a time.*

(3) ***KISS (Keep it simple, stupid.)*** *Lawyers hate non-legal training, and if you make them attend training that is longer than 90 minutes, they get really cranky. Instead of trying to cram all that could be taught into 90 minutes or forcing our lawyers to submit to day long sessions, we found it more effective to develop training programs that are unique and specific to the individual teams on just those areas in which that*

2 A Rhem (2012) "Knowledge Management in Law Firms" retrieved from: http://knowledgemanagementdepot.com/2012/03/23/knowledge-management-in-the-legal-profession/.

3 *Ibid.*

4 S Palomaki and F Wagner, "Legal Project Management from the Inside: 10 Things Law Firm Leaders Need to Know About Implementing Legal Project Management" (2011) *Law Practice Today*, American Bar Association.

team wants help. By approaching the training this way, our lawyers really hone in on the areas where they want to focus. They don't learn everything, but they learn what they want to know, they use it and they get results. Then, they come back for more.

(4) ***Encourage debate.*** *We hired an outside consultant to jump-start Sutherland's PM initiative. Throughout the training course, the consultant both anticipated and enjoyed the debates that occurred during the session and was able to use those discussions to emphasize key points on many concepts. We learned that our lawyers got the most out of PM training when we opened up the discussion and encouraged them to debate the concepts and best practices. Our lawyers fiercely debated the appropriate time to talk to clients about a change in scope, how much to involve associates in the overall project plan, what the best practices are for team meetings and communication, and how to share a post-project review with the team. And, as is usually the case in the law, there is no right answer. The 'right' answer is team, practice and client specific. What works for one team may not work for the other. The most critical piece is that the team and the client are on the same page. Listen to the debate, and you will be better positioned to help your lawyers where they need it most.*

(5) ***Do ONE thing Better.*** *Every lawyer, every practice, every client and every team has different strengths and weaknesses. Still, there is always one thing the team can do better. Encourage everyone to be involved in identifying inefficiencies, our team members have ownership in the solution, and everyone works together to improve the process.*

(6) ***Talk about Task Codes.*** *Task codes can be a sticking point for project management efforts in law firms. The codes are intended to systematically categorize legal work by grouping relevant tasks for a matter. Executed correctly, the codes can provide a platform for tracking the scope and budget of a matter based on task (eg, case assessment, pre-trial pleadings, discovery, trial preparation). Task codes can also provide historical data that allows for better budget forecasting. There can be a few challenges with using task codes, however. Using codes requires the lawyers to know and understand how to segment their time without overlap and all team members must use the codes consistently. Without consistent standards and definitions, the data that results is 'garbage in, garbage out'. Our approach is to let the client's objectives dictate how task codes will be used and then to implement them for the specific team.*

(7) ***Follow up and reward success.*** *Once a team has identified an inefficiency, how will you know if they have improved? Following up with them at regular intervals – a couple of weeks, 30 days, etc – will ensure everyone stays motivated. Ask them how they are progressing. Did the solution work the way they thought it would? Has improving one area created a more inefficient process somewhere else? Have they developed a best practice that can be shared with another team doing similar work? In addition to following up, recognizing success is essential. Make sure firm management is aware of the progress the team is making. Helping the lawyers along the way and promoting them internally when they succeed helps everyone achieve their client goals.*

(8) ***Be resourceful.*** *An area for improvement we identified was better sharing of resources. In conjunction with our knowledge management (KM) initiative, we are working with teams and individual lawyers to pool the resources they use repeatedly, making them easily accessible to anyone who may need them. We are identifying various templates and tools considered to be 'best practices' and making them available in our KM system. Sharing across the firm helps everyone do a better job for their clients.*

(9) ***Use Technology.*** *When we began the PM initiative, none of the available software products had been fully tested. Since we had the capabilities internally to create our own tool, we took the 'build it yourself' approach. We knew we wanted a platform that would help our lawyers better track the progress on matter scope and budgets, ensuring there were no surprises for the client at the end of the month. We also knew we wanted the flexibility to customize the platform for each client or individual matter.*

(10) ***Include Your Clients!*** *Conducting client feedback interviews proved by far the most effective tool we have to hear what clients really think about our firm and its services. Clients want the best service possible, and they want to help their favorite outside counsel be the best they can be.*[5]

The practice of legal project management varies from law-firm-specific practices to corporate law entities when it comes to the approach to legal work. In recent years clients have begun demanding more alternative fee arrangements, greater predictability, improved accountability, and, above all, cost containment from their law firms.[6] Project management (specifically legal project management) is a disciplined, systematic, task-based approach to work process that can provide law firms with some key tools to respond to client demands. The knowledge that is gained and reused in the legal project management paradigm is essential to gaining efficiencies and the cost containment law firms and legal entities are looking for.

4. KM in legal project management

Knowledge is generated throughout the execution of a project. KM within projects is intended to make relevant knowledge available to the project team throughout the execution of the project. Project management methodologies usually define standard project phases, processes, templates or actions that are repeated in the course of different projects.

The legal project management execution addresses why the project idea exists, the problem(s) it is addressing, the products or the deliverables of the project, who will take part in the project and how will people working on the project be organised, as well as the project location and deadlines. KM as a part of the legal project management process will document and share decisions and assumptions regarding resources, time, quality requirements, costs etc. KM will also document and share domain knowledge: knowledge about the industry, technology, processes, current situation, business products and services (ie, the software development lifecycle);

5 *Ibid*, pp1–3.
6 *Ibid.*

institutional knowledge: knowledge that a project team or member has about the organisation (ie, organisation structure, reporting structure); and process knowledge: knowledge about the project tasks, methodologies, timelines, structure, deliverables and processes (ie, project plan) as well as sharing and transferring knowledge through mentoring and lessons learned (which are documented after every phase and at the end of the project).

According to Lisa Kellar Gianakos, Director of Knowledge Management at Pillsbury Winthrop Shaw Pittman and author of "The Intersection of Knowledge and Legal Project Management":

> *KM professionals understand the process of law practice, project management, finance, and technology. They also tend to be analytical and logical thinkers. Furthermore, in many firms the KM professionals have already built bridges to both lawyers and multiple staff departments. Since LPM is a collaborative effort, those bridges turn out to be very important in the difficult LPM change management process.*[7]

Lisa Kellar Gianakos also quotes Toby Brown. Brown is a well-known LPM evangelist with a strong history in KM. "In his keynote on the Economics of Law and the Future of KM, he discussed why, for KM to remain a vital function for firms, it needs to be focused on solving the core challenges facing firms."[8] KM applied to LPM is one of the vehicles for KM to remain in front of law firms in the foreseeable future. The project development lifecycle enables many traditional KM goals to become closely aligned with those of legal project management (cultivating efficiencies, delivering better predictability; improved communications, and process improvement). It is with this understanding that KM enables project team members to reduce rework and squeezes the time that it takes to plan project execution. Sharing lessons learned and advanced practices is key to helping others excel in the legal project management process and execution.

5. Capturing knowledge in legal project management execution

When executing LPM within the firm it is essential to the continued success of the firm's project management practice to capture and reuse the knowledge gained from project management. A practice that will facilitate this is to capture lessons learned and best practices that can be leveraged in future projects. This KM method for sharing and transferring knowledge can be accomplished through the following techniques for knowledge sharing:

- Conducting after action reviews (capturing lessons learned),
- Identifying/participating in communities of practice.
- Working in collaborative settings.

5.1 After action reviews

An after action review (AAR) is a facilitated session conducted with a team or group after completion of a piece of work or project. The objective of an AAR is to capture

---

7 LK Gianakos (2013), "The Intersection of Knowledge and Legal Project Management", p1. Retrieved from: https://info.legalsolutions.thomsonreuters.com/signup/newsletters/practice-innovations/2013-mar/article4.aspx

8 *Ibid*, p2.

the knowledge gained by the team as a result of the performing/executing the work.

An AAR:

- makes learning conscious and explicit;
- identifies valuable lessons that may be helpful to future teams;
- enhances team openness and cooperation; and
- allows closure at the end of the project.

(a) Some AAR facts

Participants: An AAR is conducted by the persons who participated in the activity being reviewed. Formal AARs may be conducted by a facilitator, but the participants should be those persons who were actually involved, not their representatives or off-site supervisors.

The AAR is conducted:

- at the end of a project;
- at the end of a particular phase in a project;
- at the end of a conference;
- at the end of a case; and
- immediately following a significant legal event or action.

Types of AARs: Formal. Formal AARs are generally conducted at a more extended break in the activity being reviewed; formal AARs may take a full day and result in a detailed report.

Informal. While an activity is in progress, or for an activity of short duration, most of the AARs in which our associates are likely to participate will be informal, consisting perhaps of an hour-long discussion at the end of a day. More likely to result in a mid-course correction than a policy shift, informal AARs enable teams to identify what is working and what needs work.

After action review steps: These steps describe the general steps in conducting an AAR and their significance. The specific steps taken in conducting an AAR will depend on how much time you have allotted, outside resources needed and/or available, the complexity of your operation, and what is expected to be accomplished.

Table 1: After action review steps

After action review steps	Comments
1. Assemble participants as soon after the event(s) as practicable.	It is important to bring people together while the results are fresh in their minds.

continued on next page

After action review steps	Comments
2. Establish rules and explain objectives.	Rules and objectives make sure the AAR stays on track.
3. Summarise events as they were planned to occur, with work and time estimates, as appropriate.	Provides appropriate timelines to events as they actually occurred.
4. Elicit discussion on how the events actually took place. Strategies to make this happen include:	
• Identify mistakes, but don't assign blame. The focus should be on the actions, not on the actors.	The AAR discussion is a process of discovery, as all team members share their perspectives on what happened and why. The shared observations of the newest interns through to the most senior associates are essential to piece together how and why some objectives were met and others were not.
• Articulate assumptions.	The explicit statement of previously overlooked assumptions often leads to better solutions.
• Address objective and subjective dimensions of the events.	Discussion subjects, including attitudes, expectations, fatigue and stress, may help to explain outcomes in addition to more objective information.
• Ask open-ended questions, not questions that have one-word answers.	Open-ended questions encourage discussion and exploration of a topic. They are also less likely to make participants defensive. Compare, "Describe your trip to the court house," with "Why did it take you so long to get to the court house?"

continued on next page

After action review steps	Comments
Big picture questions include: • What went well, and by what standard? • What could have gone better? More detailed questions may address: • Why actions were taken? • How associates responded to situations? • When actions were taken relative to other events? • What alternative actions might have achieved better results? • What is required to replicate good performance?	To follow up on what went well/what could have gone better, ask participants to assign a numerical rating to an action. Subsequent discussion on how to improve the rating may lead to the kinds of details that will enable the team to improve overall performance.
5. Record results. List the associates who participated, what learning was achieved, what changes are planned, and what practices will be strengthened.	Some of the observations of the AAR will need to be shared with higher and lower levels of the organisation.
6. Establish the expectation of AARs as a regular, re-occurring feature of your organisation's operations. They should not be considered a sign of failure.	As a group activity, the AAR can promote group cohesiveness and identity. Through repetition, it makes individuals more reflective practitioners.
7. AAR pitfalls that must be avoided: • Allowing performance critiques. • Lecturing. • Over-analysing minutiae. • Griping, complaining and general negativity. • Allowing stronger personalities to dominate the review, keeping others from participating.	Address the pitfalls when executing the AAR to ensure success.

5.2 Communities of Practice (CoP)

Communities of Practice (CoP) are groups of people who share a common interest in a particular domain area, and who interact regularly to learn how to perform aspects of the discipline better. CoPs are formed by people who are engaged in a collective learning experience, who usually interact often to learn, share and to better perform their craft.

A CoP:

- can exist online via discussion boards, wikis, news groups or in real life via meet-ups or other group settings;
- CoPs consist first and foremost of practitioners; specialists who perform the same job or collaborate on a shared task;
- CoPs often form spontaneously, driven by the need of the members for operational knowledge; and
- CoPs are also deliberately encouraged where it is known there is a need for knowledge transfer.

6. Working in collaborative settings

Working in a collaborative setting encourages the sharing and exchanging of ideas. Having spent many years as a KM consultant working in this type of environment, I can attest first hand to the effectiveness this type of workspace provides when it comes to collaborating. It is my experience that collaborative workspaces are ideal for a maximum of 12 people. Too many people and there will be an abundance of 'side bar' conversations going on that the whole group could, but will not, benefit from.

The key features that make for a collaborative office space:

- An open plan and other design features (eg, high-traffic staircases) that encourage accidental interactions.
- More common areas than are strictly necessary – multiple cafeterias, other places to read and work that encourage workers to leave confined offices.
- Emphasis on areas that hold two or more people, rather than single-occupancy offices.
- Purpose-free generic 'thinking' areas in open-plan spaces, which encourage workers to do their thinking in the presence of other people, rather than alone.

7. Summary

Legal project management is at the early stages of adoption within law firms and legal service delivery today. The use of professional support lawyers (PSL) that have a background in project management in addition to law would be an ideal resource to lead project management efforts. Project management is a collaborative discipline. As law firms embrace a culture and environment of knowledge sharing and collaboration, certain KM methods such as after-action reviews and communities of practice will be infused within the legal project management initiatives.

This will support traditional KM goals of cultivating efficiencies, delivering better predictability; improved communications, and process improvement to become a part of the legal project management execution. It is with this understanding that the sharing of lessons learned and advanced practices will enable project team members to reduce rework and be more effective in executing client needs. Overall, the positive effect of legal project management infused with KM will encourage the entire team in supporting the exchange of knowledge and the effective execution of the process and procedures of legal project management.

Client-facing knowledge management

Raffael Büchi
Bär & Karrer

1. From product to client service as the differentiating factor

When knowledge management became a topic for law firms in the 1990s, the focus was on the products lawyers deliver. Consequently, knowledge management was mainly an inward facing function. KM's main objective was to support the lawyers in delivering their products: oral and written legal advice and legal documents – memos, contracts, submissions, claims etc.

As KM and supporting technology has evolved, the lawyers' products have become less of a differentiating factor. The Internet has revolutionised legal research and most of the larger firms now have a powerful search engine and a central repository for know-how where lawyers may find templates or good precedents. Know-how providers such as *Practical Law*[1] offer everything a lawyer needs to produce a document: practice notes, checklists, templates, even a peer review and legal query service. As a consequence of this development, legal products have become similar. Clients take it for granted that the documents lawyers deliver are of good quality. Documents and legal advice alone hardly make lawyers stand out anymore.

Instead, client service has become one of the most important differentiating factors in today's legal market.

This chapter discusses the role that knowledge management – the systematic and continuous collection, organisation, development and dissemination of all relevant knowledge[2] – may play in the context of client service. It further explores client-facing knowledge management in business development and marketing.

2. The core elements of client service: the playing field

Core elements of what clients perceive as service are:

- availability, responsiveness and speed; as well as
- a specific understanding of the client's needs and requirements, for its business and environment.

Other areas of increasing importance are ancillary services such as:

- supplying the client with information;

1 http://uk.practicallaw.com/
2 This definition of knowledge management is based on Schulz/Klugmann, *Wissensmanagement für Anwälte* (Aufl, Köln 2006). See n 14.

- personnel support by providing the client with secondees;
- training and continuous education of the client's staff; and
- advice on organising the client's legal and compliance function, including advising on in-house contract and knowledge management.

In all these areas, KM may play an important role. Client service is a large and growing field for knowledge management.

2.1 Availability, responsiveness and speed

Good knowledge management is one of the most important driving factors for responsiveness and speed. Lawyers have to be able to quickly tap into the know-how relevant to the matter at hand, be it through accessing his or her own collection of precedents, a know-how system with templates and precedents, an intranet with wiki-style know-how or by asking the right specialist within or outside the firm. In the latter case, the 'know-who', the knowledge about the experts – the know-how carriers – combined with the availability and responsiveness of these experts, decides the reaction-time. A culture of sharing know-how,[3] referring work to better suited colleagues and willingness to support each other is a fertile ground for fast service delivery; silo mentality, reluctance to pass on work to more specialised colleagues and poor accessibility are inhibitors. Although knowledge management may, at first glance, not be perceived as client-facing in connection with availability, responsiveness and speed, a firm's approach to KM does have a direct and significant impact on these key elements of client service.

2.2 Understanding the client's demands and needs

Under this title, several elements with importance for KM may be distinguished.

(a) Monitoring the market for legal services

Whereas businesses in other industries are constantly monitoring their respective markets, their competitors and the products and services offered by competitors, many law firms do not systematically observe developments in the legal industry and market trends, especially outside the jurisdictions they cover. Those who do might detect opportunities and risks earlier than their competitors and adapt their strategies accordingly, for example, vis-à-vis clients or with respect to recruiting talent. Knowledge about developments in other law firms may help to build up or expand relationships with these firms and increase referrals.

KM may be involved in gathering and processing such information, screening publications[4] and clients' guides[5] and passing on relevant information to those it concerns.

---

3 On the importance of KM culture see Schulz's chapter on Getting lawyers to contribute content to KM systems and to use KM resources.

4 Eg, *The Lawyer, The American Lawyer, Legal Week, Legal Business*, or *JUVE*.

5 Eg, *Chambers, The Legal 500, IFLR 1000*.

(b) *Knowledge about the client's business and environment*

KM tools and personnel may also be deployed to improve the law firm's knowledge of the client's business and its specific environment. Smaller firms may have to be satisfied with an intranet page featuring industry know-how and linking to useful websites. KM in bigger firms may send regular industry updates to partners focusing on certain sectors, for example, in the form of an industry blog.

(c) *Obtaining client feedback*

Many law firms offer 'solutions and services tailored to our clients' needs', at least on their marketing material. The number of law firms that ask their clients for feedback in a systematic and structured way may be significantly lower. This is surprising: client feedback makes it easier to take measure, to fully understand the clients' needs and to optimise client service. KM lawyers are well positioned to take part in obtaining client feedback. They understand the products and services offered by law firms and are well suited to put themselves in the perspective of clients. As an additional advantage, KM lawyers, as opposed to partners, do not have to develop their own business and may therefore be more neutral and less biased. Law firms may ask clients for feedback as part of an After Action Review (AAR),[6] after completing a matter, upon reaching certain milestones or as part of high level relationship meetings, or both.

Technically, CRM solutions (see below) may be used to process client feedback.

2.3 Supplying clients with information, intelligence and thought leadership

Adapting Wayne Gretzky's famous quote:[7] Clients wish to know where the puck is going to be and from where body or cross-checking will come. Law firms that earn the reputation of supplying clients with such information and intelligence will have a decisive competitive advantage. These firms may become the trusted early detector of (legal) risks and opportunities and become almost irreplaceable. To be able to achieve this position, the firm must be 'close to the client'. What does this – slightly overused – term mean?

(a) *'Close to the client' – what it means and how to get there*

As a principle, the more a law firm works for a client, the closer to the client it will get. The more work a client allocates to a law firm, the more attention the firm will give this client. As a consequence, law firms with clients that generate recurring work should rather focus on a limited number of key clients than spread themselves too thinly. Clients on the other hand are well advised to reduce the number of their external legal advisers to a panel of law firms. Not only will the panel firms be more willing to agree on discounts, provide support by dispatching secondees and by rendering ancillary services (as discussed below), the panel firms will also get closer

---

6 A structured review or de-brief process (originally developed by the US military) for analysing 'what' happened, 'why' it happened and 'how' it can be done better by the participants and those responsible for the project or event (see https://en.wikipedia.org/wiki/After-action_review).

7 "I skate to where the puck is going to be, not where it has been." The Canadian Wayne Gretzky, active in the NHL from 1979–1999, is regarded as the greatest ice hockey player ever ("The Great One").

to the client. With every matter or transaction a law firm advises on, its specific client know-how increases. The better the law firm's specific client know-how is, the more efficient its services for this client should become – a virtuous cycle for the client and the law firm.

What can law firms do to increase their chances of being in the circle of a client's chosen law firms? The simple answer is, they should sharpen their profile. As trivial as this may sound, many law firms don't seem to give their strategic positioning much thought. Sharpening the profile typically means reducing the scope, focusing on a limited number of practice areas, industries or on a special type of client and increasing the quality of client service, strengthening their presence and building on the reputation within the chosen scope. Less is more.

Once firms have achieved a preferred position, regularly aligning their profile and business strategy[8] with the specific needs of key clients is paramount. As shown above, asking key clients for feedback should be an institutionalised element in continuously fine tuning the firm's strategy.

(b) How KM may contribute

Supplying clients with information and intelligence is an obvious field of (client-facing) knowledge management. In many law firms, KM personnel is involved in preparing client briefings and newsletters. To stand out and provide value to clients, these briefings and newsletters should be more than backward looking summaries of recent legislation or court decisions. They should contain forward looking elements, making clients aware of opportunities and risks, pointing out possible practical implications of legislation and judicature. Clients expect thought leadership, not merely chewing the cud. Only lawyers with broad and current experience and a deep understanding for the business of their clients are able to provide such contents. Consequently, KM lawyers that are expected to write valuable client briefings and newsletters have to be embedded in the practice teams. In larger firms, they may collect and develop specific industry or client know-how.

Smaller firms with a minimal number of central KM staff should not rely on KM to provide the contents of client briefings and newsletters. A central KM function won't be immersed in practice enough to provide thought leadership. It may, however, contribute to the quality of client briefings and newsletters by supporting the authors with research and by reviewing and proofreading.

2.4 Providing clients with secondees

(a) A great opportunity to foster relationships with clients

Law firms are normally not overly enthusiastic when clients ask them[9] to second lawyers to cover peak periods or support with special projects. The seconded lawyer will be missed by his team which has to cope with the additional workload,

---

8 See Schulz/Kuth's chapter on Organising KM in a law firm.

9 In panel review processes of large corporations, the availability of (free!) secondees may be a criterion, see Tabby Kinder, "Exclusive: Shell slashes global panel from 250 firms to six", *The Lawyer*, April 19 2016.

profitability takes a hit and the seconded lawyer might like the new job too much and jump ship. Against this backdrop, law firms may be tempted to send underperforming lawyers. However, if the client is not satisfied with the secondee this strategy will backfire.

With a more positive approach and accompanying measures, a secondment is a great opportunity to get closer to the client, deepen the relationship and to increase client and industry know-how. Again, KM is well suited to play an active role.

(b) Success factors

To make the most out of a secondment, the secondee should be carefully chosen, prepared for the task and 'monitored' during the stage with the client. Apt secondees are good project managers, good communicators, have above average people and networking skills, a genuine interest for the client, its business and its people and generally make a good impression. Technical skills should be sound but are not the prime prerequisite.

Can KM lawyers make good secondees? The answer is definitely 'yes' if KM lawyers embedded in practice – or industry – teams are seconded. Know-how lawyers that manage and structure know-how rather than produce contents will typically be less suited, unless, of course, they are seconded to the client to advance projects that require their specific skills and experience. As an example, a client's legal department may want to introduce knowledge management, reorganise a contract database, create structures and platforms for know-how exchange or build a special training program for top talents. For such projects, KM lawyers in central functions may be the best possible fit.

From a law firm's perspective, an advantage of sending KM lawyers as secondees is the fact that their temporary absence typically matters less than the absence of a fee earner – financially as well as in terms of coping with the daily work load. KM work and KM projects may be postponed more easily than client work. Another advantage may be that KM lawyers have a more sensitive eye for client know-how that the law firm could benefit from, know-how about the client but also know-how regarding how the client has developed.

As a preparation, the secondee should – in cooperation with the law firm:

- find out as much as possible about the client, its business and the secondee's future team;
- define the objectives of the secondment; and
- develop an action list: for example, people to meet, connections to make, tasks to fulfil, know-how and specific information to obtain.

During the secondment, the law firm should be in regular contact with the secondee track progress towards the objectives and items of the action list. After the secondment, the secondee may add to the firm's client and industry know-how by making an internal presentation and by contributing to written knowledge, for example, on the intranet.

2.5 Supporting clients in risk detection and management, compliance and training

Within the large realm of supporting clients in organising knowledge and expertise, risk management and compliance are fields where knowledge management is of particular importance. The knowledge relevant for the risk management and compliance function includes knowing and understanding applicable laws, regulations and official instructions and relevant news. Also included is the knowledge about risk carriers such as states, regions and individuals.

To support risk management and compliance, this knowledge, the relevant experience within the organisation and know-how regarding the knowledge bearers and their environment needs to be systematically and continuously collected, organised, developed and spread.

(a) Possible measures

The following measures may make a significant positive impact on the client's risk management, compliance or in-house legal function:

- identify suitable sources of information;
- standardisation and automation of processes and documents;
- debriefings, after action reviews, sharing worst practices (admitting and discussing mistakes);
- technology, for example for document automation, intranet, blogging;
- exit interviews;
- 'master-apprentice' relationships;
- know-how exchange platforms on different levels, for example on roundtables; and
- improvement of the on-boarding process and of the basic training of new joiners.

As far as these measures are closely linked to client-facing KM, they are discussed below.

Identify suitable sources of information: In helping clients to identify suitable sources of information for risk management and compliance purposes, KM lawyers are on their home turf. Publicly available overviews of the regulatory environment in various jurisdictions,[10] often in Q&A format, written by law firms[11] may give compliance officers and in-house lawyers of international corporations a good sense of what is important and where the risks are. From a marketing perspective, pointing out these free sources of information to clients makes particular sense if the law firm is among the contributors, that is, has written the chapter(s) pertaining the jurisdiction(s) it operates.

10 Such as ICLG – International Comparative Legal Guides (https://www.iclg.co.uk/), or *Practical Law*'s global guides (http://uk.practicallaw.com/resources/global-guides); access to Getting The Deal Through (https://www.gettingthedealthrough.com/) is restricted (in-house lawyers may get free access but have to login nevertheless).

11 The contributing law firms pay to provide the contents. This is counter-intuitive for many lawyers, but makes sense if the publication is frequently visited by clients and potential clients (it is equivalent to paying for a shop window on a prominent location).

Standardisation and automation: Standardised processes and documents reduce the room for errors. That's why professionals dealing with high risks or risks with potentially catastrophic consequences such as pilots follow very strict standard procedures. KM may help to determine standard processes. Standardising documents (producing templates) is one of the oldest fields of knowledge management. If standardised documents are used, the room for uncontrolled drafting and adventurous own production of documents is reduced.

Document automation takes it one step further: rather than using templates and filling in gaps, users of automated document assembly systems answer a set of questions. As the questionnaire is completed, a document – or a set of documents – is produced automatically. There is no margin for errors. For those responsible to review, the task gets much easier: rather than reviewing documents they may review the answers on which the documents are based.

It is obvious that automation has great potential on various levels.[12] However, the software does not automate documents itself. Buying the software is only the first, easy step. The actual programming of the documents to be automated is complex and time-consuming. It can only be done by lawyers that are automating on a regular basis, at least once a week. If fee earners are responsible for automation, chances are high that they will not have enough time to do it and that the effect of the investment will evaporate. Document automation is thus an ideal field and additional skill set for KM lawyers.

Document automation may also be client-facing.[13] Law firms may offer to automate documents which are often used by the client, either using their in-house lawyers or other staff such as the salesforce. The automated documents may be stored within the clients' or the law firm's sphere. As attractive as it may seem for law firms to be able to offer automation services for clients, it may be sensitive for the clients to make use of these services: if they rely on a law firm to do the automation (and to maintain the automated documents), they have placed themselves in a situation of dependence, especially if the documents are stored within the sphere of the law firm. As a consequence, clients may decide to automate their documents themselves or to rely on specialised providers rather than on law firms.

Debriefings and after action reviews: In debriefings or after action reviews with the client, KM lawyers may assume the role of moderators and, if need be, minute-takers. They are also ideally positioned to feed the outcome into the law firm's central know-how repositories, for example the intranet, and to advise the client as to the conclusions of debriefings that may be processed on the client's side.

Technology: If KM lawyers are experienced in using technology that the client uses

12 A leading provider of legal document assembly software claims to offer "a variety of solutions for law firms that want to drive efficiency for fixed fee work, retain key clients with better quality and consistency of documents and win new clients with innovative client services", www.contractexpress.com/document-automation-solutions/Law%20Firms/?gclid=CIOEloHjocwCFQtAGwodJp4H-A.

13 As indicated in the provider's claim quoted in n 12 above: "win new clients with innovative client services".

too, or considers purchasing, they may support the client in evaluating the technology and, if purchased, in making the best use of the technology. As KM lawyers consult the client, they have an opportunity to demonstrate that their law firm has a modern approach and cultivates knowledge sharing and developing. If the client manages a major project which draws a lot of resources (such as the introduction of document automation, see above), KM lawyers are well positioned to help make the project a success. For this purpose, KM lawyers may be seconded to the client (see above).

Know-how development and training: Providing technical training about certain legal topics to the client, for example to its in-house legal team, to compliance personnel, to the sales force or to management, is a traditional ancillary service law firms may render. The presenters hope to sharpen their profile as legal experts and lawyers of choice. The preparation for such appearances should not be taken lightly: if presentation skills are below the expectations of the audience and the lawyers leave a mixed impression, even technically brilliant lawyers may remove themselves from the reckoning. Consequently, law firms should send lawyers who have good presentation skills. They don't necessarily have to be partners: an associate with a flair to teach makes a much better impression than a partner with deplorable presentation skills. Obviously, talented presenters among a law firm's KM lawyers may also be perfectly suited to train clients' personnel.

Apart from supporting clients in training their staff in technical legal matters, law firms may also advise clients on setting up or improving and expanding an internal education and training system. KM lawyers are well positioned to render such structural and organisational advice. Master-apprentice relationship, know-how exchange platforms, training of new joiners: even simple organisational measures may have a significant positive impact. Allocating a senior team member to each junior new joiner as a coach and mentor, making an effort to take junior team members to meetings and involving them in discussions enables learning by watching and listening: the traditional master-apprentice relationship is an extremely effective teaching and training model. Roundtables are forums in which participants may share their experience without much preparation. Experience shows that such roundtables work best if participation is not compulsory, not associated with major efforts and if participants use it to share know-how rather than war stories (mainly trying to impress). Whereas roundtables with participants of different seniority and experience are particularly interesting and educational for juniors, experienced participants often find expert roundtables more worthwhile.

3. Knowledge management in business development and marketing

The systematic and continuous collection, organisation, development and dissemination of all relevant knowledge[14] not only increases the efficiency and quality of legal products and services but also facilitates and professionalises marketing and business development.

---

14 See n 2 above for a definition of knowledge management based on Schulz/Klugmann.

3.1 CRM – the KM tool for business development

Customer Relationship Management (CRM) tools are essentially KM tools for business development. They typically support lawyers in collecting, organizing, categorising and developing contacts, prospects and leads and in sharing the knowledge with others for the benefit of the law firm. Through a CRM tool, lawyers may maintain the quality of client data centrally and in a coordinated way, log their client related activities, register future events and appointments, set reminders, or create lists for marketing purposes. A culture of sharing contacts and information about these contacts creates a fertile ground for cross-selling, extending business and for acquiring new business. It also enables law firms to interact with clients and other business partners in a coordinated, structured way. From a client's perspective, in an ideal law firm all lawyers would share all know-how without constraints and egoistic considerations, be it related to products and services or be it related to clients. In this Unicorn LLP all lawyers would refer all work for which one of his or her colleagues is better suited to this colleague. A client would always get the best possible service and could always count on fully benefiting from the firm's size.

3.2 Possible roles of KM lawyers in business development and marketing

KM lawyers with a focus on knowledge management processes and structures may also apply their specific knowledge management know-how in the field of business development and marketing. With the purpose of supporting business development and marketing they may focus on industry know-how, client intelligence (as managed with a CRM tool) or on the legal market and its developments. As experts of finding the right sources of information, efficiently using information and making information accessible within the firm, such KM lawyers may easily switch their field of practice from law to business development and marketing. This does not mean that they are business development and marketing experts but, relying on their knowledge management skills, they are capable of supporting these experts.

(a) Detecting business development opportunities

In defining and adapting their strategy, law firms should continuously be on the lookout for new business development opportunities. What practice areas are evolving? What are the implications of technical, economic, social and political trends, developments, events and incidents on legal advice? KM lawyers may help monitor the environment in which law firms do business. They may, for example, regularly do research on competitors or law firms in other jurisdictions and analyse what they offer. KM may also be responsible for reading publications that cover the legal services market, screening them for new practice areas or new ways of practising in established fields.

(b) Pitches and beauty contests

In many practice areas, law firms regularly have to participate in pitch processes to win new business. Legal departments of large clients have made it standard to select a panel of law firms through rigorous 'beauty contests'. Whether pitching for a specific transaction or aspiring to become a panel firm of an attractive client: the (non-billable) work related to such exercises is significant. Since producing pitch presentations, filling out questionnaires and writing fee quotes is often repetitive, good KM is essential for an efficient use of resources. KM lawyers embedded in practice teams are well suited to create the specific contents of pitch presentations, central KM functions may help answer questions and give an overview of the firm's services.

(c) *Submissions for client directories and awards*

If KM lawyers have a broad overview of the firm, its practice areas, services and key players they are well positioned to draw up submissions for client directories such as *Chambers & Partners, Legal 500* or *IFLR 1000*, be it for rankings or for awards. Their legal background and their detailed understanding of a law firm's business makes it easier for them to succinctly describe work highlights and differentiating factors in submissions, without using platitudes.[15] They may also support researchers – often non-lawyers – in identifying the relevant interview partners and in making sense of their answers to the researchers' questions.

Since KM lawyers don't have their own business to nurture, they are not prone to pouring grit into their own mill. Without self-interests it is easier to defend the interests of the firm and of all its lawyers equally.

(d) *Finding the right lawyer within a firm*

For the reasons described above, KM lawyers with business development responsibilities are also well suited to advise existing or potential clients, but also other firms referring work, from a neutral point of view as to what lawyer or what team is best suited to attend a matter. If the scope of a potential new matter is unclear, KM lawyers in business development functions may attend the first meeting or call to make an initial assessment of the issues at hand and to involve the right lawyers. Depending on the matter or request, such a preliminary triage may be more efficient than using fee earners' time as from the very beginning.

(e) *Creating contents on the law firm's website*

Based on their legal background and understanding of the law firm's business, KM lawyers may contribute to the contents of the law firm's website, for example by helping to draw up the description of the services and practice areas, by drafting press releases and feeding the deal ticker or by listing publications.

(f) *Knowledge management related to publications and their distribution*

Lawyers are offered endless opportunities to participate in publications, contribute to global guides, and to place firm and individual profiles or advertisements. To separate the wheat from the chaff and to know which publications are serious and which are worthless, specific knowledge management is needed. The organisations selling these

15 As Chambers & Partners phrase it on their submission template: "Be specific. Avoid generalities such as 'client service' or 'breadth of expertise'. Give us a focus on what is special or unique about this department."

'unique opportunities' play on the vanity of lawyers, the lack of specific know-how and on the often astonishingly uncoordinated approach of law firms to these topics.

Law firms are well advised to centralise everything connected to sponsored publications and to placing profiles and advertisements. Sponsored publications, publications the authors pay for, are counterintuitive to many lawyers ("what do you mean: I have to pay for the article I write?") but if the distribution platform is right it may make just as much sense as it may to pay for a shop window on 5th Avenue or Oxford Street. Certain publishers and platforms are distribution machines, receive millions of clicks a year and give detailed feedback on reader stats. Participating may leverage the effect of a law firm's publications significantly and allow targeted marketing. Other publications and platforms may claim to be read by 'decision makers' but prove shallow and implausible. To generate the respective know-how and to decide on a strategy, careful and time consuming research and a certain amount of experience is essential. Personal, long-lasting relationships with key personnel of the publishers help to get good deals and to keep up to date with industry developments. Only law firms with a competent central contact for publishers have a chance to stop their business developers from contacting lawyers directly. The efficiency gains of dealing with all the publications only centrally are considerable. Publications that prove to be worthless but still contact lawyers should be prevented from emailing anyone in the law firm by blocking their URL.

Again, KM lawyers with their topical understanding and their know-how as to what may be interesting to readers are well suited to being central contacts for publications. KM lawyers with special writing skills may also review articles before they are published to ensure a certain level of uniformity and quality.

4. KM principles of universal validity

Whether KM faces clients or serves the business development or marketing function, the following key principles apply to all KM projects:

- Analysis of needs and definition of objectives first – no size fits all.
- Always ask first: what does really add value?
- Content[16] is just as important as good technology.
- Keep it simple and start small (quick wins).
- Involve internal experts and listen to them.[17]
- Experienced, higher ranking experts should be responsible for KM in the field of their speciality.
- Analyse what's already there first (IT, know-how) and use it wherever possible.
- Allocate enough resources (particularly time) to drive KM projects, appoint or hire a dedicated knowledge manager.[18]
- Cultivate a tolerant culture in which mistakes may be addressed frankly and constructively.[19]

---

16 See Schulz's chapter on Getting lawyers to contribute content to KM systems and to use KM resources.
17 See Schulz/Kuth's chapter on Organising KM in a law firm.
18 See Schulz/Kuth's chapter on Organising KM in a law firm.
19 See Schulz/Kuth's chapter on Organising KM in a law firm.

- Focus on less experienced team members – they will benefit the most.
- Vary the intensity of your KM efforts, for example by periodically organising know-how competitions.

These principles are interrelated: KM initiatives will only be successful if there is a real need for them and it is clear what they aim to achieve. Internal experts have to be involved when exploring needs and defining objectives, not only because they have crucial insights and experience but also because the likelihood that they will support KM initiatives is much higher if they have shaped them. As a consequence, centrally devised KM measures are doomed to fail: in knowledge management, no size fits all. What may make sense for one jurisdiction, one industry, one practice area, one culture or one team may not make sense to others. KM solutions should not be off the shelf but tailor made.

KM has to deal with one ubiquitous counterforce: the lack of time (and often enthusiasm) of those that should be involved and drive KM initiatives and an unfavourable position on the priority list. In view of this counterforce, KM projects should be as simple and easy as possible. They should start small, for example in cooperation with a few enthusiasts, and provide quick wins. Large, ambitious projects to be rolled out in the entire organisation are bound to fail. Since everybody's capacity and patience for KM work is limited, it is crucial to focus on what really adds value, such as measures that support new joiners or junior team members to get up to speed and avoid mistakes. It's much easier to win senior team members over for knowledge management initiatives if they see a direct benefit,[20] as a result of the KM initiative, they will have to spend less time training and supervising juniors.

In a tolerant culture in which mistakes, insufficiencies and possibilities for improvement are addressed and discussed openly, KM finds fertile ground. By contrast, finger-pointing, face-saving or self-marketing is counterproductive.

Last but not least: as important as technology may be for certain KM initiatives, it will never alone contribute to success. As an example, even the most powerful search engine will only be able to find contents, not to create it. Spending a lot for technology raises the stakes: the costlier a KM initiative, the greater the frustration if it does not fulfill expectations.

5. Conclusion

Client service, business development and marketing offers are a wide playing field for KM.

Well-developed knowledge management has a direct positive impact on client service by:

- making it easier for lawyers to react quickly and deliver speedily; and
- supporting the lawyers in their understanding of their clients' needs and business.

---

20 Lawyers will typically ask themselves "what is in it for me?", see Schulz's chapter on Getting lawyers to contribute content to KM systems and to use KM resources.

KM staff may also play an important role in rendering ancillary services to clients, such as supplying them with information and supporting them in risk detection and management, compliance and training. KM lawyers are well suited to advise clients on the organisation of knowledge sharing, on standardising and automating document production and on implementing IT tools for know-how purposes.

Business development and marketing are also part of the wide playing field for KM. KM staff may be involved in CRM and in detecting business opportunities and pursuing them. Due to their legal background and understanding of a law firm's business, KM lawyers are well suited to 'sell' the firm, for example by:

- creating pitch documents;
- writing submissions for rankings and awards; and
- contributing contents for the firm's website.

Furthermore, KM lawyers may play a central role in marketing by publishing legal articles or chapters of commentaries and guides.

Whether in the traditional realm of legal knowledge management or in the client-facing field, in business development and marketing, to avoid failures, the fundamental KM principles should be observed.

Knowledge management in mergers and acquisitions

Anthony J Rhem
AJ Rhem & Associates, Inc

Situations often arise to cause organisations to merge or be acquired. The effect of these mergers will and often does lead to a loss of valuable knowledge from both sides of the merger/acquisition equation. This loss of knowledge is due to positions being consolidated and/or eliminated, other personnel taking early retirement packages or other financial incentives.[1] The question is how do we identify who the key knowledge holders are and what knowledge do they hold? Also, has it been determined that this is viable knowledge to the 'new' organisation going forward and what is our plan to retain, capture, or acquire this knowledge?

All of these questions can be answered with a comprehensive KM strategy that includes a human capital management component, geared to identify viable initiatives that will address these questions.[2] One such initiative will be to develop a knowledge map of the organisation to be acquired. A knowledge map is a mechanism used to identify key knowledge and the knowledge holders of the organisation. Once these maps are completed, further analysis is needed to determine the process, procedures and initiatives necessary to prioritise, retain, and/or acquire knowledge that may leave. Often organisational knowledge is the reason certain mergers happen. KM is the mechanism to transition individual knowledge to corporate knowledge and facilitates its availability for all employees. Understanding who are the critical knowledge holders and their relationships as well as their roles, responsibilities and work products are all components of sound human capital management.[3]

This understanding will lead to determining which positions and personnel perform duplicate functions, which will lead to knowing the employees that should be dismissed. Not only do you have to determine which personnel perform duplicate functions, but also who is more valuable through his/her experience, education, and importance to the organisation going forward. The human capital management component of the overall KM strategy is also an investment in employee selection and development. This contributes to the organisation meeting its goals and objectives of not only the merger but for the new organisation on an ongoing basis. In addition, we must keep in mind that executing a KM strategy with a human capital management component can be the catalyst to increased adaptability, enhanced worker performance and having the ability to do more with your existing personnel resources.

---

1 AJ Rhem, *Knowledge Management in Practice* (Boca Raton, FL: CRC Press, 2016).
2 *Ibid.*
3 *Ibid.*

1. **Knowledge mapping**

At a time when organisations need to 'know what they know' and use that knowledge effectively, the size and geographic reach of many of them, along with the proliferation of data, information and knowledge make it especially difficult to locate existing knowledge and get it to where it is needed. Once you let employees leave you run the risk of pertinent knowledge leaving with them. The focus of the knowledge mapping effort should centre on the employees within the organisations. Mapping responsibilities, expertise, and the work products employees produce will gain an understanding of the know how within the organisation and if that know how is valuable to the organisation going forward. The knowledge mapping deliverable is an extension of the people side analysis of the M&A transaction.

2. **Constructing the knowledge map**

To assist in identifying key experts to retain during the employee decision stage of the M&A, producing a knowledge map of your organisation will be greatly beneficial. Creating a knowledge map is an excellent tool to facilitate the identification of the key knowledge holders, knowledge gaps and identify areas where knowledge is eroding. However, performing a knowledge mapping exercise should focus on a particular department, functional area, or specific organisation domain and gradually be built upon until an entire knowledge map of your organisation exists.

Before starting to develop the knowledge map (see Figure 1: Knowledge map example), ensure the intentions are clear. This includes understanding the purpose and scope of the knowledge map. The thing to keep in mind is that there is never a single map for every purpose. Knowledge mapping is about relationships (people-to-people and people-to-content), and how these relationships interact within the organisation.

To construct the knowledge map, you will go through a process that includes interviewing employees to understand how they work, the processes they utilise, the content they create and access as well as the people they interact with. This is done because knowledge is found in processes, relationships, policies, people, documents, conversations and through links to suppliers, competitors and customers. This information is used to graphically represent these relationships into a map. However, instead of creating a static map, in which several views of the knowledge would need to be created, I suggest using software to create an interactive map. An interactive knowledge map will provide different perspectives of the relationships and the knowledge each employee has.

3. **Steps for developing the knowledge map**

Knowledge maps are depicted by a network representation of individuals, their relationship to information and other individuals. Each individual is further described with properties identifying their areas of expertise (or know-how), job roles and interest (see knowledge profile). The steps for developing a knowledge map include:

- *Select domain area:* Selection of the area of the business to begin mapping will allow for better focus and understanding. The knowledge map can continue to evolve until the entire organisation is captured.

Figure 1: Knowledge map example

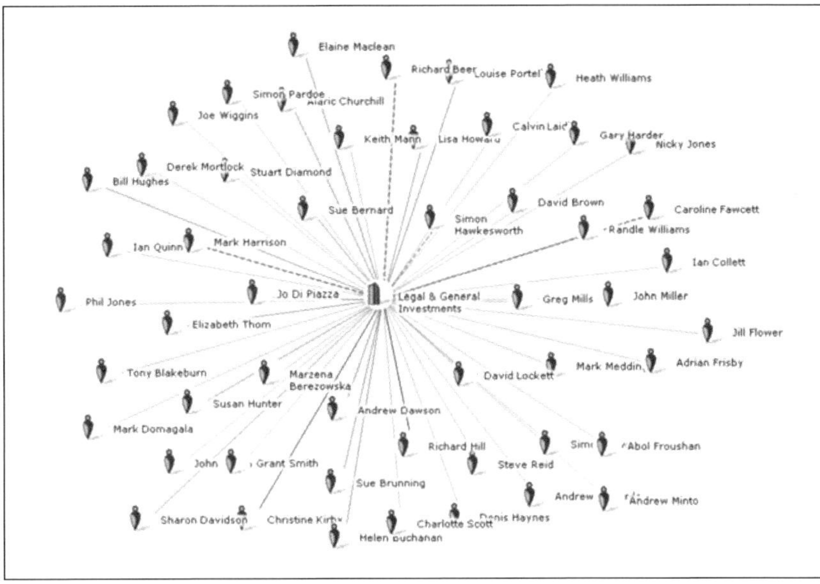

(Source: Created by Market Visual (http://www.marketvisual.com/): http://tinyurl.com/legalknowledgemap)

- *Identify key ideas:* Identify what the knowledge map will identify. This can be limited to people-to-people, people-to-content or both.
- *Construct preliminary map:* Using the list of concepts, construct a preliminary knowledge map, linking concepts with links. Note that concepts are usually nouns, links and verbs.
- *Review the knowledge map:* Check the map to ensure all concepts are depicted and that the relationships between concepts are meaningful and complete. Check also for overall organisation of the map level of complexity, and interconnectedness (that concepts are interrelated, that is, no concept is isolated).
- *Modify the knowledge map:* Adjust the knowledge map according to the results of the review.
- *Finalise the knowledge map:* Complete all adjustments to the knowledge map.

4. Knowledge profile

A knowledge profile (KP) (see Figure 2: Knowledge profile example) records skills, tools, practices and social networks, it highlights competencies, identifies gaps, helps with learning programs to address deficits, realise opportunities and heighten awareness for the owner and colleagues. A KP will provide detailed information about each knowledge holder associated in a knowledge map.

KPs may focus on the individual where they form a key part of your personal knowledge management (PKM) system or are aimed at a 'collective' view of a team,

Figure 2: Knowledge profile example

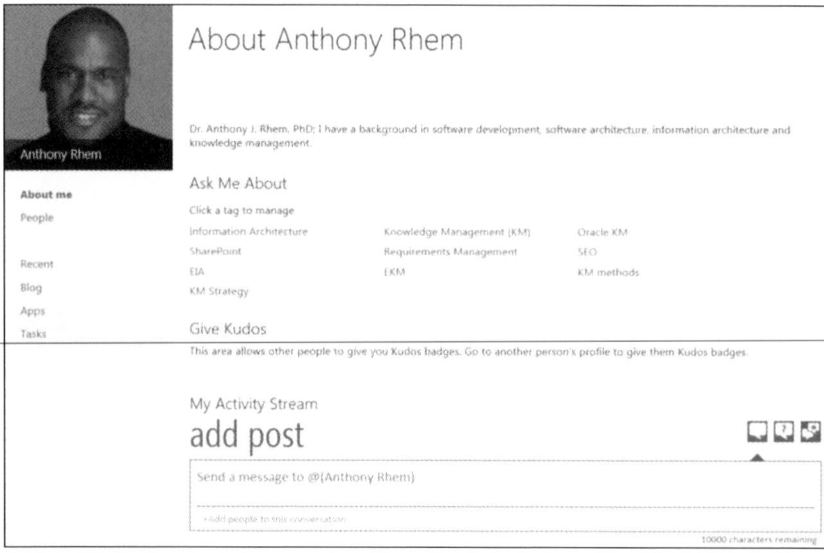

group, community or firm. Profiles may be constructed via manual or automatic means, be highly structured or very informal and are maintained by the end-user or compiled from test batteries and questionnaires by expertise profilers and competency specialists.

A knowledge profile goes beyond determining information needs, guiding information seeking behaviour and considers the adoption and use of tools, the condition and functioning of (personal) social networks and learning desires. Successful KPs focus on the future, they reflect current skills and activities above past positions, awards and educational achievements, providing some indication of where and how the person can best contribute to organisational and team goals.

Knowledge profiles are often a key element in knowledge mapping, knowledge audits, CRM and play an increasing role in advanced search, expertise location, agent-based work assignments, customer selling strategies and portal user-interfaces. Related information is found in the yellow pages, expertise directories and academic resumes, but the knowledge profile is distinguished by a list and evaluation of relationships (promotes flow), preferences and proficiencies with communication systems/tools and applicable tacit knowledge strengths.

5. The people side of the M&A

The people side of M&As as pointed out by Dr Mark Braverman in his research entitled: "The Human Side of Due Diligence: Protecting the M&A Investment" centres around applying KM principles, practices and policies to produce a high performing, highly effective workforce (Braverman, n.d.). Corporate mergers are about more than numbers and market opportunities, which is why CEOs need to think about the long term fit of the corporate cultures as well as the financial and market aspects. Here are four bases to touch on the 'people side' of merger and acquisition due diligence that CEOs should never overlook.

5.1 Employees

Employees become naturally fearful when mergers and acquisitions are rumoured. Will the employees retain their jobs? Even if they do, will they be the kind of jobs that they are used to? They are all too aware that the executives exiting from their company, once it is acquired, will receive sweetened deals in the forms of settlements, a responsible position in the new organisation, or a combination of both.[4] In some cases, employees are hired on a contingency basis in the new organisation and if they do well, they are retained long term. The key here for both the acquiring and the acquired organisations is to know what exactly is going to happen to the employees on both sides of the merger and to be transparent about it.

5.2 Boards

Who is going to sit on the board after a merger or acquisition completes? Often, the acquired organisation gets at least one seat on the acquiring company's board.[5] For the CEO, this can be easier said than done. Do you alter your board organisation to include more seats? How will the votes be distributed? Will all board positions be voting positions? Are incumbent board members replaced? This should be a major political line item in any merger or acquisition evaluation.

5.3 Customers and other stakeholders

There are those outside of both companies who have been loyal customers and stakeholders for years. What is going to happen to them once the two companies merge? The Chief Marketing Officer (CMO) and Chief Executive Officer (CEO) should be integrally involved in this area of strategy, because you could very well lose customers as a consequence of ineffective 'advance messaging' to them on what is going to happen to services, products, retail outlets, etc.[6]

5.4 Operations

Most organisations know how important it is to get IT in on early evaluations for potential mergers or acquisitions because different organisations invariably have different systems, and at some point, these systems must come together.[7] However, it is equally important to pay the same amount of attention to daily operations. How similar are both business and IT governance standards (and work ethics) between the two organisations? Are operations in manufacturing, sales, and the back office sufficiently similar so that work processes do not have to be redefined and employees retrained?

---

4 M Braverman (nd), "The Human Side of Due Diligence: Protecting the M&A Investment". Retrieved from: www.bravermangroup.com/services/OrgConsult/text/The%20Human%20Side%20of%20M%26A.pdf.

5 *Ibid.*

6 *Ibid.*

7 *Ibid.*

6. Communication

Communication can help employees to manage the merger syndrome because it informs them of the changes in their environment, thus reduces uncertainty and ambiguity. Communication is the most valuable commodity for the successful implementation of a merger or acquisition. The specific communication objectives change for every phase of integration. As the deal moves through its phases, information changes and the circle of knowledge grows. Nothing is a secret for long, and leaders must be prepared, not only for what they know is coming, but for the unexpected. Leaders should follow a phased approach to communication, in which planning is sensitive to continuing information flowing from multiple organisational levels about the progress of integration. Information flow in a company is one of the most important aspects of a merger that must be understood and consistently adhered to. The trust level in the organisation must not deteriorate. An environment must be maintained where people feel they can be straightforward and share information/knowledge with other colleagues. When this environment is compromised, people will often feel that they are afraid to disagree with higher management, let alone new management.

Communication is a requirement for financial success, because low morale, high turnover, direct costs in workers' compensation and healthcare expenditures and lowered productivity will all have consequences for the level of return on investment. Leaders cannot assume they can and will know everything. But they do have a responsibility to put into place the structures that will maximise their awareness as they go forward. Leaders who confront change effectively are rewarded with superior business performance on the part of their employees. When employees believe their employer is effectively managing change it is perceived as a gain for shareholders. Conversely when employees believe their employer is NOT effectively managing change it is perceived as a loss for shareholders. Proper planning for the management of people issues in a merger or acquisition should be a top priority.

7. Productivity

After a merger or acquisition, employees who feel uncertain about their job security and are mistrustful of leadership regarding the sale may be unmotivated and averse to risk. Planning for who among your employees will continue on after the merger or acquisition is a key ingredient for success. More often than not, however, this planning is limited to a narrow fixation on payroll and percentages; a shrinking in the employment rolls is often part of the plan, not only in a merger where synergies are expected but in an acquisition as part of the striving for efficiencies. Formulating a retention plan, leveraging information uncovered as the result in creating a knowledge map will change the typical focus to a small handful of top people, a few people at the middle and lower levels, creating a climate where valuable staff are vulnerable to poaching by competitors.

An acquisition or merger can create conditions in which a company is at risk for losing those people who may be critical to immediate and longer-term business success by virtue of their management skills, knowledge of business systems and processes, and intellectual capital. This can have consequences, not only downstream, but for the transaction itself. Organisations considering mergers or acquisitions should have these 'people centric' line items on their merger and acquisition checklists, but many do not. The political fallout from a corporate move like this can be major, which is why organisations that perform their due diligence with attention to people as well as to markets and numbers succeed most often.

8. Leveraging KM in the company valuation

Investors in a company that is aiming to take over another one must determine whether the purchase will be beneficial to them. In order to do so, they must ask themselves how much the company being acquired is really worth. Naturally, both sides of an M&A deal will have different ideas about the worth of a target company: its seller will tend to value the company at as high a price as possible, while the buyer will try to get the lowest price that he can. There are, however, many legitimate ways to value companies. The most common method is to look at comparable companies in an industry, but deal makers employ a variety of other methods and tools when assessing a target company. Here are just a few of them:

8.1 Comparative ratios

The following are two examples of the many comparative metrics on which acquiring companies may base their offers:

- Price-earnings ratio (P/E ratio). With the use of this ratio, an acquiring company makes an offer that is a multiple of the earnings of the target company. Looking at the P/E for all the stocks within the same industry group will give the acquiring company good guidance for what the target's P/E multiple should be.[8]
- Enterprise-value-to-sales ratio (EV/sales). With this ratio, the acquiring company makes an offer as a multiple of the revenues, again, while being aware of the price-to-sales ratio of other companies in the industry.

8.2 Replacement cost

In a few cases, acquisitions are based on the cost of replacing the target company. For simplicity's sake, suppose the value of a company is simply the sum of all its equipment and staffing costs. The acquiring company can literally order the target to sell at that price, or it will create a competitor for the same cost.[9] Naturally, it takes a long time to assemble good management, acquire property and get the right equipment. This method of establishing a price certainly wouldn't make much sense in a service industry where the key assets – people and ideas – are hard to value and develop.

8.3 Discounted cash flow (DCF)

A key valuation tool in M&A, discounted cash flow analysis determines a company's

8 Coveo (2013). "Measuring Return on Knowledge in a Big Data World." Coveo, San Mateo, CA. Retrieved from: www.coveo.com/~/media/Files/WhitePapers/Coveo_Measuring_Return_on_Knowledge_in_a_Big_Data_World.ashx

9 *Ibid.*

current value according to its estimated future cash flows.[10] Forecasted free cash flows (operating profit + depreciation + amortisation of goodwill – capital expenditures – cash taxes – change in working capital) are discounted to a present value using the company's weighted average costs of capital (WACC). Admittedly, DCF is tricky to get right, but few tools can rival this valuation method.

9. Knowledge value equation

The need to make the most of organisational knowledge, to get as much value from it as possible, is greater now than in the past. Companies are finding themselves with piles of information within multiple channels, locked away in silos, different systems, different departments, different geographies and different data types, making it impossible to connect the dots and make sense of critical business information. New computing models like cloud and social business are exacerbating organisations' ability to collect, analyse and process data. The data is there, but it isn't being harnessed in the right way to increase our collective knowledge. And it is our collective organisational knowledge that gives us the edge over our competition.

For a potential merger, understanding the value of the organisation to be acquired is critical to positioning a price that is both equitable and acceptable to the acquired company. If your organisation is positioning itself to be sold, understanding how KM can increase the overall value of the company is essential to obtaining a fair price. So, how do we leverage KM to understand the value of the organisation? One such way is to apply the concepts presented in the knowledge value equation by Mark Clare.[11] This equation aligns with the third method/tool used when assessing a company (stated above), which examines the use of discounted cash flow (DCF) and presents an equation: KM value = F (cost, benefit, risk) = total DCF created over life of KM investment. The equation states that the value created from managing knowledge is a function of the costs, benefits and risks of the KM investment (project or strategy) in leveraging and protecting the knowledge.[12]

The knowledge value equation (KVE) simply states that the value created from managing knowledge is a function of the costs, benefits, and risks of the KM initiative. Thus, mathematically stated:

> KM value = F (cost, benefit, risk), which equals total discounted cash flow (DCF) created over the life of the KM investment.[13]

This formula attempts to quantify the intangible impacts of KM, relating it back to cash flow. This includes improved problem solving, enhanced creativity, and improved relationships with customers. KM projects produce a stream of benefits over time. This will enable KM projects to be evaluated based on a series or stream of cash flows. In doing this, we must understand the concepts of time value of money and DCF. To take the intangible aspects of KM and turn them into a series of cash flows that can be discounted over time, we must first start with ways to increase DCF.[14]

10 M Clare, "Solving the Knowledge Value Equation" (2002) 5(2) *Knowledge Management Review.*
11 *Ibid.*
12 *Ibid.*
13 *Ibid.*
14 AJ Rhem, *UML for Developing Knowledge Management Systems* (Boca Raton, FL: CRC Press, 2005).

10. Knowledge value tree

An important concept identified in determining the knowledge value equation is to build a knowledge value tree (see Figure 3: Knowledge value tree). A knowledge value tree makes the connection between knowledge and value in an organisation more visible by understanding the relationship and connection of KM functionality, business impact, and financial impact.[15] This viability of the value of knowledge in the organisation can be directly tied back to understanding what competitive advantage your organisation has in its marketplace, its percentage of that market, and the potential to capture additional market share. An examination of corporate valuation can be found in the book: McKinsey and Company Inc's *Valuation: Measuring and Managing the Value of Companies*. I believe that this is an important factor when considering buying an organisation as well as if you are positioning your organisation to be sold.

Figure 3: Knowledge value tree[16]

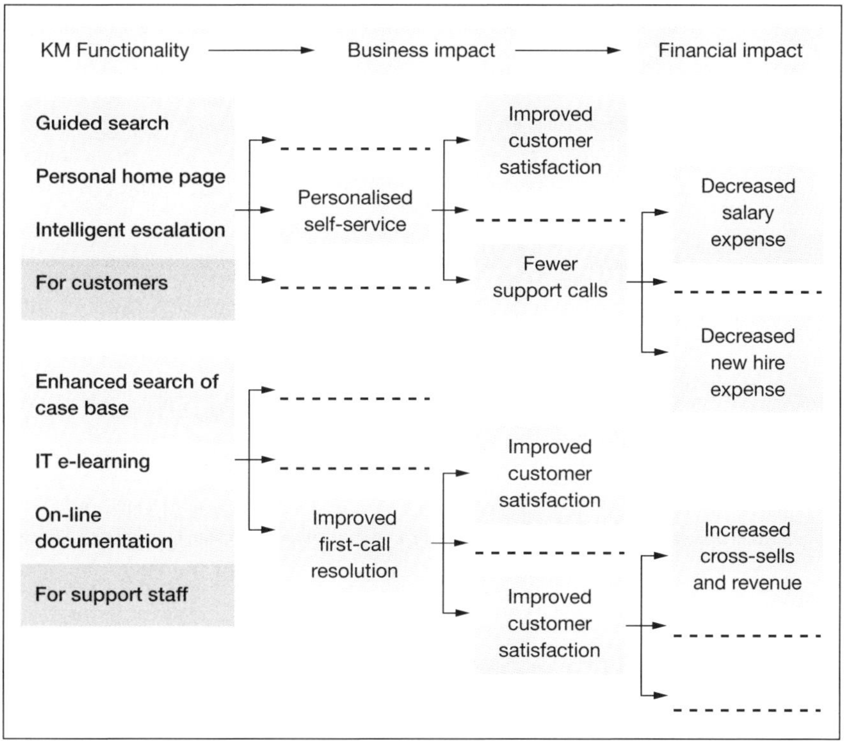

The knowledge-value tree is a treelike graphical representation that is used to make the connection between knowledge and value more visible. The mapping is as follows:

15 See n 10.
16 See n 10.

KM functionality → business transformation → DCF → value.[17] As a result of an M&A transaction there is a link between the change in business metrics and one or more aspects of DCF. A change in business metrics will have an effect on one or more of the drivers of DCF. The presentation of knowledge value trees has to be convincing to business stakeholders and senior management. This has to be positioned in order to show how we would achieve a ROI on the intangible benefits of a KM investment (ie, KM functionality → processes and practices → business metrics → DCF drivers → value).[18]

Knowledge-value trees also provide a mechanism for determining where and how economic value is being created. Discovering these knowledge-value drivers is one of the central tasks of KM. Knowledge-value trees and the calculations associated with them involve some assumptions.[19] To reduce the risks associated with these assumptions we must consider the following:

- Use financial reports and other summary documents to make informed judgments.
- Review all assumptions with the appropriate business experts.
- Quantify risks associated with your assumptions by determining how a change in the assumption influences the total DCF.
- Use computations, rather than absolute evaluation by developing a set of scenarios that look at a range of assumptions.
- Use models to frame assumptions whenever possible. The assumptions that go into knowledge value trees should be based on the best business data and experience available.

11. Aligning KM with M&A activities

During the execution of the M&A there are several areas in which KM will play a key role. The following table provides a synopsis on where KM aligns to address specific M&A activities.

M&A activity	KM method/activity
Retention of employee knowledge (1)	Executing the capture, cataloguing and storing of knowledge (including work products) of essential employees that will be leaving as a result of the M&A transaction
Retention of employee knowledge (2)	Establishing a knowledge portal will enable individual knowledge to be stored and included as part of the corporate knowledge base where it can be accessed across the firm and this will facilitate the retention of the firm's knowledge

continued on next page

17 See n 10.
18 See n 10.
19 See n 14.

M&A activity	KM method/activity
Identifying cost consolidation/ savings	The use of knowledge mapping will identify duplicate jobs, functions and processes that can be eliminated or streamlined to produce areas of cost savings
Training and learning	Implementing knowledge transfer, sharing, collaboration processes, policies and tools will create an environment where employees can learn from each other, share best practices, and provide practical training for less knowledgeable employees before, during and after the M&A transaction
Retention of the 'right' employees	The use of knowledge mapping will identify the 'right' expertise to keep within the new organisation. Knowledge map will facilitate the identification of the key knowledge holders, knowledge gaps and identifies areas where knowledge is eroding
Obtaining company intellectual property, financial statements, manuals, historical information, evidence of government and regulatory compliance, and other pertinent information related to the M&A due diligence	KM will provide the ability through information architecture techniques (content organisation, taxonomies, and metadata) to properly locate, label, and catalogue information to be accessed to complete the M&A due diligence

11.1 KM in M&A – a practical checklist

The following is a checklist for incorporating KM principles during the execution of M&A activities.

✔	Complete a KM strategy that includes a human capital management component
✔	As a major initiative coming out of the KM strategy produce a knowledge map, understanding who are the critical knowledge holders and their relationships as well as their roles, responsibilities and work products

continued on next page

✔	Determine synergies – synergies are the magic force that allows for enhanced cost efficiencies of the new business
✔	Incorporate people-centric policies and procedures – mergers are about more than numbers and market opportunities, which is why CEOs need to think about the long term fit of the corporate cultures involved in the transaction
✔	Execute a holistic communications plan – leaders should follow a phased approach to communication, in which planning is sensitive to continuing information flowing from multiple organisational levels about the progress of integration
✔	Utilise the knowledge value equation to contribute to the determining the valuation figures – this equation examines the use of discounted cash flow (DCF) and presents an equation: KM value = F (cost, benefit, risk) = total DCF created over life of KM investment

12. Why mergers and acquisitions can fail

It's no secret that plenty of mergers don't work. Those who advocate mergers will indicate that the merger will cut costs or boost revenues by more than enough to justify the price being paid. It's not as simple as just combining computer systems, merging a few departments, eliminating redundant suppliers, and the merged company will be more profitable than ever! Historical trends show that roughly two thirds of large mergers will lose value on the stock market. The motivations that drive mergers can be flawed and efficiencies from economies of scale may prove elusive.

Most research indicates that M&A activity has an overall success rate of about 50%[20] Chief executives of mid-market companies (generally speaking, businesses with between $20 million and $300 million in revenue) should keep those odds in mind as deals are offered to them.[21] The consequences of a failed merger or acquisition are far greater for a mid-market company than for large corporations. Large companies usually have enough resources to move on and maintain their business. Most mid-market companies lack the finances or bandwidth to absorb a bad deal.

As with most transactions they look great on paper, but few organisations pay attention to the details, that is, how the deal will actually work once all the paperwork is signed. This includes: thoroughly assessing the culture of your target acquisition, and determining if it is compatible with your company's culture, understanding if the deal is in line with your corporate strategy in order to determine

20 Robert Sher (2012) "Why Half of All M&A Deals Fail and What You Can Do About It." Retrieved from: http://www.forbes.com/sites/forbesleadershipforum/2012/03/19/why-half-of-all-ma-deals-fail-and-what-you-can-do-about-it/.

21 *Ibid.*

what knowledge is necessary for the new company to successfully execute its strategy and identify who the key knowledge holders are that support the strategy moving forward.[22]

Meticulously and diligently screening possible M&A deals may increase your odds of success. However, consider the odds and remember to pay attention to details such as: is the deal priced so that you can afford to put the necessary resources into the integration while still having a return on investment, is the acquisition, along with all the costs and risks associated with it, a better choice than all other alternatives, how does the organisation retain the key knowledge holders, what are the gaps in knowledge the organisation needs to fill, and how will the gaps in knowledge be mitigated. Mid-market CEOs who can't do the homework will be better off reconsidering the transaction altogether.

13. Conclusion

13.1 Knowledge and organisation culture

An organisation's culture evolves from many sources. Culture is manifested in policy and procedures, organisational structure, and everyday behaviours, both formal and informal. These sources are the originators of knowledge within the organisation. Knowledge is the differentiator when it comes to increasing competitive intelligence and creating a competitive advantage. Knowledge can be interpreted within and outside of the organisation in many ways. Included in this interpretation is how knowledge is exchanged between geographically dispersed employees, suppliers and partners. The ability to blend (or align) the culture of the companies involved in an M&A transaction is critical to its success. Also critical to the success of an M&A transaction is understanding how the knowledge assets of different organisations' cultures will fit together. This understanding is essential in combining diverse sources of knowledge during a merger and/or acquisition.

14. Keys and advice for leveraging KM in M&A transactions

This section highlight keys and advice for successfully executing KM activities that support an M&A engagement. The following are keys to leveraging KM in M&A transactions:

- Planning for who among your employees will continue on after the merger or acquisition is a key ingredient for success. Therefore, understanding what knowledge is needed and who are the key knowledge holders when planning employee and/or business function consolidation (or elimination) or constructing a knowledge map is a useful tool in this analysis.
- Before conducting a knowledge mapping initiative, it is important that all employees complete a knowledge profile. This will provide the knowledge map with the necessary details of the employees in order for the knowledge map to accurately reflect the knowledge 'key' holders of the organisation.
- Plenty of mergers don't work, it's not as simple as just combining computer

---

22 *Ibid.*

systems, merging a few departments, eliminating redundant suppliers and the merged company will be more profitable than ever! So, do your homework!

The following is advice to follow when leveraging KM when executing M&A transactions:

- If your organisation is positioning itself to be sold, understanding how KM can increase the overall value of the company is essential to obtaining a fair price. Leveraging the knowledge value equation will be an essential tool in the valuation process.
- When utilising the knowledge value equation build a knowledge value tree. A knowledge value tree makes the connection between knowledge and value in an organisation more visible by understanding the relationship and connection of KM functionality, business impact, and financial impact.
- Another point of emphasis when calculating the return on knowledge is to understand that it is not a simple task, and yet it is important that organisational leaders think about increasing return on this critical asset.

Layered client portals for development of client relations

Boyd Hendriks
Informationland

---

1. Introduction

It is true that technology brings the competitive edge to law firms. Client portals, the interface between law firm and client, are much more than technology, they are the system in which case files, information and knowledge are shared. They imply strong administrative discipline and well overthought information flows.

Once you start sharing knowledge and information via portals outside the case documents, or around themes relevant for the client, there is a high expectation of the quality of the content. This content must first be generated on a representable high quality. So besides technology, that can be acquired at a cost, it needs serious knowledge and information management. The law firm must be ready for this. How? Not easy. But it is easier, once the underlying business case is understood.

This business case can be the driver for development or improvement of processes and disciplines necessary. Over the last years, client portals have developed from basic data rooms to sophisticated knowledge exchange platforms. We have seen an increase of possibilities with portals and their added value for client relations. In spite of its significance and the fact that this is something we all agree on, the Return on Investment (ROI) of client portals is not well documented. Most client portals connecting law firms with their clients are confidential. Large scale research and benchmarking are therefore missing.

Nevertheless, it is understood in general that the added value is based on five points:

- The development of the client relation.
- Making additional services possible such as:
  - virtual helpdesks;
  - access to libraries and exclusive know how collections; and
  - training and seminar overview for clients, etc.
- Positioning of the law firm within the client organization.
- Cross selling of other legislative areas within the client relation.
- Earlier engagement in strategic thinking.

The rule of thumb is that an active use of the client portal normally has a linear relationship with the profitability and duration of the client relationship. It is therefore worth our while to invest in this. The financial costs might be fair, but the organisational efforts can be huge, depending on the current state of internal KM.

In this article we will discuss the building blocks of client portals. We will learn that successful portals can be built up over three distinct levels. Only a few years ago a portal connecting a law firm and a client was always a representation of a document management system, with very little extra to it. It had case files and core documentation, in the case of due diligence it often harboured large quantities of data, background documents and files. Security was and still is key.

The latest development is an intuitive, knowledge-rich, well designed interface, overlaying the traditional portal. It is more attractive, easy to navigate through and appeals to a wider user group within the client organisation. Lately we experimented successfully with trials of a third overlay as a general landing page that shows a relevant blog in the centre, which is of interest to the largest user group in the client organisation. In general terms each portal level is a landing page in its own right. From the top to the lower level there is increasing security necessary. Also, the deeper the portal, the more exclusive or confidential the content is. To explain the difference between the portal levels we will shortly name and describe each level briefly and later discuss them in more detail.

The deepest, most secure client exclusive portal, is the 'knowledge portal' with case documents, related information and client exclusive knowledge. It is well structured, file-driven and highly secured.

Overlaying the knowledge portal we find the 'intelligence portal', with knowledge and information of direct relevance for the client, but not related to any case. The intelligence portal provides us access to the knowledge portal, to exclusive seminars, analysis and opinions, blog and newsletter archives etc.

The highest portal level is the 'client blog'. Exclusive, but with client organisation-wide access. It provides opinions, newsletters, announcements, access to the help-desk, library services etc. The client blog will have certain overlaps with the law firm blogs open for the general public. We will now discuss each level in more detail.

2. The knowledge portal

This is the deepest and most confidential level of the client portal. This is where client case files are stored as in a traditional document management system (DMS) and knowledge and intelligence documents are shared that are directly related to client affairs. The core qualities of KM are applied here and expressed in levels of: completeness, relevance, accuracy, confidentiality, reliability, actuality etc.

The knowledge portal is the most applied level and is currently in most portals the only level present, with its DMS look and feel. Ideally it consists of two separate tabs. One tab gives access to current client files and related archives, and the second tab gives access to strategic and legal knowledge, selected and sometimes personalised for the client. Frequently the knowledge files show a subdivision of themes and topics as agreed with the client.

It is common practice that client access to the knowledge portal is arranged on an individual level in combination with read-only or full-writing rights. This means that each individual user experiences the core level of the portal differently, in content and therefore in added value. In other words, no access to certain folders mean that these remain invisible.

Figure 1: Three different portal levels, seen from the client perspective

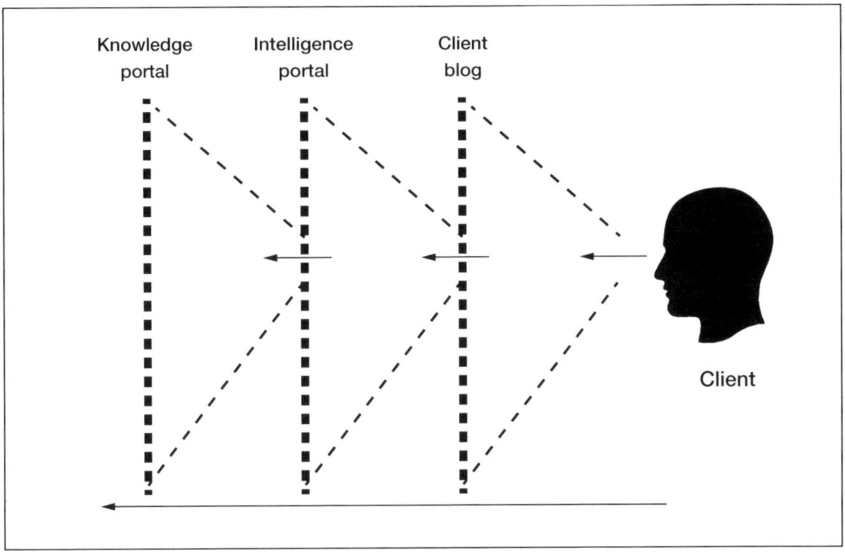

In this level, importantly, is the access to financial planning, often presented in a management dashboard, that shows engagement, progress and costs at any particular moment. This type of transparency and reporting is very much sought after by clients.

With regard to navigation in the knowledge portal it is important that the files are arranged in a specific structure. This might be different than in your DMS and is normally adjusted to the client's requirements. For metadata it is recommended to work with a short and practical list only.

Structural in-house testing has shown so far that navigation along a logical structure of a maximum of three, but mainly two layers deep, will give good and quick selection results, especially when applied in combination with Boolean-search operators like 'and' or 'not'. These search results are often much stronger than searches based on selection of metadata. Abstracts do support selection within the search results, but keep in mind that abstracts are simply as good as their abstractor. Often these roles change hands over time, as a result of a possible shift of the context, so that the use of abstracts in search and selection might produce less reliable results.

Most metadata structures also show an unbalanced development over the years. This is based on accidental historical choices or shifts in focus points over time. Searching metadata that represents content rather than topics often gives a false impression of completeness or reliability. Time allocated to abstracting or metadating is therefore often not giving the expected return. We observed that systems that force the use of metadata are normally fooled by their users when these are obligatory and skipped when they are optional.

It is a powerful experience for a client to have access to a strong file system with well overthought structure and quality content, without the administrative burden on their side. The client team has instant access to an up to date document set and a reliable KM system for wider use. This by itself will give more depth and broadness to the relationship.

In comparison with law firms, legal departments of client organisations in general lack a strong support structure. They often lack well equipped in-house library services, know-how employees or support lawyers. The structural and timely build-up of theme-based knowledge is therefore often missing. This gives additional value to the relationship from the client's perspective. The law firm positions itself strategically in-line with key themes that are relevant to its client by publishing top content on the knowledge portal.

Themes are often temporary in character, in line with developments of law and regulation or with the strategic agenda of the client organisation. Often theme-specific core knowledge is written by the firm and expressed in articles, white papers, discussion documents, blogs etc. Sometimes it is written especially for the client and its environment, like relevant scans or assessments. It is completed with directly related case law or jurisprudence, policy documents, the expected rules and regulations etc.

Specific and high valued, maybe even exclusive knowledge and intelligence, given to the client via the knowledge portal, might cannibalise certain work that is now picked up by the client's own legal team. This fair risk must be seen as an investment. It is likely that higher-end and more profiled work will be granted in return. We will discuss the ROI later in the conclusions.

3. The intelligence portal

This is the newest level of client interaction and built in web technology. It is often the landing page from which one can access the knowledge portal with the case files. The traditional client portal has been around for a while, as has blogging technology and the application of blog sites. Both needed to mature and law firms in general had to appreciate the important opportunity that arose to engage with client organisations on a knowledge-exchange/partnership level, before serious dashboards could be designed and piloted.

The content of the intelligence portal is contextual to the underlying knowledge and case files on the knowledge portal. It prepositions the law firm in new areas of client interests and supports broadening of the relationship. It kick-starts dialogues with trusted clients on new terrains, without a negatively perceived sales flavour. It expresses expertise based leadership and creates opportunities for earlier client engagements on new themes. The intelligence portal is in the position where non-sales, knowledge driven cross selling takes place.

The urge for good content for the intelligence portal demands a strong role for information, know-how and KM in law firms. The information sources that are publicly available to all or commercially obtainable with reasonable costs, should first be reworked and enriched. There is a risk that the content of the intelligence portal is too general and can be found elsewhere. Users will often shy away after experiencing this regularly. This means that information not created by the firm itself, and therefore in origin not exclusive, should be reworked by the principles of an information value chain. At the start of this value chain input is given by well filtered information from relevant sources. Timely spotting of developing themes is a requirement. Law firms with a reactive business model will find themselves more often in a disadvantaged position, in which price rather than pre-position is leading. Law firms with an intelligence portal are taking the lead by introducing new themes, initiating dialogues and pre-positioning themselves with thought leadership.

Cost cutting as we have seen in the previous years has often weakened the information services or library practice from many law firms. Involvement from senior fee earners or partners is too costly to play a significant role in content creation. On the other side, the lack of legal schooled information professionals not helping to feed the process of effective writing or blogging can take place. During the last years we have seen investments from top firms in the information centres. Those who invested will see a cost effective involvement in the new economy of knowledge sharing.

4. The client blog

Recently we have seen the development and application of a client blog as a first landing page or highest level of portal. It is organisation-wide, but client exclusive. It overlays the intelligence portal and has a larger more general user group within the client organisation. Short articles, professional opinions and the latest specialised blogs and vlogs can all be found on the client blog. It is especially fit for large client organisations with a diverse network relationship with the law firm. The blog will lead to more general and higher-level positioning and cross-selling. The client organisation as a whole is engaged and informed about seminars, courses and activities in a more general agenda function. The knowledge map gives an overview of law firm-wide expertise, rather than the constellation of active case or project teams, as is the case on the intelligence portal. There is no active archive function underlying the presented newsletters and blog items. Being the most general landing page, the client blog will give access to the intelligence and knowledge portal.

5. The information value chain

Besides creating content for portals, we also rework and enrich information from external sources. To explain what we mean with reworking and enriching information we can best look at the information value chain (see Figure 3). This shows the different steps of information development, starting with input from unsorted information coming from external sources, all the way through to information-based recommendation.

Information is dealt with by different professionals in the law firm. These are situated either centrally at a library or knowledge centre, or locally near partners or fee earners. Centrally, the legal librarians, the know-how staff and the knowledge support lawyers are working with the first three steps of the information value chain:

- Filtering of information, based on search strings/Boolean logic.
- Clustering the filtered information by theme or topic.
- Relevance ranking of information per cluster.
- (Also alerting and abstracting is done centrally.)

Figure 2: A general overview of the content of the individual portal levels

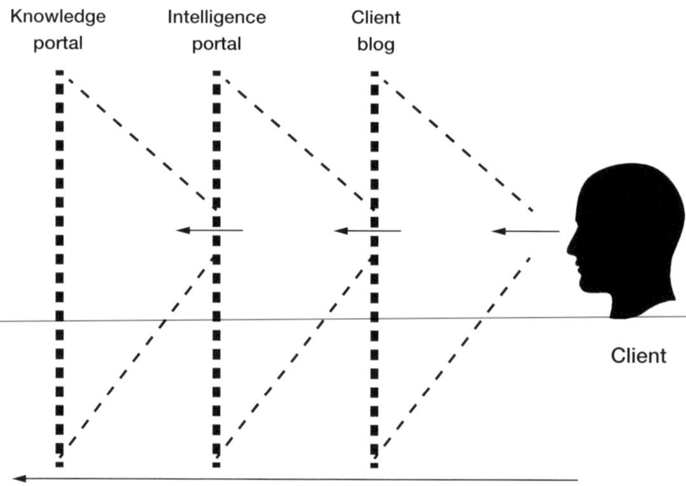

Knowledge portal
- Confidential material
- Current case files
- Latest versions
- Archive
- Financial planning
- Management overview
- Access and security on personal level
- Direct access to pre-filtered knowledge
- Personalised knowledge areas

Intelligence portal
- Small, specialised user groups
- Controlled access
- Key knowledge driven
- Personal or team agendas
- Milestones and progress dashboard
- Team knowledge maps
- Access to filing section
- High relevance
- Targeted, reworked news
- Newsletter and blog archive and search
- Specific cross-selling

Client blog
- Large, general user group
- Controlled access
- Wider knowledge definitions
- General agenda
- General cross-selling/ positioning
- Law firm knowledge map
- Access to deeper portal levels
- General relevance
- Less targeted news
- Latest newsletters
- Blogs, vlogs and opinions

All steps so far can also be provided for by publishers or external information service providers. This needs frequent guidance and quality checks. Any step from analysis upward is mainly done by professional support lawyers or fee earners and the results should be fit for publication on the client portal. Copyright law restricts forwarding of unaltered texts from external providers or publishers. The three 'content generating' steps are:

- analyses of clustered information;
- conclusions based on the analyses; and
- recommendations based on the conclusions.

The output feeds the client information needs and is part of the knowledge based relationship with your firm.

Figure 3: The value chain of information

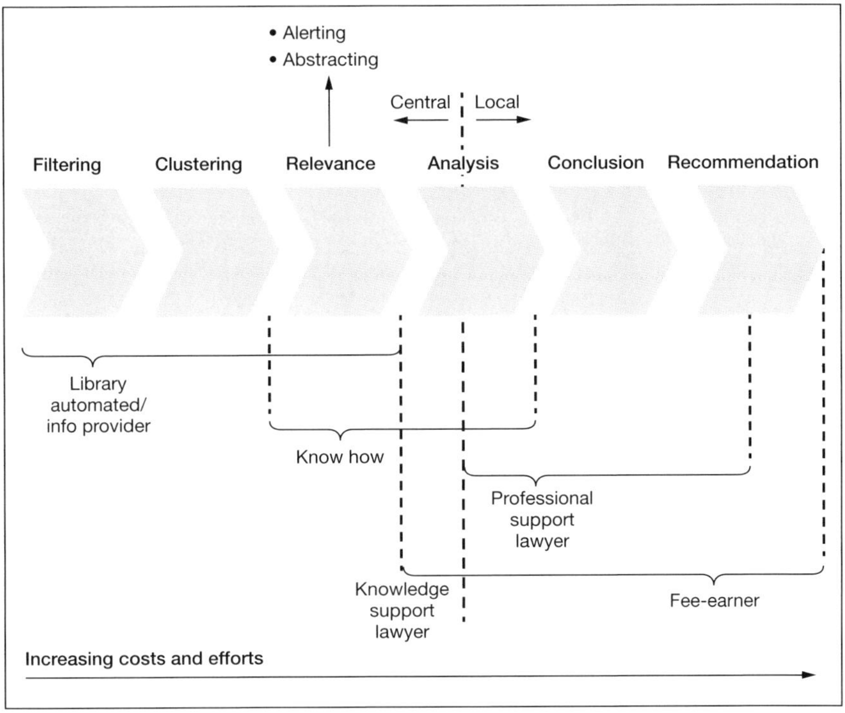

6. Qualities of information and information exclusivity within client portals

On different levels within the portal structure different degrees of information exclusivity occur. This difference in quality comes at different costs, related to a difference in effort:

- general reworked;
- client specific; and
- client exclusive.

Figure 4 (below) shows which categories occur on which portal level. Take note that no general information from common sources is placed unaltered on any of the portals. This will avoid the risk that the portal is experienced as a general repeated source and steers it away from copyright breach.

7. Difference in users and effects on business

It is important to understand how the number of users vary over the different portal levels, the position they have and the effect on the business of their portal use. No fixed numbers are given, but in general a description of the user group per portal level can be given as follows:

- Knowledge portal: the number of users normally equals the size of the client

Figure 4: Information exclusivity over three portal levels

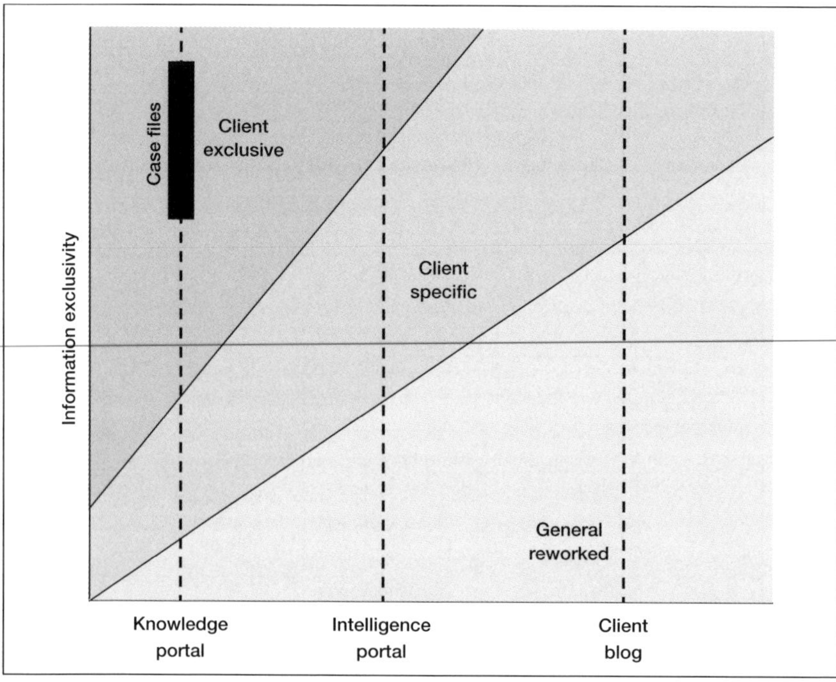

team that has direct but infrequent email contact with the law firm. They are personally known by the firm. The user experiences direct availability of core documents and knowledge, and is via portal or other channels always in a direct dialogue with the firm. There is a strong urge to put most quality control on this portal level.

- Intelligence portal: has a wider but limited user group of all client team members, higher management, identified decision makers and those known by the firm with a direct interest in the themes or services discussed. Restriction of users is based on the level of confidentiality and personal or strategic value of the content published on the intelligence portal. The identification of all users of this level is known individually. The use of this portal level creates loyalty from clients and possibly generates recurring business.
- Client blog: has the highest number of users. They are not known individually but via a single sign-on they are known to belong to the client organisation, but their identity and position will remain unknown. A strong position of this portal level is that there is a higher probability of contributing to cross selling and expanding services for clients.

8. Levels of confidentiality and security

The client finds logical access via a natural flow running from the general to specific, or from client blog to knowledge portal. With each level the security increases and, in general, so will the confidentiality. Access to the client blog can be arranged by a corporate-wide sign-on, leaving the users unidentified but their relationship with the client organisation without doubt.

Figure 5: Difference in confidentiality and security over the three portal levels

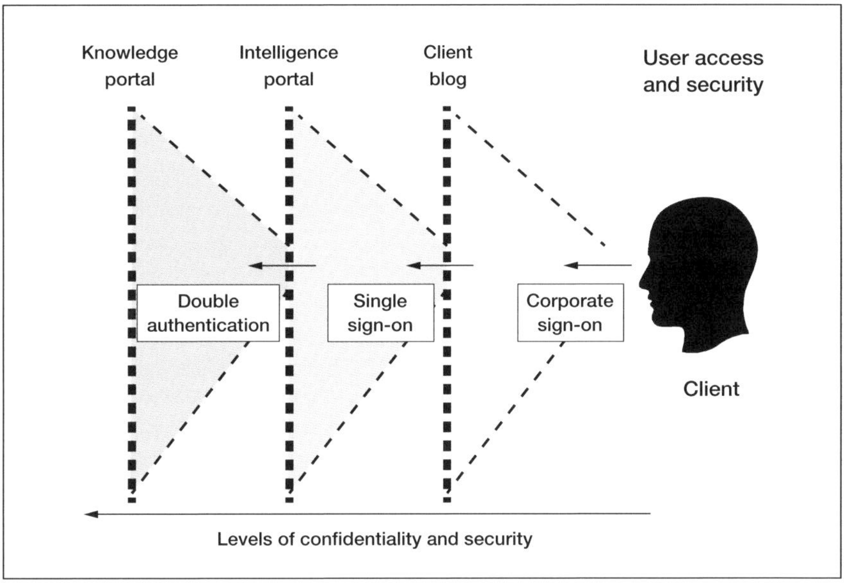

The client blog will give access to those with the right identity to the intelligence portal via a single sign-on. Individual users are recognised on this platform, but the content will not differ between users, as there is no difference in rights.

The client blog and the intelligence portal will give access to the knowledge portal via double authentication. This secure access will double check any identity by requesting a code sent by email or SMS. Individuals will be recognised by the portal and reading/writing rights are arranged for each user/folder. Each level of the portal can also be reached via a bookmark of the browser interface, but will always require the right level of access.

9. Conclusions

With the introduction of the attractive and intuitive intelligence portals and client blogs, overlaying the traditional DMS-like client portals, there is serious potential in developing a knowledge-based relationship between law firms and their clients. It will lead the way to extended business models in which traditional legal services are extended. This extension can range from legal knowledge support, research, information services and outsourcing to more strategic consulting. The position of the three different portal layers may lead to real alternative fee arrangements.

It is complicated for law firms to widen their services outside the current and proven ones. With the advanced portals discussed here, the law firm has a show window within the client, with the right user group, with the right content, in the right context. The business case for the length and depth of the relationship is quickly made when knowledge exchange is involved. But the power of thought leadership leads to more strategic engagement, often starting at an earlier moment than the traditional start of regular legal engagement.

This in-depth partnering with the client, being part of the earlier strategic orientation, innovation or risk assessment, is the moment when financers and strategic consultants usually start their engagement. Law firms with a knowledge driven connection might very well deserve an early, lucrative seat at the same table, with increasing follow-up business as a logical next step.

Showcasing outside the library walls: growth through collaboration

Emily Allbon
City, University of London

1. Introduction

At a time when libraries in all sectors are facing threats: whether from within their own organisations or on a national scale, the challenge to prove value is a continuing one. Information professionals are fighting on many fronts; dodging bullets designed to take chunks out of budgets and slash staff numbers with no regard for expertise, and it can be difficult to keep focused and remember what makes librarians unique.

Under this barrage we need to bring in reinforcements – champions. However, these cannot be disconnected colleagues in the wider business singing out praise from afar, but by necessity active collaborators. Collaboration is absolutely core to the success of an information service and those who manage it.

This chapter seeks to explore collaboration in various ways, questioning what it is about the skill set of an informational professional that makes them such a useful partner. We'll be looking at examples of those who have left the profession to see which skills they prize most from their previous career. This may seem an odd approach, but it is one I hope will demonstrate the enviable transferable quality inherent in this skill set. We'll also look at collaboration more broadly to see examples of this in action – librarians collaborating with other teams in their organisation, but also with those externally. These examples are not drawn from the corporate sector – it is markedly more difficult to collaborate externally in a competitive environment but I hope you will find the examples interesting nonetheless. There are some imaginative projects out there!

Proving worth is important, whatever the size of your organisation, institution, firm or company. Worth will go some way to securing you greater visibility and an increased likelihood of influencing the wider business. In today's climate the strategy for this is often very statistics-driven – numbers being generally the key language decision-makers value. However, narrative can also be very powerful when engaging the wider community, who in turn will be useful advocates for you.

The Pro-Vice-Chancellor for Student and Staff Services at Aberystwyth University, Rebecca Davies, is a strong advocate for the power of collaboration of this type. She notes that a successful, collaboration-rich library and information service will:

- be part of the shift to open-access scholarly communication;
- be entrepreneurial and mutate services, take risks, and learn from (regular) failures to confront disruptive technologies; and
- collaborate within and outside our professional and institutional boundaries,

working as part of multi-service teams and with organisations and businesses outside our perceived sector walls.[1]

Rebecca's third point here is absolutely crucial – collaborating with 'outsiders' sends a very strong message about the expertise within the information profession: by working together with non-librarians, our circle widens and influence extends. In Higher Education (HE) the landscape has altered tremendously, with an emphasis on convergence and bringing more and more services together under the same umbrella management.

It is challenging to distinguish our work in this environment, particularly when the services we offer are less visible than a decade ago. The dominance of online, and the subsequent change in how academic staff teach, students learn and the means by which both research, mean we have needed to develop new competencies. Across all library sectors, except public, the less people need to visit our physical spaces, the more focus we need to place on ensuring the work we do is evident.

Faculty used to rely almost exclusively on the library for the scholarly materials they needed for research and teaching, and librarians guided faculty to and otherwise facilitated the discovery of these materials. As scholars have grown better able to reach needed materials directly online, going to or using the library is not essential to carrying out research and so faculty are turning to other options.[2]

2. What's in it for me?

Survival is one thing but actively seeking collaborations has the potential to take your career in many different directions. My own experience as a law librarian who collaborated resulted in many opportunities: being asked to write papers and present at conferences all over the world, becoming a member of the editorial board of a non-library journal (*The Law Teacher*), being awarded various prizes from the library profession and externally, and getting the chance to connect with the full range of those from my discipline: students, academics, other librarians and lawyers in practice. However, this can only happen if you're prepared to move out of your comfort zone and seek connections in the wider world, outside of your library, your institution, your profession and possibly your country.

As law librarian at City University of London, where I worked for 14 years before changing to legal academia, I created a website for law students called Lawbore.[3] This began life as a simple gateway site; pointing students to quality legal resources freely available online, but over the years has developed into a bit of a beast, with community elements, skills tutorials, events roundups and a careers blog.

It has grown organically in the sense that I used my experiences with those I met in my work as inspiration for its features, and ideas would spring from my contact

---

1 Rebecca Davies, "The Changing Higher Education Context" in Melling and Weaver *Collaboration in Libraries and Learning Environments* (2013), pp10–11.

2 K Guthrie and R Housewright, "Repackaging the Library: what do faculty think?" in "Climbing out of the box: Repackaging Libraries for Survival, Special Issue" (2010) 51(1) *Journal of Library Administration* 77–104.

3 Lawbore http://lawbore.net.

with both the students and academics. As time went on however, I became braver and began to look at actually involving them in the content, getting their buy-in, but also learning from them. I'll touch on a few elements of this work under the headings below. However, we'll also be looking at the many other collaborative 'stories' that have captured the imagination of their organisations and beyond.

3. Librarians and academic staff

As a librarian I reached out to my academic colleagues on various occasions to collaborate with me in developing new resources for Lawbore, but I'll just detail two for you here. The first was *Talking Essays* – within HE feedback is always problematic: students think they don't get enough of it, academics aren't always convinced students read and take on board the feedback they receive. I worked with my academic colleagues to select a mix of assessments (varying standards) in the core areas of law, recording audio feedback and then making each snippet available as a hotspot in each essay so students could get a real feel for what works and what doesn't.

The second was Learnmore,[4] the skills part of the site, which housed online tutorials, talking slideshows, articles and video content around legal writing, research, mooting, careers and exams. I had created lots of content but the mooting area was incomplete. (For those of you unfamiliar with this activity, law students participate in moot competitions, representing one of the parties in a fictional case which has gone to appeal.) There were barely any resources on mooting online and I felt Learnmore could really fill a gap; it was something I was often asked about as a librarian. I approached a new academic who taught on a Legal Method module and together we organised the filming of many moots, trawling through footage to find short clips to illustrate points and getting students to share their tips with us online. This proved very popular and we were excited to receive the Routledge/Association of Law Teachers (ALT) Teaching Law with Technology Prize in 2013.

4. Cross-institutional collaborations

The long-running Library Impact Data Project,[5] funded by JISC and managed by the University of Huddersfield, is an impressive example of many libraries working together (Huddersfield collaborated with seven other university libraries). The first phase of the project looked at whether links could be made between library use and attainment and the second focused on whether connections could be drawn between library use and retention.

Collaborations around data and library analytics are likely to increase – with librarians working with researchers, IT specialists and publishers to exploit the increasing quantity of freely available data in order to make connections and reveal new findings.

4 Learnmore http://learnmore.lawbore.net/.
5 See the JISC Activity Data project blog for further information: https://library3.hud.ac.uk/blogs/lidp/.

5. Librarians and learning technologists

At Regent's University London, an innovative Christmas-themed open online course "The Twelve Apps of Christmas"[6] was developed by a small team of learning technologists and a librarian. The aim was to engage their colleagues at the university in thinking about how they might use free-to-use applications (apps) in support of teaching, so was targeted firmly at academic staff and others with a teaching role at the university: e-learning teams and librarians. Each day a new app would be introduced to participants, along with reading content and a 10-minute activity to complete. There was also a discussion forum where experiences of use could be shared, along with alternatives suggested. Apps chosen for the programme included Poll Everywhere, Padlet, Dragon Dictation, Turnitin, Wunderlist, Prezi, Simplemind+ and Padlet.

With over 500 participants signing up from across the world this collaborative project has received much acclaim, both within the university and externally, and the team are working on other projects for the future.

Many university librarians work with their e-learning and educational development teams to develop workshops for academics, students and researchers.

6. Libraries and the community

One of the most well-publicised partnerships of recent years can be found in the West Midlands: the fabulous golden library named The Hive. The hybrid university and public library in Worcester has drawn together the community – becoming a central point for a vast range of information and services, with an average of 2,500 daily visits.[7] The partnership between the University of Worcester and Worcestershire County Council has continued to flourish, with complementary strategic plans and a focus on making a contribution across all sectors of the local population. Provision of a business centre was considered key from the start; and representatives from local companies and the Chamber of Commerce were invited along to explore with the university and county council how they might go about developing such a centre for the business community. The centre (relaunched in 2014) has developed many new partnerships, as well as a full annual programme of business-related events.

Although not strictly a collaboration, the University of Aberdeen has an impressive outreach programme to local schools, employing two full-time Learning and Outreach Officers to work with schools and local community groups, sharing their special collections with the community.

A music venue is likely to top any list of 'most unexpected library partners' but the Sir Henry's/University College Cork[8] (UCC) project is one of the most exciting collaborations of recent years. Sir Henry's, a Cork nightclub and live music venue,

---

6 Andy Horton, "The Twelve Apps of Christmas: How collaboration between librarians and learning technologists brought success to an open online course" SCONUL Focus 65, pp18–22. http://www.sconul.ac.uk/sites/default/files/documents/5_18.pdf.

7 Stephanie Allen, 'The Hive: the joint University of Worcester/Worcester public library that's open for business" SCONUL Focus 65 pp23–28.

8 Martin O'Connor gives an interesting interview via UKlibchat: https://uklibchat.wordpress.com/2015/03/31/feature-23-a-recent-interview-with-a-librarian-and-his-experience-of-collaborating-outside-libraries/. More information about the Sir Henry's exhibition via the UCC website: http://www.ucc.ie/en/about/uccnews/fullstory-481342-en.html and the Sir Henry's blog: https://sirhenrys2014.wordpress.com/.

had a firm following from both the dance and rock crowds, during its 25 years of business. The club closed in 2003. A tweet was the trigger for three individuals to come together to organise an exhibition at UCC celebrating the influence of the club on the Cork community: Elaine Hogan, an academic at UCC, Martin O'Connor, librarian at UCC and Stevie G, a DJ and promoter. The efforts of this trio brought together the community, encouraging them to donate memorabilia and stories to the exhibition, which ran from July to September 2014. Like the Hive, this collaboration reached diverse sections of society, not only regular library-goers.

7. Librarians and other university teams

Learning spaces is one area where there is a lot of movement in terms of sharing ideas across the institution: projects led by the library to manage and develop learning spaces outside of the library, but with collaboration from IT, Facilities, Student Services, the Students Union and the students themselves. Bradford University, University of Bolton, Teeside University, University of Portsmouth, University of Exeter and the University of Cumbria are such examples. The Information Commons at the University of Sheffield represents a joint venture between the library and Corporate Information and Computing Services.

There are various examples of librarians working with Careers teams on employability projects and also teaming up with Academic Support and Study Skills teams.

Bit of a cheat inclusion here, but in my role as an academic at City University London I set about revitalising student induction in September 2015 by collaborating with our Academic Support Advisor. In order to focus students' attention to the importance of academic writing and to give them the opportunity to get to know each other and the local area, I designed six trails around London, each taking in four buildings of legal significance.[9] The students had a basic introduction to writing skills before setting off in groups to find locations, answer research questions and take some selfies of their groups out and about. Later that week they had very interactive writing workshops with us, before writing a short piece based on something they'd been inspired by on their travels. They were given feedback and the 21 winning pieces were announced. Although not library-related, some aspects of this would be really simple to adapt for library induction.

8. Librarians and students/alumni

So many examples of collaboration here; working with students to create resources as well as 'training them up' to communicate your message to their peers is a sensible strategy. Students listen to other students and that is a powerful thing.

LSE have achieved great things with their SADL project:[10] Student Ambassadors

---

9 See an example trail and student selfies: http://blog.lawbore.net/2015/10/exploring-the-law-with-our-new-llb1-students/ as well as examples of the student submissions: http://blog.lawbore.net/tag/exploring-the-law/.

10 Maria Bell and Jane Secker, 'Transitions from School to Higher Education: Understanding the Needs of Undergraduates at LSE" in *Information Literacy, Lifelong Learning and Digital Citizens – Second European Conference, ECIL 2014*, Croatia, October 20–23, 2014, pp309–318. See also http://blogs.lse.ac.uk/lsesadl/.

for Digital Literacy which was the result of a partnership between the library and the Learning, Technology and Innovation (Lti) team. The project is aimed squarely at undergraduates, with a select few being chosen as ambassadors, who undergo four digital literacy workshops during the year. They are let loose on their peers; delivering the content in workshops themselves. It's wonderful to imagine the digital literacy message infiltrating the student body from within!

The University of Hull recruits student 'Skills Leaders' to help out with their workshops, as well as employing them to critique their materials and web usability.

An innovation at The Hive is that they partner up with students to assist them in their recruitment process for new professional library posts. The benefits of this are striking; first, by giving students ownership – passing on a feeling of them having a stake in the library service, but also allowing the interview activities to be much more innovative and meaningful. Seeing how candidates interacted with students during a work-related task was invaluable.[11]

Lawbore has always recruited students to work as creative partners; each year a handful are taken on as 'legal journalists' where they write event reviews, comment pieces and reflections on experiences.[12] Like the experience from The Hive, this gives them ownership and increases the sense of community at City, as well as giving the students the valuable opportunity to see their work published online.

Retaining links with students after they graduate is also important as we bring them back for interviews on the site, and to speak at events. Many of these graduates come back to us when in practice with opportunities for current students, for example *pro bono* work. Two of our students every year get the chance to write for the fantastic UK Human Rights Blog[13] (written by the barristers at the chambers of One Crown Office Row) as regular contributors, thanks to one of our alumni, Adam Wagner.

One summer we used a group of students who had just finished exams to film a whole series of tips and tricks which would be useful to the incoming cohort. They also filmed a video glossary for us, holding up lots of different legal sources (law reports, encyclopedias, statutes, textbooks...) and talking through why they are important and when to use them. Like the LSE example, we recognise that students appreciate the wisdom of their more experienced peers.

9. Librarians and publishers

Law students always have difficulties reading cases – it is a daunting business opening up 40 pages of dense text and working out what each section means and where you can best focus your attentions to decipher the judicial reasoning. I approached the Incorporated Council of Law Reporting (ICLR) to see if they would be willing to work with me on creating a resource for Lawbore to assist new law students. We used the same technology as *Talking Essays* and Paul Magrath, Head of Product and Online Content, narrated a journey through a case, highlighting why each section might be important in their research.[14]

---

11 Sarah Pittaway, "Students as partners in recruitment" SCONUL Focus 65 pp40–43.
12 See posts on *Future Lawyer*: http://blog.lawbore.net/.
13 UK Human Rights Blog https://ukhumanrightsblog.com/.
14 Anatomy of a law report http://learnmore.lawbore.net/index.php/Anatomy_Of_A_Law_Report.

10. Our skills – both desirable and transferable?

We can see from the many examples in the previous pages that collaborations with others outside the library profession can have many positive benefits, but what strategies can we use to show what excellent project partners we are?

Keen to understand what skills we should prize most closely I spoke with individuals who have left the information profession to pursue other vocations, curious to find out what they still utilise in their new role and how well these competencies have translated across sectors. Here is a snapshot!

Case study 1

Previous roles (as a librarian)

Academic Librarian, Academic Services Manager, Information Science Research Fellow

Current role

Research Policy Manager (Publications) within Research Office at a UK University

This individual is responsible for advising the University on research publication strategy and providing evidence to support that strategy. They also act as secretary to the Research Quality Enhancement Sub-Committee.

Skills learnt in their library roles which are still useful in the current post include diplomacy, liaison, information management, an understanding of the scholarly communication process, web development and training.

Case study 2

Previous roles (as a librarian)

Researcher at *The Guardian* and later at Lehman Brothers

Current role

Director, Anti-Money Laundering, Deutsche Bank

Unsurprisingly, this former librarian draws heavily on the organisational skills learnt early in their career. In this heavily scrutinised sector, they need to know they and their team can lay hands on information which might be required at very short notice by senior management, law enforcement teams or the regulators. This can be challenging as the information takes many forms; correspondence, management information, transcripts of interviews or bank account data.

They also note how important it is to know how to harness and store the knowledge of colleagues when conducting an investigation into processes.

Case study 3

Previous roles (as a librarian)

Law Librarian – Cardiff University, Director of Library & Information Services, BPP

Current role

Head of Student Technology & Learning Resources, Pearson College

This former law librarian's recent roles are akin to a CIO role – they see this as being a post which listens to the business, works out what technology and information requirements need to be met and then articulate this to the appropriate teams. When pressed on how their previous profession might have given them a grounding for this type of role, they note how librarians excel at working out the relative values of things and are able to converse easily with technical teams. They also note that the fundamentals learnt whilst managing libraries – staff management, budget controls and contract negotiation have all been pivotal in preparing for this current role.

Case study 4

Previous roles (as a librarian)

Library Assistant, Collection Development Librarian, BPP

Law Librarian – Kings College London, Ebook sales specialist – Proquest

Current role

Director of Information Sales, Geoscience World

This former librarian notes three formative experiences which have assisted in their current role. Working in the ebook industry involves presenting at conferences, and to libraries, in order to sell different ebook acquisition strategies (eg, PDA), as well as completing tenders and dealing with consortia. They highlight those invaluable induction sessions they gave as a subject librarian, and how well they were prepared for presentations and public speaking. Their knowledge of how library budgets function has also been a huge advantage in the role. Finally, they cite dealing with argumentative law students as great preparation for this position in this new industry.

Case study 5

Previous roles (as a librarian)

Information Officer – Freshfields and later at the FSA

Current role

Senior Knowledge Manager for Global Corporate Finance Business (at one of the 'Big Four' auditors)

This individual works with country leaders in the business to help define a knowledge strategy for their business, by looking at size, focus and priorities in both the short and longer term. Key is working to understand what markets and clients they want to attract, how they need to collaborate with colleagues in other geographies and what resources will be necessary to meet these targets. As you might expect, all of this has to also align with the knowledge strategy of the business as a whole – ensuring that colleagues are aware of how everyone works and what they do in order to avoid silos.

They note three valuable skills from librarianship that have paid dividends in their current role; helping people articulate what they need, getting to grips quickly with complex ideas and information and advanced communication skills. In relation to the articulation point, early experience at Freshfields is cited here: [this] 'helped me to develop skills in making sense of an immediate requirement and understanding a situation, fleshing it out and also predicting what might be needed in the future'.

They observe that early roles taught them how to analyse a situation, extract what is needed to support the client/team and disregard anything irrelevant. With regards to communication they point out that in a global business you will be dealing with teams you rarely meet. Having the skills to communicate with individuals you manage from afar is vital, as is an understanding of cultural issues and potential sensitivities in this context.

Case study 6
Previous roles (as a librarian)
Research Librarian, Trainer, Library Manager at Slaughter & May, Denton Wilde Sapte and Baker & McKenzie.
Current role
CSR Manager, Baker & McKenzie

As a CSR Manager this former librarian manages the law firm's charitable partnerships and coordinates the *pro bono* programme. They also organise all staff volunteering opportunities, direct sustainability activities and have responsibility for managing a proportion of the social mobility work experience programmes.

Like interviewees numbers 3 and 5, they emphasise how important the ability to clarify people's needs is within the role, a skill which was refined over years of enquiry desk work. In the current context an example might be dealing with an initial approach from a charity and working out where to direct this and what element to focus on. They note how, as a librarian, they were positioned as a 'hub' – revelling in the role as a connector within the organisation, where people came with queries and problems. It has been important to carry this into this new role, bringing together groups of volunteers. Finally, they state how much they continue to rely upon research skills for benchmarking and keeping an eye on what other organisations are focusing on.

11. Conclusion

What these brief profiles demonstrate is that these former librarians have in no way shed their past lives: the skills they gained in the profession have stuck with them and remain valuable to them and their organisations today. Although there is some crossover, there is also diversity in the qualities highlighted. From these six snapshots and the collaborations earlier on in the chapter we see librarians as great communicators, innovators, managers of budgets, people and spaces. We see them as experts in needs analysis, as leaders, as people who can pinpoint organisational issues and provide imaginative solutions. Above all though, those who work in the information profession are facilitators; making connections, seeing gaps and joining up the dots within an organisation – there is no better collaborator.

Organising KM in a law firm – coordinating processes and resources

Martina Kuth
CMS Hasche Sigle
Martin R Schulz
German Graduate School of Management and Law (GGS)

1. Introduction

In this chapter, we would like to provide an overview of some key aspects of organising KM in a law firm, and provide the reader with some recommendations regarding the necessary structure, process and resources.[1] Our thoughts and suggestions result from our practical experience as well as from our studies of the subject. We suggest taking a joint approach from the perspective of different information professionals involving important KM stakeholders and interest groups.

After linking some typical organisational issues to the law firm's KM strategy, we suggest following the well-known distinction between explicit and implicit knowledge for organisational issues of law firm KM as well. For organising explicit knowledge (such as agreements or documents produced in legal transactions) we provide a checklist for some typical elements and features of a KM database. For organising the so-called implicit knowledge (eg, lawyers' insights and experience), we provide some ideas for visualising and expressing such experience by looking at specific knowledge processes like identifying and acquiring relevant knowledge, as well as collecting and distributing it. Since success of any KM organisation will depend on its regular and consistent quality control, we put special emphasis on how to establish effective content management procedures in order to keep knowledge resources up to date.

Last, but not least, we also refer to the question of the right mix of resources, and in particular to the question whether or not law firms need so-called professional support lawyers (PSL) to perform the relevant KM tasks.

2. Linking organisational issues to the law firm's KM strategy

As indicated in other parts[2] of this book, it is necessary to align KM activities and projects with the law firm's specific business model and its business strategy. This

1 Analysing all aspects of the subject would obviously require much more room, and we do not purport to be able to cover every detail. Some parts of this chapter have been already covered (partly in more detail) by Martin Schulz and Luis Felipe Mohando, "Precedent databases and Knowledge Management" in Hermann J Knott (consulting ed), *Risk Management in Law Firms: Strategies for Safeguarding the Future* (Globe Business Publishing, 2014) pp117–128.

2 See eg, Lustigman's chapter on implementing KM strategy in practice and Schulz's chapter on getting lawyers to contribute content to KM systems.

also applies to the question of how to design and structure the KM program. Organising KM in a law firm will certainly depend on individual factors like the size of the law firm, its specific business focus and its international scope of activities. Nevertheless, we believe that organising an effective KM system will always raise a number of general issues and challenges which need to be addressed.

2.1 Involving important KM stakeholders and interest groups

When organising legal information and know-how, it is advisable to involve important KM stakeholders and interest groups in the first place. Involving the following KM stakeholders and interest groups is important not only for identifying potential gaps in existing know-how resources, but also for defining roles, responsibilities and requirements to be met when implementing and maintaining the KM system.

(a) Lawyers (and their clients) as a primary interest group

Given that law is a knowledge-intensive business and lawyers are typical 'knowledge workers',[3] this group would of course include lawyers as a primary interest group. Depending on the size of the law firm there might be a designated team of partners and associates being charged with certain KM tasks and functions. However, also in smaller law firms there is always a need from fee earners for making relevant information and knowledge resources available in an accurate, convenient and current form. Taking the trend of 'client-facing KM'[4] into consideration, another important interest group is that of the law firm's clients. From an integrated and holistic KM perspective, however, including the client's view is restating the obvious. KM programs and activities should always promote the capacity of the law firm and its members to best serve their clients on a sound and up to date legal basis.

Therefore, it is important to involve lawyers, for example a representative group of them, when planning the original design and structure of the KM organisation. This applies also in cases where the law firm seeks advice by consultants in order to ensure that any structural proposals are customised and tailor made to the specific needs and requirements of the law firm. Furthermore, lawyers should always be represented when the KM program is readjusted or updated in order to cover new features and developments.

(b) Integrating information professionals

It is also important to involve information professionals such as law librarians and PSL when planning and developing the KM organisation. Law librarians have traditionally played a crucial role in law firms. In many small and medium-sized law firms, they still represent the key source of legal information management providing services like the selection, acquisition, maintenance and delivery of relevant knowledge.[5]

Bigger law firms often also employ PSL[6] as information professionals with law

3 See eg, Gretta Rusanow, *Knowledge Management and the Smarter Lawyer* (2003), describing a law firm as a "knowledge based business" at p7. See also Martin Schulz and Marcel Klugmann, "Creating a Culture of Knowledge Sharing in Law Firms" in KD Althoff *et al* (eds), *Professional Knowledge Management, Lecture Notes in Artificial Intelligence* (Springer, 2005), p386.

degrees and some years of legal practice who will typically perform some similar functions to law librarians. For example, typical tasks for a law librarian would not only include cataloguing, indexing and classifying legal information,[7] but also answering enquiries from fee earners (including hard copy and online search and delivery of relevant material), as well as providing news on legislation and new case law. Answering legal enquiries from fee earners and providing updates on new law will often also form an important part of the job profile of PSL. In those law firms which offer taxonomies as a guideline for their know-how databases (as an additional feature to a full text search function), PSL may also be required to help build and update a legal classification scheme (based on their training in legal terminology and structure).

(c) *Considering links to business services like HR and business development*

In addition to the KM interest groups described above, it might also be useful to consider other business services when designing the KM program and structures. This applies in particular to HR and to business development.[8] As indicated, there are close links between several HR and BD activities to KM activities and projects. In order to enable an open and constructive exchange of ideas and experience among KM, HR and business development (BD), it seems useful to consider the goals and functions of these business services. Examples for joint activities would include integrating KM resources into HR programs (like learning and development) and using KM resources to identify current legal developments in order to update key clients.[9] Effective exchange of knowledge and experience between KM and HR as well as KM and BD may facilitate the attraction of new clients as well as the retention of existing ones.

2.2 Combining elements of codification and personalisation strategies

The question of how to organise and structure KM should be considered a necessary element of the law firm's KM strategy.[10] As indicated, the task of developing a KM strategy is a crucial factor for building an effective KM system.[11] Accordingly, all necessary KM investments and activities should always match the business strategy of the law firm.[12] The required alignment with the business model applies to the original organisational design and structure of the KM system as well as on its future development.

---

4 See Büchi's chapter on client-facing knowledge management.

5 See Jules Winterton, "Law Libraries and their Users" in *BIALL Handbook of Legal Information Management*, 2nd edn, pp1; Martina Kuth, "Between Book and Database: Meeting Information Needs in a Law Firm's Library" (2014) 14 *Legal Information Management* 115–120.

6 *Cf* Ann Hemming, "Knowledge Management" in *BIALL Handbook of Legal Information Management*, 2nd edn (n 1), p223; see also Matthew Parsons, *Effective Knowledge Management for Law Firms* (Oxford University Press, 2004), pp64–65.

7 *Cf* Diana Morris, "Cataloguing and Classification" in *BIALL Handbook of Legal Information Management*, 2nd edn (Routledge, 2014), pp231–238.

8 See eg, Abbott's chapter on human resources and Büchi's chapter on client-facing knowledge management.

9 See Büchi's chapter on client-facing knowledge management.

10 See Lustigman's chapter on implementing KM strategy in practice. See also Schulz and Mohando (n 1), pp120–121; Rusanow (n 3), pp46–50; Matthew Parsons (n 6) pp77–95.

11 See Rusanow (n 3), pp261–288; Parsons (n 6) pp77–95.

12 Schulz and Mohando (n 1), pp120-121.

With regard to the focus of the KM strategy, it is helpful to follow the traditional distinction between a so-called strategy of codification and a so-called strategy of personalisation.[13] A codification strategy is focusing on explicit knowledge which is typically codified in written documents like memoranda, agreements, examples of transactions, and legal briefs. Such a KM strategy focusing on codified knowledge will thus seek to systematically collect, classify, store and distribute these written knowledge components.[14] A KM strategy with a focus on personalisation will, on the other hand, concentrate on building an effective framework to allow lawyers and other members of the firm to effectively communicate and exchange their know-how and experience (the so-called 'implicit knowledge').[15] Since both explicit knowledge (ie, standard forms, memoranda or documents from important transactions), as well as implicit knowledge (in the form of experience), are very valuable knowledge assets for day-to-day legal practice, law firms should ideally combine both strategic approaches when developing their KM strategy.

3. Organising explicit knowledge – some structural guidelines

In most law firms, a digital KM database will form the core structural part of the KM system for organising explicit knowledge. This KM database typically represents a kind of a 'virtual library' and serves as the gateway and pathfinder to all explicit knowledge and as the central knowledge repository. In our view, this should apply regardless of where the knowledge collections and information resources are physically or digitally stored, and would include resources on the law firm's intranet, online research tools and websites, digital knowledge collections, as well as books and other hardcopy information material on the shelves of the library. The following issues and questions are important when structuring the contents and functions of the KM database.

3.1 Building a KM database – typical contents

The following list is not exhaustive but covers some typical contents in a 'KM database', in the form of online as well as hardcopy sources, and covering primary as well as secondary legal sources such as:[16]

- legislative materials (including EU law and foreign law of relevant jurisdictions);
- case law (court decisions, decisions by administrative authorities etc);
- commentaries, handbooks on the practice of law, guidelines etc;
- information by and on relevant industry sectors and authorities (eg, in the area of banking, financial services or insurance companies);
- publicly available information sources on markets and clients;
- best practice documents;

13 See Morten T Hansen, Nitin Nohria and Thomas Tierney, "What's your Strategy for Managing Knowledge?" (1999) *Harvard Business Review* 106; see also Parsons (n 6), pp161–173.

14 *Cf* Rusanow (n 3), p308.

15 For developing a KM strategy for law firms see Rusanow (n 3), pp261–288; Parsons (n 6) pp77–95.

16 See also Rusanow (n 3), pp75–80; Guy Holborn, "Sources of Legal Information and their Organisation" in *BIALL Handbook of Legal Information Management*, 2nd edn (Routledge, 2014), pp53–73.

- examples from transactional work of fee earners (so called precedents); and
- standard forms developed by fee earners.

As follows from the strategic approach outlined above, the scope and content of the KM database need to be tailored to the business needs of the law firms and to the demands of important KM interest groups including librarians, PSL and other information professionals.

3.2 Useful features and functions of the KM database

When organising explicit knowledge resources, another aspect to be considered at the start of the project is the functionality of the KM database. Taking the user's perspective first, the following questions are relevant:

- How user-friendly is the system (addressing issues of easy and convenient access and navigation)?
- Is there a table of contents/taxonomy tool (helping users to get an overview of know-how resources, to navigate and to find related content)?
- Are various search options offered (eg, full text search, search by metadata, search within the classification scheme)?
- How can knowledge and information be stored (options for adding additional information to documents or for references to external sources)?
- How can knowledge and experience be shared and distributed effectively (clarifying different forms of users' rights like simple access, edit rights etc. Deciding on different form of distribution like 'pull' and/or 'push' functions)?
- How can knowledge and information be updated (addressing the implementation of review cycles and content management)?

All these questions need to be answered when designing the initial structure as well as new features and functions of a KM database. In order to make the user's needs and requirements part of the process it seems advisable to involve a selected group of the stakeholders indicated above (lawyers, PSL, librarians and representatives of other service functions) in developing and testing new functions and features. For example, when discussing different forms of search options in the KM database, it might be useful to include a classification tool for the visualisation of interrelated content (eg, the tax aspects of an M&A deal) – such a classification tool could supplement a 'Google'-like search option.[17] A combination of a full text ('Google-type') search function with a classification search, that is an option to navigate through a taxonomy of legal subjects, can help users to find interrelated issues (eg, in corporate and tax law). It can also help to avoid the so-called 'content silo' trap – describing a phenomenon amongst lawyers to focus too closely on their own area of legal expertise.[18]

---

17 *Cf* Schulz and Mohando (n 1), p125; Martin Schulz, "Content Management – A Fine Art – And a Knowledge Paradox" (2008) *Knowledge and Information Management Legal* 17–20. For the functions and use of taxonomies see Vainikainen's chapter on taxonomy and informal tagging; Christine Miskin, "Taxonomies and indexing" in *BIALL Handbook of Legal Information Management*, pp246–253.

18 See Martin Schulz *ibid*, Content Management, p18. See also Rusanow (n 3), pp241–242.

In addition to the users' needs, it seems advisable also to take the needs and interests of information professionals (like law librarians and PSL) into account in order to facilitate their tasks in operating and maintaining the KM database. For example, knowledge managers and information professionals will appreciate a variety of tools and design options, like the ability to:

- tag know-how items with metadata (like author, applicable law, language) before storing those items into the KM database.[19] Using these metadata methodically will have a positive impact on any searches in the database (provided they are used consistently);[20]
- link know-how items to other information sources (internally and externally);
- use various search options (full text search, search for metadata etc); and
- use a (legal) classification system or taxonomy in order to categorise know-how items and to guide users.

For law librarians, PSL and other information professionals these specific tools and features will help them to accomplish their task as effective 'knowledge brokers' answering information requests and enquiries from the fee earners and managing the contents of the KM database.

4. Visualising implicit knowledge – some recommendations

Building a strong KM database with useful functions and features is an important step for organising KM in a law firm, but is only half the battle. As outlined above, a KM database will be the traditional repository for explicit knowledge, and many law firms have spent much time and effort to build, buy and maintain huge repositories for their codified knowledge resources. However, knowledge exists not only in explicit forms, but also quite often in the form of implicit or tacit knowledge stored in peoples' heads.[21] In order to be able to also embrace this form of knowledge, and in particular the experience and insights of lawyers, it is important to include some additional tools and techniques when organising KM in a law firm.

4.1 Looking at key knowledge processes

As a starting point, it is useful to see KM not as a static system, but as a dynamic process. When thinking of possible ways how to externalise[22] and visualise lawyers' implicit knowledge in the form of experience and insights, one should therefore think of relevant knowledge processes.[23] There are several process-oriented KM

---

19 For the use and function of 'tagging' see Vainikainen's chapter on taxonomy and informal tagging. See also Diana Morris, "Cataloguing and Classification" in *BIALL Handbook of Legal Information Management*, 2nd edn (Routledge, 2014), pp31–38; Christine Miskin, "Taxonomies and indexing" in *BIALL Handbook of Legal Information Management*, pp 246–254.

20 Schulz and Mohando (n 1), p125.

21 See Rusanow (n 3), pp72, 111, 119–120; Parsons (n 6), pp161–173. As far as possible, this implicit knowledge should also be captured, made explicit and shared by writing it down in manuals, practice notes and guidelines, which are then stored in the database.

22 In their landmark book *The Knowledge Creating Company* (Oxford University Press, 1995), Ikujiro Nonaka and Hirotaka Takeuchi describe the so-called 'externalisation' as the process for making implicit knowledge explicit.

models discussed, but we will focus on the following important processes: knowledge identification and acquisition, knowledge exchange and distribution, knowledge preservation and development.[24]

(a) Knowledge identification by mapping knowledge and experience

One useful way of mapping knowledge is a taxonomy (as defined above) which includes not only documents but also pointers to experience. A useful tool to visualise experience, skills and competencies of lawyers and other experts is an expert directory (sometimes called 'yellow pages') answering the following questions:

- Do you know all relevant personal skills and qualifications of the law firm's members (professional qualifications, language skills, specific knowledge about clients etc)?
- Are these personal skills and qualifications recorded systematically?
- Do you also include links and related information to external experts and institutions?

(b) Knowledge acquisition through hiring and developing experts and skills

Knowledge acquisition is often realised by buying other companies, for example with specific know-how or innovative technology. Another option, being relevant also for KM in law firms, is to hire experts in order to complement existing or to develop new knowledge resources. The following questions may be helpful:

- Do we have enough lawyers in each practice area to serve the needs of our clients?
- Can we acquire additional skills and competencies, for example by education and training tools?
- If not, can we meet additional requirements by the lateral hiring of experts?

(c) Knowledge exchange by providing communication and learning tools

As outlined above, the task of exchange and distribution of explicit knowledge can be accomplished by providing convenient access and search tools in the KM database. In contrast, enabling the exchange and distribution of experience requires a framework of communication and a culture of trust, answering the following questions:

- Are there flexible and convenient ways to talk and to exchange insights and experience (eg, lunchtime meetings on interesting cases and transactions, practice group events including discussions on recent legal developments)?
- Is there a systematic process to learn from past transactions and proceedings (eg, by using so-called after action reviews, deal debriefings etc)?

---

23 See Thomas H Davenport and Lawrence Prusak, *Working Knowledge* (Harvard Business School Press, 1998), pp52–106; David Skyrme, *Knowledge Networking* (Butterworth Heinemann, 1999), pp59–70.

24 In addition to the references cited in the preceding fn, see also Gilbert Probst, Steffen Raub and Kai Romhardt, *Managing Knowledge: Building Blocks for Success* (1999), pp27–216. They developed a popular process-based model defining so-called 'building blocks of knowledge management' to structure key knowledge processes, consisting of knowledge identification, knowledge acquisition, knowledge development, knowledge distribution, knowledge preservation and knowledge use. See also Martin Apistola and Petter Gottschalk, *Essential Knowledge and Management Issues in Law Firms* (Universal Publishers, 2011), pp175–184.

- Do we promote and foster an atmosphere of open feedback and constructive criticism (in order to encourage colleagues and employees to raise and discuss critical issues)?
- Are 'lessons learned' from deals and transactions being made part of the education and training formats for lawyers?

(d) *Knowledge preservation talking to leaving colleagues*

In order to avoid loss of valuable knowledge, law firms should also consider as systematic a process of knowledge preservation. In addition to IT security measures to prevent loss of data from the KM database, managing the loss of experience from leaving lawyers and other law firm members seems much more difficult. The following questions may serve as a guideline for addressing the issues:

- Do we know who is leaving the law firm and when? What is the effect on client relationships and practice development?
- Do we have tools to ask leavers for know-how to be left with the law firm (eg, by conducting so-called exit interviews etc)?
- Do we systematically document and record the results from exit interviews and make them available to our colleagues?

4.2 Creating an atmosphere of collaboration and constructive feedback

As follows from the suggestions indicated above, the key for visualising implicit knowledge is to create a collaborative framework enabling lawyers and other members of the law firm to communicate with each other and to exchange their insights and experiences of daily legal work and experience. Such a framework will require an atmosphere of open and constructive feedback. This can be achieved by creating a so-called 'knowledge sharing culture',[25] where people are encouraged to help each other by sharing knowledge and experience (in contrast to a rather competitive climate where everyone works only for his own profit – ignoring the benefits of KM). However, in many law firms a 'go-it-alone-mentality' and the 'not-invented-here-syndrome' still exist. These problematic attitudes need to be and can be overcome by a clear KM strategy and by dedicated law firm management, KM staff and the (gradual) persuasion of fee earners. In addition, also non-legal staff should be persuaded that KM is always a valuable task. Undoubtedly, administrative staff possess various skills (eg, knowledge about local authorities, language skills etc) which may be of value to the KM team and to the law firm as a whole.

5. Organising quality controls – the art of content management

The success of any KM organisation will depend on its regular and consistent quality management control.[26] This applies to all knowledge resources including tools used to structure explicit knowledge as well as to visualise and externalise implicit knowledge. Thus, content management, which means a systematic process of careful

---

25 For the importance of the 'knowledge sharing culture' see Rusanow (n 3), pp187–220; Parsons (n 6), pp96–116; see also Schulz and Klugmann (n 3), pp386–391.

26 Schulz and Mohando (n 1), pp126–127. See also Schulz (n 17), pp17–20.

selection, evaluation and updating of knowledge resources, must become an integral part of any knowledge collection.[27]

5.1 Criteria relevant for quality management and control procedures

In order to manage content effectively, law firms should consider the following questions:

- What type of content is worth storing (eg, precedents, interviews with experts, checklists)?
- How are storage requirements defined and controlled (eg, how should documents be classified and archived)?
- What are appropriate review and updating procedures (defining time periods and 'lifecycles' for regular updating)?
- Who is in charge for review and updating of knowledge (creating a system of shared responsibilities)?
- Who is in charge for controlling the validity and effectiveness of content management?

Since the primary goal of content management is to secure the usefulness and quality of the collected knowledge, it should start with a thoughtful and strategic selection of content.[28] This requires definition of some necessary criteria typically associated with high-quality information and knowledge serving as a guideline for the necessary content management and quality control procedures. Such criteria should include, among other things:[29]

- accessibility (checking whether content is presented in a user-friendly format);
- accuracy and correctness (checking whether content is valid and free from errors);
- clarity and scope (checking whether content can be easily understood by users);
- topicality (checking whether content is current and updated regularly);
- relevance to the practice (checking whether content includes useful hints for legal practice);
- reliability (checking whether content comes from trustworthy sources); and
- security (checking whether content is protected against loss or unauthorised access).

5.2 Establishing systematic review procedures

In addition, it is necessary to establish consistent review and control procedures on a regular basis.[30] As part of implementing an updating process one can create so-called 'knowledge lifecycles' including regular review dates.[31] At the review date, the task of updating knowledge can be delegated either to lawyers or to PSL and other

---

27 Schulz and Mohando (n 1), p 126 with further references. Rusanow (n 3), p 242.
28 Schulz and Mohando (n 1), p126.
29 See in general Martin J Eppler, *Managing Information Quality*, 2nd edn (Springer, 2006) pp69–85. With regard to legal KM see Schulz and Mohando (n 1), pp126–127; Schulz (n 17), pp17–20.
30 See Rusanow (n 3), p242; Schulz, (n 16), p19.
31 See Schulz and Mohando (n 1), pp126–127.

information professionals. In order to secure buy-in from legal practice, however, the responsibility for review and updating should not only be left to PSL and information professionals. On the contrary, lawyers should always be involved, for example when deciding on the reusability of knowledge resources.[32]

5.3 Checking the legal issues

Irrespective of the kind of knowledge (explicit or tacit), certain legal requirements have to be checked before documents may be stored in the KM database or before implicit knowledge is visualised.[33] For example, exemplary documents from transactions will often contain confidential information and it is very important to erase such information systematically before storing any documents in the KM database.[34] Other legal restrictions may result from license law or from copyright issues.[35] In addition, when lawyers' competencies appear in an expert directory, it might be necessary to obtain their consent in order to avoid the violation of data protection rules or confidentiality requirements. The legal framework is dynamic and therefore, every KM activity needs a thorough examination for any legal requirements.[36]

6. Which persons to involve – finding the right mix of resources

Last, but not least, organising knowledge in a law firm also includes the issue of whom to involve for performing knowledge management tasks. Again, this question should be included in the KM strategy as part of the necessary KM budget. Thus, the issue of appropriate staffing will again depend on individual factors like the size of the law firm, its specific business focus and its international scope of activities.

6.1 Need for knowledge managers and information professionals

As follows from the various and sophisticated KM processes described above, a KM system requires a lot of time and effort to become and remain effective and valuable. Since fee earners will only be able to devote part of their time to KM related activities, it is generally a good idea to delegate certain tasks to information professionals and knowledge managers such as law librarians and PSL. Whether or not a law firm needs PSL, that is fully trained legal professionals, to perform KM tasks depends primarily on the size of the law firm as well as on the intended scope and budget of the KM program. Accordingly, the need for PSL is also a strategic question, which should be addressed when developing the law firm's business and KM strategy.

6.2 Employing PSL – some benefits and costs

Although there are many different forms of KM organisation, depending of the individual business model of each law firm, one can find two typical models of organising KM activities:[37] under the first model, practising lawyers perform KM tasks in addition to their fee-earning activities. In these law firms, lawyers will not employ

---

32 Schulz and Mohando (n 1), p127.
33 Schulz and Mohando (n 1), p124.
34 *Ibid.*
35 *Ibid.*
36 *Ibid.*

PSL for KM tasks, but will often ask law librarians (or a group of them) to support KM projects. The advantages of this model include practical relevance of KM contributions as well as a consideration of current needs resulting from daily legal practice. Some major disadvantages, on the other hand, result from the fact that client work will often take priority over KM activities and establishing quality control mechanisms for knowledge resources may become a significant challenge.[38]

In contrast to the first model of lawyers as knowledge managers, other (and typically bigger) law firms employ 'special KM forces' like PSL to perform KM tasks,[39] quite often in cooperation with other information professionals such as law librarians. As an advantage of this model, KM tasks can be delegated to professionals according to their specific knowledge and experience. For example, PSL can use their legal education and practical training for valuable (yet time consuming) tasks like analysing new legal developments, updating standard form documents, or designing training sessions for their colleagues.[40] These contributions by PSL can be effectively combined with special knowledge of other information professionals, and in particular with the knowledge of law librarians, for example by training users in the efficient use of knowledge tools.[41] However, the second model requires investing in qualified staff, and developing a career path for different types of information professionals.[42] Furthermore, delegating KM tasks to PSL, librarians and other information professionals, might lead to the wrong impression that KM might generally be delegated. In order avoid this impression; management should always involve lawyers (on a representative basis) in all strategically relevant KM projects and activities. If PSL act as knowledge brokers coordinating the efficient retrieval and use of knowledge resources, they can help and complement the services of law librarians as their fellow information professionals.

7. Conclusion and guidelines

In sum, organising KM in a law firm is a complex and a dynamic concept, which requires adjusting the concept in alignment with the business model on a regular basis. The differences between explicit and implicit knowledge require a flexible approach when organising key knowledge processes such as identifying, acquiring, sharing and updating relevant sources. Although the task of visualising implicit knowledge is much harder to achieve than storing explicit knowledge, it should not be neglected. If lawyers and information professionals (like PSL and law librarians) take a joint perspective and collaborate effectively, they can create an effective framework for exchanging experience and insights. KM is a continuous journey rather than a short trip. Thus, we would suggest including information professionals also in the future development of KM and relying on their multi-faceted experience on how to organise and structure knowledge resources in a law firm.

---

37 For a description of these models see Schulz and Mohando (n 1), pp121–122.
38 Schulz and Mohando (n 1), p127.
39 See Schulz and Mohando (n 1), p121; for the use of PSL see also Parsons (n 6), pp64–65.
40 See Schulz and Mohando (n 1), pp121–122; see also Büchi's chapter on client-facing knowledge management.
41 Schulz and Mohando (n 1), p122.
42 Schulz and Mohando (n 1), p122 with further comments in n 34.

About the authors

Stephanie Abbott
Director, Janders Dean
stephanie.abbott@jandersdean.com

Stephanie is the leader of Janders Dean's APAC Knowledge Management & Innovation Practice. She is a dynamic and innovative senior consultant in legal knowledge management, change and organisational development.

She has been working with law firms and in-house legal teams in the areas of knowledge management, process improvement, technology and learning for over 13 years in Hong Kong and Australia. Stephanie understands the diverse cultures and dynamics of the Asia-Pacific region, and combines deep experience in her field of expertise with a strong commercial and practical sense. She has held senior organisational development and knowledge management roles in major international law firms, such as Mayer Brown and Gilbert + Tobin. As part of the Janders Dean team she has advised regional and international law firms, in-house legal teams and government organisations about their knowledge and legal service transformation strategies.

Emily Allbon
Senior lecturer in law, City, University of London
e.allbon@city.ac.uk

Emily Allbon was law librarian at City, University of London for 14 years, before joining the City Law School as a lecturer in 2014. She now teaches various modules on the undergraduate programme including Legal Method, English Legal System and Land Law as a senior lecturer. As a librarian her work was recognised both internally at City (she was given the Robert Kitchen Award 2012 for her "outstanding contribution to the University") and more widely, with highlights including being named Wildy/BIALL Law Librarian of the Year 2012, receiving the Routledge/Association of Law Teachers Teaching Law with Technology Prize 2013 and being given a National Teaching Fellowship from the HEA in 2013.

She has written extensively on issues of legal information management, legal skills teaching and student engagement and has just published her first student textbook: *The Insider's Guide to Legal Skills* (Routledge, 2016).

Raffael Büchi
Head of know-how and business development,
Bär & Karrer
raffael.buechi@baerkarrer.ch

Raffael Büchi is head of know-how and training/continuous education as well as business development at Bär & Karrer. He is responsible for the firm's know-how system, its website, its intranet, its publication strategy as well as for all the submissions for rankings and awards. Furthermore, he is a member of the steering committee of the Bär & Karrer College, the internal training program for associates. In the field of legal knowledge management he also advises clients of the firm and organises workshops.

He regularly publishes on topics within his specialisation. He is a speaker at the workshop series 'Compliance in Action' of the ZHAW (Zurich School of Applied Science). On January 20/21 2016 he chaired the international knowledge management conference KM Legal Europe in Amsterdam. Raffael Büchi was one of the Presiding Judges for the STEP Private Clients Awards 2015/16.

Silke Gottschalk
Operational head of compliance,
Luther Rechtsanwaltsgesellschaft mbH
silke.gottschalk@luther-lawfirm.com

Silke is the operational head of compliance at Luther Rechtsanwaltsgesellschaft mbH. She is responsible for the firm's conflict check and compliance system including AML-proceedings. As a former IP/IT lawyer, she is especially interested in IT-driven knowledge management technologies such as enterprise search systems for law firms. Silke is a regular speaker at the IBA annual conferences and current chair of the IBA law firm management committee subcommittee on knowledge management and IT.

Boyd Hendriks
Managing director, Informationland
boyd@informatieland.nl

Boyd Hendriks (1959) is managing director of Informationland, a consulting firm based in The Netherlands and the United Kingdom. He has a long track record with top law firms developing their knowledge management and IT strategies, and lead their teams to new roles in the changed business models of their organisations. He developed the first knowledge exchange portals in accountancy and pioneered with knowledge management in finance and health industries. Boyd lectures knowledge management and innovation at the University of Applied Sciences in Amsterdam.

Martina Kuth
Librarian and coordinator, Library and Information Services, CMS Hasche Sigle
Martina.Kuth@cms-hs.com

Martina Kuth has a diploma in librarianship (Dipl-Bibl) and a Master in Library and Information Science (MA LIS) accredited by CILIP. She has been working as a one person librarian in legal company libraries since 1987.

Currently she runs the library of the CMS Hasche Sigle in Frankfurt am Main and coordinates the Library and Information Services in all German CMS-offices.

She volunteers for the board of the Arbeitsgemeinschaft juristischer Bibliotheken und Dokumentationsstellen (AjBD), which is a section of the International Association of Law Libraries IALL, and is a member of various German professional associations.

Martina authored the first handbook on One-Person-Librarianship originally written in the German language as well as various articles. Furthermore she is an associate of the editorial board of b.i.t.online, a leading journal for librarianship and information science.

Allie Lustigman
Knowledge & information manager,
Charles Taylor
Allie.Lustigman@ctplc.com

Allie Lustigman MsC, MCILIP is the knowledge & information manager at Charles Taylor, which is a leading international provider of professional services including end-to-end management of insurance companies like The Standard Club, a third party liability shipping insurer. The information service includes the provision of legal and commercial research, knowledge management, information resource management, current awareness and intranet management. Before joining Charles Taylor Allie worked in the legal sector at Magic Circle and top city law firms.

She is a Chartered librarian and member of

the Chartered Institute of Library and Information Professionals (CILIP), and the British and Irish Association of Law Librarians (BIALL), sitting on their public relations committee.

Allie regularly publishes articles on the topics of intranets, knowledge and information management.

Luis Felipe Mohando
Head of knowledge management, Sorainen
felipe.mohando@sorainen.com

Luis Felipe Mohando is head of knowledge management in Sorainen. As part of the knowledge management team he designs, implements and manages systems and procedures enabling Sorainen legal teams to organise, share and use know-how and experience.

Luis Felipe joined Sorainen's M&A and private equity practice bringing his international experience from the tax department of Ernst & Young in Buenos Aires, and from building up and heading the Corporate and M&A team in Leverone & Mihura Estrada.

He read law at Torcuato Di Tella University in Buenos Aires, additionally holding LLM degrees from New York University, the National University of Singapore and Torcuato Di Tella University. He was called to the Buenos Aires bar in 2002 and the Madrid bar in 2010.

Between 2012 and 2015 he was the Chairman of the IBA law firm management committee subcommittee on KM & IT.

Porcia Newell
Licensed attorney
porciabeasleynewell@gmail.com

Porcia Newell is a licensed attorney with over 10 years of experience in the financial services industry. She has provided legal support to some of the largest banking institutions in the US, including Wells Fargo and Bank of America. Most recently, Porcia's work has included drafting bank policies and procedures, and tracking state legislative updates for enterprise-wide compliance purposes.

In addition to her work advising corporate clients, Porcia also led a consumer advocacy law practice based in the San Francisco Bay area. Her practice areas included civil litigation and trust and estate planning.

Tara Pichardo-Angadi
Head of knowledge (EMEA), Norton Rose Fulbright LLP
Tara.Pichardo-Angadi@nortonrosefulbright.com

Tara Pichardo-Angadi has a law degree from King's College London and a Maîtrise from the University of Paris 1 – La Sorbonne as well as a post-graduate diploma in legal practice from the College of Law.

Upon qualification, Tara joined the Paris asset finance team of Norton Rose Fulbright. Tara became a Knowledge Lawyer in October 2004, where her role encompassed keeping the finance team updated on changes in law (both French and English), drafting and maintaining our French law precedents and answering queries on both French and English law and training, including ensuring compliance with Paris Bar regulations.

Tara became Head of Knowledge in the EMEA region in November 2012, including managing stakeholders' knowledge requirements, developing knowledge plans, feeding into the global knowledge strategy and managing local knowledge teams, budgets and projects. Tara regularly assists clients as regards their training and access to knowledge.

Anthony J Rhem
President/Principle consultant, AJ Rhem & Associates, Inc
tonyr@ajrhem.com

Dr Anthony J Rhem, PhD is a management consulting and IT professional with over 30 years of experience and since 1990 has served as president/principle consultant of AJ Rhem &

Associates, Inc, a privately held Management Consulting and IT firm located in USA, Chicago, Illinois. Dr Rhem holds degrees in business management, computer science and knowledge management. As a consultant, strategist and adviser Dr Rhem has worked with Fortune 500 corporations in retail, communications, financial, insurance, legal, healthcare and the military (US Army and US Air Force) in implementing strategies, policies and solutions centred on information technology and knowledge management. As a professor and corporate instructor, Dr Rhem has trained hundreds of personnel across many corporations, law firms, government and military agencies in the principles, practice and application of strategic management, information architecture, software engineering and knowledge management.

Martin R Schulz, LLM (Yale)
Professor of German and international private and corporate law, German Graduate School of Management and Law (GGS), Heilbronn, Germany
martin.schulz@ggs.de

Dr Martin R Schulz is a professor of German and international private and corporate law at the German Graduate School of Management and Law (GGS) in Heilbronn, Germany. He studied law at Goethe University in Frankfurt/Main and Yale Law School, New Haven/USA, holding a doctorate in law from Goethe University and a Master of Laws Degree from Yale. His publications and main areas of expertise include international corporate law, corporate compliance and knowledge management for lawyers. Before joining the GGS faculty, Martin R Schulz worked full time as an attorney-at-law and as a knowledge management lawyer for a renowned multinational law firm. In addition to his academic activities, he joined the Frankfurt office of CMS Hasche Sigle as Of Counsel in November 2015.

Gerard J Tanja
Partner, Venturis Consulting Group
gerard.tanja@venturisconsulting.com

Gerard Tanja is a partner at Venturis. He holds an LLM and PhD degree in law, and has a MBA from the University of California. Before establishing Venturis, Gerard worked at the University of Leyden, was legal adviser to the Minister of Foreign Affairs and was, before moving to Clifford Chance (World Firm Management Committee), General Director of the TMC ASSER Institute for International Law.

At Clifford Chance, Gerard was responsible for HR development and know-how management.

At Venturis Consulting Group, Gerard specialises in strategy formulation, merger consulting and KH management projects. He has been involved in a number of international law firm mergers, has assisted several Anglo-American firms with the establishment of their European offices and has undertaken a series of strategic reviews of European offices. In addition, he has been heavily involved in a number of law firm restructuring and governance initiatives and KH implementation initiatives in the Benelux and Germany.

Jonna Vainikainen
Business process manager, Castrén & Snellman Attorneys Ltd
jonna.vainikainen@castren.fi

Jonna Vainikainen is a business process manager and works in the Knowledge Management Team at Castrén & Snellman Attorneys Ltd in Helsinki. She has a specialist qualification in management.

Jonna's responsibilities include, among other things, business process and master data management as well as the development of project management. She is also actively involved in business development projects and strategy process development. In addition, she provides induction training and other training for the firm's personnel.

Jonna specialises in business with an ICT emphasis, focusing on consistent personal and corporate development.

Related titles in the same series

Globe Law and Business

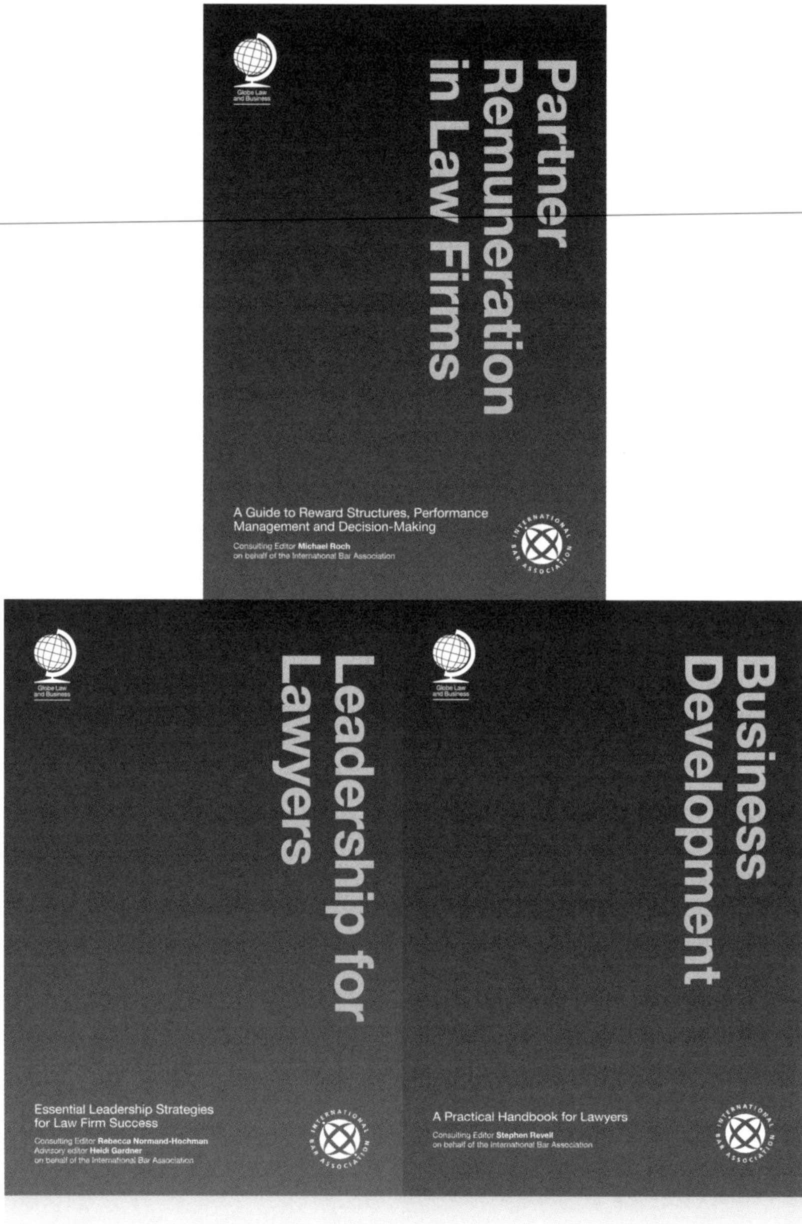

Go to **www.globelawandbusiness.com**
for full details including free sample chapters